Powerfully
Likeable

Powerfully Likeable

A WOMAN'S GUIDE TO EFFECTIVE COMMUNICATION

Kate Mason, PhD

HARMONY

NEW YORK

Harmony Books
An imprint of Random House
A division of Penguin Random House LLC
1745 Broadway, New York, NY 10019
harmonybooks.com | randomhousebooks.com
penguinrandomhouse.com

ISBN 978-0-593-79720-4
Ebook ISBN 978-0-593-79722-8

Printed in the United States of America on acid-free paper

1st Printing

First Edition

BOOK TEAM: Production editor: Abby Duval · Managing editor: Allison Fox ·
Production manager: Maggie Hart · Copy editor: Martin Schneider ·
Proofreaders: Rachael Clements, Marisa Crumb, Jil Falzoi, Taylor McGowan,
Natalie Richman · Indexer: Gina Guilinger

Book design by Jo Anne Metsch

The authorized representative in the EU for product safety and compliance is
Penguin Random House Ireland, Morrison Chambers, 32 Nassau Street,
Dublin D02 YH68, Ireland. https://eu-contact.penguin.ie

*This book is for all of you mentioned within
and for all of you reading—thank you*

We spend too much time teaching girls to worry about what boys think of them. But the reverse is not the case. We don't teach boys to care about being likeable. We spend too much time telling girls that they cannot be angry or aggressive or tough, which is bad enough, but then we turn around and either praise or excuse men for the same reasons.

—CHIMAMANDA NGOZI ADICHIE

One of the criticisms I've faced over the years is that I'm not aggressive enough or assertive enough, or maybe somehow, because I'm empathetic, it means I'm weak. I totally rebel against that. I refuse to believe that you cannot be both compassionate and strong.

—JACINDA ARDERN,
former Prime Minister of New Zealand

CONTENTS

INTRODUCTION / xiii
Power and Likeability:
Getting to Know Both Sides of the Binary

ONE / 3
The High Price of Being Agreeable—
and How Not to Pay It

TWO / 26
"It'll Only Take Two Seconds":
Why Imposing Syndrome Makes Us Play Small
(and How to Beat It)

THREE / 55
Communicating Power and Authority
Through Our Voices and Physicality

FOUR / 89
Kill Your Confidence:
Find Your Power

FIVE / 112
Asking Great Questions and
Giving Great Answers

SIX / 134
Locating Our Powerful Likeability
When Our Batteries Are Low

SEVEN / 149
Recasting Difference as Strength

EIGHT / 177
The Downsides of Preparation and
the Importance of Rest

NINE / 207
Overcoming Fear: Navigating
Conversations Under Threat

TEN / 237
Failure Privilege: Why It's Not Available to
Women and What to Do About It

CONCLUSION / 259
Beautiful Works in Progress:
Living a Powerfully Likeable Life

ACKNOWLEDGMENTS / 263

NOTES / 267

INDEX / 277

All names are unreliable in this book.

*In some cases, clients and friends have been
happy for me to use their real names;
others have requested anonymity.*

Power and Likeability:

Getting to Know Both Sides of the Binary

t's the year 2000. We survived Y2K, Britney's *Oops! . . . I Did It Again* is huge, and George W. Bush has been narrowly elected president. I am seventeen years old, and my acne and I have just sat down after speaking at the National Debate Tournament. Look, I hear you. Debate is not cool, but this was what I lived for. I felt truly alive when I was speaking, as if I was exactly where I was meant to be—weaving ideas together, watching them land, and persuading an audience to believe my case. I've loved debating since I was ten years old, when I would get so nervous that I'd turn bright red and physically shake—you could see my palm cards tremble from afar.

Absolutely everything about debate sang to me: the strict rules of engagement, the logic, the skill of making a compelling argument, and the democratic way everyone got the same amount of time to speak. I remember wondering, *Why wouldn't you love this? Why isn't everyone doing this?* I had spent months preparing for this tournament, highlighting

The Economist issues and doing countless practice debates, and I felt I had done a great job, standing shoulder-to-shoulder with my beloved male teammates.

After the debate, a well-respected retired coach we had never met gave our team members some notes. My teammates were congratulated for their "gravitas" and "presence"; their deeper voices and serious faces were seen as authoritative and commanding, and their arguments were complimented for their clarity and impact. When the coach came to give me feedback, she sighed and said, "Kate, you just can't be angry about *everything.*" On the one hand, she was right. In that one galling moment, I learned that tone and variance are crucial to being a compelling speaker.

Manner, it turns out, really matters to our likeability. The ways we use our voice, tone, and affect can contribute positively to a perception of warmth and approachability, for instance. In the inverse, our manner can be construed negatively, coming across as aloof, detached, or, in the extreme, downright aggressive.

But the other emotion I felt when the coach gave her feedback that day was fury. I had debated with the same level of intensity as my teammates, but it hadn't landed the same way. I knew my arguments were sound and my logic was strong, but she didn't comment on *what* I had said, only *how* I had said it. This type of feedback, of course, wasn't new to me.

Throughout my debating career, I was consistently told that I was too aggressive, too unsmiling, too arrogant, or too intense. And so I tried to change. I slid up and down the scale of masculine and feminine communication styles, trying to find a place where I could still be me. For example, I toyed with being a gentle, feminine speaker while simultaneously trying to emulate all the successful, mostly male speakers I had ever seen. Imagine me, if you will: five-foot-six, blazer and pencil skirt, lips ablaze with Cotton Candy Lip Smacker, loudly arguing, "Ladies and Gentlemen, time and again, I have asked the opposition to come up with even one way they are protecting human rights, and instead all we can hear is *shrieks of silence!*" and then smiling sweetly and returning to my seat. This did not, as you might be able to tell, go smoothly.

I craved an external demonstration of my autonomy, strength, and potential, but it didn't get me what I wanted. When I was playing feminine, I was perceived as too soft or easily beatable; when I was too masculine, I was "too much." Oops, I did it again. And again, and again.

Today, I am a coach, and I help leaders at organizations such as Netflix, Uber, Google, Microsoft, and many more elevate the way they present themselves and boost their signal, impact, and value. I know that my early struggle to find a comfortable way to communicate with authority but still be liked by a crowd is a familiar story to so many of us—because I observe it in my clients daily. I see recurring communication patterns that affect everything from who gets heard to who gets promoted. In fact, many women in these organizations still feel as if life has two doors: the powerful one or the likeable one.

WHAT IS THE POWERFUL/LIKEABLE BINARY?

You are probably well acquainted with these doors. Behind each one is a set of B-movie characters: the Ice Queen and the

Bad Bitch on one side, and the Girl Next Door and the Nice Doormat on the other. You can choose door one or door two, but switching after you have decided is almost impossible.

As women, we usually discuss these doors, this one-way choice, when we consider the process and struggle to gain power at work. We strategize before meetings, second-guess in bathroom stalls, text outfit options to our best friends, run through scenarios in our heads, and try to anticipate every possible variable of our performances. We know in our bones that we must choose between being powerful or likeable, and also that we're destined to lose, whichever way we jump.

This shrinking, reductive binary of powerful versus likeable is a disaster, if you haven't already noticed. What is especially vexing is that we experience penalties that men don't—and it is incumbent on us to figure out how to solve this inequity when *we didn't even ask for it in the first place.*

But here we are! And worse, when we are boxed in, we are guaranteed to lose because we have no way of showing our true selves or capabilities. This is dire for us because it makes us feel small, unimportant, and unworthy. It is also a significant loss for our organizations, families, and communities. Because we have chosen to be, say, the Girl Next Door, we might acquiesce to unreasonable demands for fear of being perceived as unlikeable or we might hesitate to give a direct order. Real power will feel foreign to us.

Or because we have chosen the route of the hard-nosed Ice Queen, we get feedback that we need to soften, that people find us off-putting and aggressive, that we're unapproachable, and that we have poor partnership skills. We find ourselves being overlooked for special opportunities or promotions, excluded from team events, or bitched about in the break room.

Women of color may experience even stronger penalties, with different cultural standards for deference, humility, and the act of pushing back, which only goes to further underscore the deltas between us and our male counterparts. Being stuck in the powerful/likeable binary also means we're stuck in the various other binaries that these doors invoke, too: quiet/loud, pleasant/aggressive, deferential/ambitious, demure/brash. All this sets us up to feel undervalued, unnuanced, and unfairly pigeonholed.

So, what happened to me after that debate? After I stopped being angry about everything (and stayed angry about that very act in my head), I made it onto the state team, against the odds. From there I was then selected to represent my national team, Australia, at the World Schools Debating Championships in Johannesburg, South Africa. We won the tournament, and I was ranked the ninth-best individual speaker in the world.

Winning a world title (yes, even a pretty dorky one) at eighteen gives one an unusual perspective, to say the least: it seemed, well, *obvious* that anything was possible with a lot of hard work and practice. I had come a long way from that shaky, red-faced ten-year-old.

But here's the thing. I think I won because I played the only game I saw around me: I was stern, adversarial, and hyperaggressive. And while I was obviously good at being those things, the experience left me with a sense of longing; I had won the tournament but had lost something of myself. I look at photos of me from that time, and I see a self-conscious and defensive-looking young woman, carefully calculating exactly how to show up and calibrating just how angry I was allowed to be. I don't see the full me. And it stayed with me, this feeling of incompleteness, of not knowing how to show up as my true self. It didn't go away because I won the trophy. If anything, it only revealed itself to me even more.

This is the challenge of powerful likeability.

What Can Powerful Likeability Look Like?

It took me some years, but I finally dialed into a mode that communicated much more of who I actually am and reconciled many of the contradictions I had felt when I was a teenager. Through painful trial and error, I learned I could embody a broader array of communicative patterns, ideas, and interests than I had previously felt I had license to. I could hold my own boundaries *and* connect with warmth; I could present myself with authority *and* have close friends. I could articulate what I wanted *and* not alienate those around me. I began to find a space for myself in which I could start to communicate and feel like I was showing off my true sense of self.

And so I headed straight to law school, intending to become an attorney, and then went on to get my PhD in literature, all the while remaining bright-eyed in the knowledge that I'd be contributing to a field that was more than ready to hear women speak. After graduating, I took a sharp left turn from the humanities into tech. I worked in the senior levels of male-dominated tech companies for more than a decade, working with exceptional men and women and coaching them to present the best versions of themselves. I assured myself that all these complex issues of communicating while female, which I'd grappled with in debate, wouldn't exist in the real world. Yet in this work, I continued to observe the gendered ways women wrestle with power and recognized many of the same double binds and tensions that had existed for me as a debater.

I learned that the male-coded style of domination and confrontation I had seen in the world of debate more than existed in the workplace—it governed it. I was talked over, dismissed, and excluded in meetings. On occasion, my ideas were stolen. It was a depressing game of bingo. And, of course, it's not limited to Silicon Valley. My friends spoke to me about the same problems in the legal profession in London, the advertising scene in New York, and the consulting firms of Sydney. They may have been wearing different outfits, but the challenges of finding comfort and communicating within a predominantly male workplace were almost the same.

From Tokyo to Toronto, San Francisco to Sydney, women balance how they present themselves to the world and how the world reflects us back. Like me in debate, the women I met and worked with struggled with how to push back, be assertive, give direction, hold their ground, and be ambitious, all while still being *likeable*.

It's not just women in the corporate world, either. Women from all walks of life struggle in a similar way. Whether it's a mother standing up for her child at a school meeting, a patient advocating for more information from her doctor, or an activist articulating her position, time and again, I have heard variations of "What if they don't like me?" and "I'm not sure if I'm ready" and "I don't want to come across as being too aggressive."

This is an intriguing paradox. These women know that likeability is one of the keys to their success, but they don't know how to exercise power without giving it up.

The good news is that likeability by itself isn't the problem—it's great! Liking people—and wanting to be liked—is a deeply human and non-criminal urge. It's the quality of wanting someone to exist in your orbit or, equally, wanting to exist in theirs. Think about the people you know whom you deem likeable: they probably have an energy that makes you want to be around them and to show up wherever they are. You might be pleased when you see a message from them on your phone or happy when you learn they're invited to that upcoming dinner. When I was working at Google many years ago, we'd ask ourselves when hiring new people, *Would I want to sit next to this person on a plane for fourteen hours?* That, to me, is the essence of positive, generative likeability: an energy that works in your favor, helping you create teams of allies and friends wherever you are. Likeability is the ability to corral people around you and your cause, and it's critical to building trust and deepening relationships. Instead of understanding likeability as something to avoid or negotiate intensely, we can conceptualize it as a compelling currency that doesn't have to be forgotten in order to access power. Likeability *is* power. If power offers us opportunity, it's likeability that lets us take it.

The problem is that we've been taught that likeability for women is different. It's not just being a good egg—it means displaying virtues like agreeability, extreme selflessness, suppression of anger, and deference, to name just a few. We're taught to not raise our voices and not ruffle feathers but to smile and laugh politely at inappropriate jokes, and so on. There's a perception that women care too much about likeability or have to concede too much to acquire it in the first place. In many cultures, likeability as a woman can be read as one who smiles, who defers, who isn't argumentative, or who doesn't take up space. If a woman shows strong emotion, pushes back, or even expresses mild disagreement, she becomes unlikeable. Or hysterical. Or too emotional. You've seen this movie before.

We're also not wrong to be concerned about being unlikeable, for study after study shows there are penalties when a person isn't "likeable enough": inequitable salaries, never-eventuating promotions, and an endemic lack of funding for our ideas. It's even been suggested that juries are more likely to believe expert testimony when the expert is likeable. I can feel your collective eye roll from here.

Power isn't a problem by itself, either. When we talk about empowering people, we mean we want to facilitate their ability and capacity to do more, to act on their own behalf, and to influence behavior and the events around them. Power doesn't have to be the loudest voice in the room or the firmest handshake. I like to think of it as the ability to stand in our own space, comfortable, unrattled, assured, and alive in any given situation. To many women, power feels obvious, and to others, it feels radical; we are all spread out on the spectrum of how much power we have been used to exerting—and how much we feel we can comfortably adopt.

We call our own power into question often, wondering what—if anything—we would say if someone were to ask us to take notes in an otherwise all-male meeting. Or when we question ourselves: *Did I sound too harsh? When should I follow up afterward?* Or my personal favorite: *Did I put enough exclamation points in that email to look friendly?* And its corollary: *Did I put too many exclamation points and look psychotic?* On the one hand, we want to be able to inhabit authority, and on the other, we're also managing our emotions and everyone else's at the same time—or at least trying to. Exhausting, no? My women clients tend to share that they're exasperated to spend so much time gauging *how* their message is landing, as well as *crafting* the actual message itself.

How Does the Powerful/Likeable Binary Affect Us?

Against this backdrop, even the most exceptionally credentialed women ask me, "How can I be seen to be in charge and be likeable? Is it possible to be authoritative while still being 'nice'? Moreover, how can I communicate all the complex parts of my personality?"

You might identify as one of these women—I work with many. Consider the following two exceptional women leaders, who have impeccable credentials, sophisticated headshots, and impressive-sounding roles. From the outside, they do not seem concerned about how they show up in the world. But when I talk with them, a different story emerges.

Take Michaela, who runs strategy and operations for a finance start-up and, as is common in tech, is the only woman on her otherwise all-male leadership team. She says pragmatically, "As I get more senior, more is put on my plate, and I'm just incapable of saying no. It always feels gendered, and I find it hard to push back, even when I know I should."

Or Hyo, who works at a large media company and emanates a sense of quiet calm. She describes how she looks to other women in her organization as role models and learns what sorts of behaviors to avoid. According to her, women who are assertive in her organization are "very negatively perceived." She says, "So I overcompensate and apologize for everything. I basically apologize for existing so that I don't seem like them."

And of course, let's not forget women who experience almost the opposite challenge. Consider the following two women, who have similar credentials and seniority and are equally troubled by how they're showing up in the world, but for entirely different reasons.

Lake is a hypercompetent business manager who is forthright and direct. She explains she recently didn't get an overdue promotion because of a perception that she "overmanages" senior executives. She tells me she's "trying to take the feedback constructively, but it's hard not to feel like it's gendered and personal."

Sadaf works in a PR agency and is a loud, serious presence. She says that one of her primary criticisms is that she can be abrupt with people when, in her words, "I'm just trying to do my job the most efficiently." She suspects her people-management feedback is the reason she's not asked to lead big client pitches, despite having seniority at the agency.

So, dear reader, just how did we get here? Is it even possible for women to be powerful and likeable simultaneously? It's not an intuitive idea—seeming bananas on the face of it—but the question itself has deep, deep roots. For hundreds of years, men have had the luxury of defining what power looks and sounds like. Classicist Mary Beard points to the fact that in Ancient Rome "public speech was a—if not *the*—defining attribute of maleness. . . . A woman speaking in public was, in most circumstances, by definition, not a woman." We've obviously carpe'd a lot of diems since then to accept the idea of women speaking in public, but still, there persists an underlying insistent bias against women who are forthright, loud, shocking, or embarrassing. Women who speak their minds are not symbolic of accepted and acceptable femininity.

Quick fixes, we know, don't work. We can't remedy decades of inequity with the things we've already tried. Two decades ago, we were told that "nice girls don't get the corner office," which frankly seems mean. Ever since, women have been consistently told to build executive presence (whatever that means) and "be more confident" or even the never-appreciated "just smile more!" Pithy, rhyming aphorisms embroidered on pillows or bedazzled on water bottles (I'm looking at you, anything that mentions the word *badass*) just won't get us there.

But the price for this hovering in binary limbo is intolerable. The societal limitations concerning what we can say, do, wear, eat, and watch inhibit our enthusiasm and capacity and force us to walk in smaller and smaller circles. We feel controlled by invisible forces that keep us tiny.

HOW TO MOVE FORWARD

In this book, I'm going to show you that in order to embody a powerful likeability, we must change the definition and play the game differently. There are as many ways to show up and communicate as there are women in the world. I'm going to give you the tools to be your true selves, the ability to communicate that self in any situation and to be as powerfully likeable as you want to be.

Here's the thing, we don't need to change who we are. Becoming a more authoritative, warm communicator doesn't mean imitating what men do; instead, it's about choosing different tools or practices to help us find and then amplify our own presence and, in turn, ourselves.

You can reject this powerful/likeable binary that you never asked for and find your own road map to being both powerful and likeable at work, at home, and beyond.

Leaving behind the powerful/likeable binary allows us to say our message with techniques that fit us best and allows us to construct a new version of power and authority. I want to help you think about how to find the answer that feels right for you and where you are in your career and life right now, by imparting tools to be the best contributor and leader possible. Not everything in this book is going to resonate with you, but just as a tool kit has lots of different tools, hopefully you'll be able to pick up the ones that feel right to you.

By reorienting our focus away from how we're being perceived and instead working on *who we are,* we can amplify what is special about ourselves and we can show up as an individual rather than as the boring stereotypes from doors one or two. This practice helps unlock our value for ourselves, our communities, and our organizations and strengthens our voice, reach, and impact. This type of warm power is an internal unassailability: the ability to steer our respective ships through still or troubled waters, navigating in the directions we wish. So we can speak and be listened to, we can contribute and be recognized, and we can ask and receive.

The primary goal of this book is to enable you to learn and practice tools that will help you engage your audience so that you can deliver the most powerful and likeable version of yourself. I've purposefully made the ideas in *Powerfully Likeable* a system by which you can adapt what you need and when, illustrated in ten chapters that move along a continuum. I begin by looking at how we even got to this point by situating the culture of agreeableness and the price we pay for abiding by it. I then move on to the different ways we can show up in our body, reimagine confidence, and avoid Imposing Syndrome. (Yes, *imposing,* not imposter.) I then want to show you how many traditionally feminine-coded attributes, such as community, empathy, and cooperativeness, can actually amplify your sense of power. Rather than being perceived as weaknesses, they can fortify our presence in powerful ways.

This book will help you reflect on the things you do and figure out whether your actions and words are based on *fear* or on *potential.* My wish is that you can reconcile that divide within yourself and find a space that feels comfortable, warm, and inviting.

I don't pretend to speak for other women's experiences, but I will help share them here through anecdotes and stories from the hundreds of women I've worked with over the past twenty years. I want to help you think about how to find the answer that feels right for you and where you are in your career and life right now.

The Book in Your Hands

Powerful likeability isn't a prescription but rather an invitation to try out different parts of yourself and see which ones serve you and make you feel good. In each chapter, I'll invite you to experiment with different ways of communicating exactly who you are: you'll see sections titled "Try this" where you can actively apply ideas to your own contexts in a way that feels appropriate and comfortable to you. I want to help you increase your volume, amplify what you already have, and build on all the hard work you've done up till now.

By the end of the book, you will know that:

1. We don't need to choose to be powerful or likeable, and we can reimagine *power* as a verb: something we do, not something we have.
2. The high cost of agreeableness has historically influenced our communication and, subsequently, our opportunity, status, and agency.
3. We can overcome Imposing Syndrome—the disease of playing small and not taking up space—and amplify ourselves and those around us.
4. Our bodies can be sites of power and authority, despite looking unlike historical models of both.
5. The Confidence Combination is a new, more authentic way of showing up. By killing our confidence and presence dysmorphia, we can find our true power.
6. By using clear logic, evidence, and debate strategy, we can ask and answer questions without appearing "difficult."
7. We can recast our differences as strengths to help us con-

nect more with people around us and open up opportunities. We can also use warmth instead of deference.

8. We can learn a new, lighter-touch preparation framework and avoid the Preparation Expectation placed on so many women. We can also learn to rest and avoid exhaustion in our communication.

9. Even when under threat, we can overcome and mitigate high-pressure situations and find calm, influential communication.

10. We can reject Failure Privilege and succeed more easily when we reconceptualize *failure* as experimentation.

Powerfully Likeable can also be your workbook: make it your own, scribble in it, bend the spine, and dog-ear the pages; by the time you get to the end, it should feel like we've written a book together, with a plan you can call your very own. By giving permission to be our full selves, we can find a third door behind which is the role of a lifetime: our best and most powerful self.

Powerfully
Likeable

ONE

The High Price of Being Agreeable— and How Not to Pay It

In which we bravely venture forth to explore why agreeableness is held in such high esteem, discover the weird communication expectations on us women, work up the courage to have a tricky conversation about potted plants, observe how people-pleasing seeps into our communications, and conduct an inventory of all the things that turn our power up (and turn it down).

Recently I caught up with one of my brilliant friends, Niki, who works in crisis communications. She told me she had done seven hard work things that day, but the one task that was proving the most challenging was figuring out how to raise a difficult conversation with her neighbor about potted plants in their shared yard. It's not that Niki doesn't know *how* to have that conversation (or that she can't handle a discussion about potted plants!), it's that it took an enormous amount of mental energy to write a note that was nice but not minimizing, warm but firm, and clear but not aggressive. Not only did scripting the note take a long time, but as she said, "I've *still* spent the rest of the day wondering if I'm a bitch."

For many of us, just like Niki, it's not the actual role we're doing that is hard; most of my clients are women at the heights of their careers who *more* than know how to do their jobs. It's much more that our system is slowed down by worrying about these extra concerns. Many of us always have these draining tabs open in our mental browser, metaphorically depleting our batteries when they could be used for so many other useful things.

The pursuit of agreeableness is exhausting.

Historically, communicating while female necessarily seems to involve balancing being amenable while also trying to pursue our goals. This skillful act of influence is a deeply powerful one: we already know something, but we have to demonstrate our competence to others so that they can see what we see and believe what we believe. Most of the time, we don't have physical props or, sometimes, even evidence; we're using our words and emotion to convey authority, credibility, passion—whatever is required in the moment—to change someone's mind or to go after an outcome. And we do all this while also not alienating or irritating or overshadowing our listener. We must be the most persuasive, most compelling, and most engaging while also being emotionally aware, non-threatening, non-triggering, and more.

While most of us don't study Interpersonal Communications 101 in college, these skills are deeply integral to how we show up at work, whether that's in the corporate world or as a teacher in the classroom, and even how we show up in our personal lives. Much of the practice of developing our authority and credibility lies in our successful ability to communicate in a compelling manner. What are the tools of communication that we can use to help give our arguments weight, structure, and credibility? How can we hold our ground and get the thing we want, while also maintaining relationships with those around us? And why does this always come back to the powerful/likeable binary?

Skilled communication so exquisitely engages the powerful/likeable binary because it requires both of those qualities from us in equal measure at the same time. In moments where we need to change someone's mind, we need to present with power—maybe it's authority, credibility, knowledge—at the exact same moment that we present a sense of warmth or friendliness. We know that, in order to respond meaningfully to someone, we can't alienate ourselves from them in the moment: more than ever, we need for them to see us as allies—or at least not antagonistic to their goals. Even better, we might be seen as empathetic or deeply understanding of their motivations.

And cute paradox ahoy! Being amenable often means that we diminish or minimize ourselves to engender closeness, which results in us losing any power we might have held in the first instance. Conversely, the very *instant* we transition to bulldozer power mode to push our idea forth with energy or brashness, we lose the likeability war. It sounds like a perfect storm, and it really is. And, of course, the penalty of seeming "difficult" is real, too. We know that being labeled "difficult" is itself a tricky label to shake once handed out or decided upon. It means we're not amenable in the ways a largely patriarchal world would expect us to be. Ironically, it often means we're raising a point that absolutely needs to be discussed.

THE UNFAIR EXPECTATIONS ON US WOMEN WHEN WE COMMUNICATE

The next questions we must ask ourselves are: *Is the communicative burden higher on women? Is more asked of us, or expected at the outset, when we offer a response?* You can probably already imagine my answer here. I'm certain this is true, in part because our literal voice is often called into question when we are in the act of communicating. There's even a special vocabulary saved up for women who communicate outside the "amenable" sphere. Consider the fact that we women don't remind, we *nag*; we don't complain, we *whine*; we don't go over time, we *waffle*; we don't laugh, we *cackle*; and when we express a strong feeling, we're *emotional, bossy, hysterical, moody, hormonal, shrill,* and other descriptors that are rarely ever used when discussing men. Even when women speak with each other, we're not sharing information, we're *gossiping, gabbing,* or *prattling.* In short, it feels like we're *fucked.*

It goes without saying that men can display a fuller version of themselves communicatively without any of this negative vocabulary being directed at them. When men are not amenable—if they shout or get angry, for instance—they're *passionate, animated,* or *engaged,* very often without facing penalty. (And sometimes they're even lauded for their emotional range!)

Like me in my debate days, when the stakes are so high and we need to communicate something of great importance, we sometimes go too hard and too fast and bulldoze our way through to the end. *See? See how right I am?* This insistence is likely doomed for failure. No one—man or woman—likes to be bulldozed over. (And trust me on this one—I have done my fair share of bulldozing.) And of course, the opposite can be true, too; we can meekly raise a point, not cutting to the heart of the issue, and the other person can leave the conversation unpersuaded and unchanged.

And of course, there are a lot of different suggestions for what to do in these response-heavy situations. I recently came across a video online about delivering your message with power. In slow-motion horror, I realized that the (female) creator was advocating literal words to use at work, a list that included phrases featuring "masculine verbs" such as "I advise," "I declare," and "I implore." All I could think of when I saw this was Elle Woods's words from *Legally Blonde*: "I object!" With respect to the featured coach, a "masculine verb"—whatever that is—is just not going to be the change you want to see in the workplace. Or in the case of "I implore"—we don't live in Dickensian times, so the less said there, the better.

One of the challenges of being amenable is that we remain heirs to many of the same old ideas and norms when it comes to assuming speech or power (not always the same thing, but often). Sure, men don't wear togas or lecture in the forum anymore, but women are importantly often still positioned as being *outside* of power. When we "break the glass ceiling" (or fall off the glass cliff or bump into a glass wall), for example, there's an assumption that we were in one place and had to move to another to have power; it was never *inherently* available to us. As author and social commentator Elise Loehnen notes, "Women are expected to 'know their place'—firmly outside, yet supporting circles of power—and abide by it."

HOW PEOPLE-PLEASING FLOWS INTO OUR COMMUNICATION

A lot of women I know describe themselves somewhat disparagingly as "people pleasers." As in, they give a long exhale and sigh, "Ugh, I'm such a people pleaser!" as if this choice is a fait accompli that can never be undone. People-pleasing is such a loaded term to me because at its core, it sounds like something you would *like* to do—please the people around you. In fact, it almost sounds definitionally true: few would argue that they want the opposite—to be a *people dis-pleaser* sounds miserable and mean.

So, what does it mean to be a people pleaser when it comes to communicating at work, and how can we know when we find ourselves in a people-pleasing pattern? Pleasing other people is exactly that: a choice. Sure, there are some rewards that come with that choice, but there is also an enormous toll it can take on our health, sanity, and career.

People-pleasing means going along with someone else's agenda or ask. It's about saying yes. Yes to accepting more childcare and household duties, yes to caring for elderly members of our family, yes to taking on another thankless task in the office that no one will see or give you credit for. Or even yes to something that's objectively quite pleasant—but you still don't want to do it. You might have said yes to something and then realized later that, in fact, you didn't want to do it, go there, or see that person at all. We say yes because it's become a signifier for likeability. Women who say yes in these contexts are helpful, amenable good girls. And women who say no are working against us.

To illustrate, I want to tell you about a time many years ago, when I first moved to San Francisco and I met a group of incredible women. I distinctly remember hoping we could become friends and imagining my life with a group like them by my side. A few weeks later, one of them—Claire—sent out an invitation to the group for a concert and dinner afterward. Success! My dream was happening! The only downside was the performance was a long opera, which was by far not my favorite genre of performance. I was torn. I really wanted to spend time to get to know this group more, but I knew I *really* didn't want to go to the opera. I replied to the thread that I wasn't much of an opera buff and asked if they would mind if I met them all for the dinner afterward, as I'd love to see them. The group of friends—who I still adore to this day, by the way—often jokingly still refer to the Opera Incident. They tell me they all would have preferred to go only to the dinner, too, but felt compelled to accept the invitation to join for the whole night, for fear of being rude or unlikeable.

Unfortunately, this idea of acquiescence is deep-seated with many women: *I'd better not be unlikeable, I'd better not make him angry, I'd better just go along with it.* Or even, *I'd better say yes to the opera, even though I hate opera.* While that impulse might in some circumstances come from self-protection against violence or unpredictability, some of it comes from adhering to anachronistic but pervasive ideas of being a "good girl": compliant and docile. "No means no" is something we were all taught, yet we oftentimes find ourselves offering a maybe or a soft yes—and then regretting it later.

Sitting somewhat uncomfortably near the idea of people-pleasing is a phrase I keep hearing, which is " 'No' is a full sentence." While a super important message for bodily autonomy and consent, this simply does not work at work. It rarely feels appropriate to respond, say, to a manager's ask by just saying no. It's plain negligent to believe this sort of thinking helps prepare people for saying no in the workplace.

So, how do we push back clearly and kindly? You could try a number of actual full sentences that might help you hold boundaries but also get you out of doing something, such as the following:

"Thanks so much for thinking of me. Normally I'd love to, but I'm at capacity at the moment—I'll let you know if anything changes."

This works for a freelancer or someone who can take on work on their own schedule.

"This sounds interesting. Could you let me know how you'd like me to prioritize my current work streams to fit this in?"

This could work for someone with a direct manager to remind them of current workload demands.

"I love that idea. Unfortunately, I don't have bandwidth to give it the time it deserves."

This could work for a cross-functional request that you don't want to take on (or even organizing a cake in the office, sigh).

The True Yes

A gentle way of unlearning some of the people-pleasing likeability you might experience is to reframe your energy around focusing on the true yes. By this I mean that it's helpful to start to pay attention to what is deeply worth saying yes to. If we're already acculturated to saying yes, then let's make it easy and work out what the true yeses are versus the socially acceptable ones we might regret later. When do you want to say yes? When do you find yourself thinking, *I want to be in that person's orbit. I could learn so much from this experience. I connect with and feel seen by them. I genuinely want to give my time, energy, or money in this way.*

Sometimes, thinking about what makes you give something a wholehearted yes can help you decide where to spend your energy and resources, and everything else, by default, is a no. For me, I'm often quick to say no. (I know, it's unusual for a woman, but here we are.) I'm usually dubious about most invitations to things, wondering what's in it for the other person and strongly preferring to protect my time and energy by not overcommitting to things. I suspect this came from a late-teenage period of chronic ill health, which meant I was somewhat forced to accept my limitations at the time and diligently watch for overexertion.

Since then, and with my health enormously improved, I still think about what sort of effort and energy I want to give to various asks—and I don't always say yes to everything at all. I've had to unlearn my fast no responses and meet the question with curiosity. Instead, I'll ask, "Who's coming? What will it be like? What do you foresee my role being?" This approach gives me time to understand the opportunity and time to honestly let my brain unclench and work out what I want my true yes to look like. Now I can say with almost 99 percent accuracy that I take meetings only with people I truly want to meet, I speak only where I truly want to be present, and I go only to places I really want to visit.

My friend Ros questioned me about this recently. She mentioned in passing that she had written an op-ed, and I asked her to send me the link so I could read it. She replied, "Oh, you're just saying that to be nice. You don't have to read it." No, I explained, if I'm asking, I really want to read it. Otherwise, I would have just said, "Oh, that's wonderful!" and moved the conversation on. This is not because I don't care about people who write or create things around me at all—I do—but I know also that I'd rather be honest about my capacity in a given moment. To me, it's a gloriously liberating feeling.

These cultural yeses, many of them subconscious or largely unquestioned, unsurprisingly filter down into how we communicate with others. Many of my clients still struggle with saying no or pushing back on requests. They know all the data just like you do. They know they should say no, and yet the struggle persists. So it's helpful to think about how to carve out practical ways of thinking through our needs and working through which tools might be most useful in finding that sense of peace within ourselves and the way we communicate that self to others.

> **Try this:** The next time you're faced with a decision, before you answer, think of what your true yes might look like. Can you make a suggestion that will help get you closer to what you'd actually like to accept? Take time to think through what exactly you'd like to give (or not give).

Calling Out the Success of Others Can Reinforce Your Own Authority

Of course, one of the lovely ways you can channel your agree-ableness and also look supremely self-assured in the moment is—wait for it—to call out the success of others around you. I know—implausible, right? But here's the insight I wish I had known at the beginning of my career: telling other women they're great and calling out their success counterintuitively works to reinforce your *own* power and authority. If you can generously and confidently give credit to someone else, it doesn't look like you are nervous about your own work or about their star eclipsing yours. Rather, it looks like you have everything under control, and you're just happy to give a friendly shout-out. In other words, there's no quicker way to show that you have faith in your own work than to calmly and genuinely call out someone else's win.

When I worked at Google, we were told that the company hired only 0.2 percent of people who applied for jobs there. Such a statistic could have created a culture of fear and sharp elbows, but most of the time it engendered a strong sense of collegiality and camaraderie. It was as if we all knew we had passed through the eye of a needle to get there, so we should automatically trust one another and get along. Some of my closest friends today are from that time in my career, and I left the company more than ten years ago. So many of those connections were formed in part, I think, because we were gener-ous and kind to one another when we were colleagues—we had each other's backs, often in times of great pressure or crisis.

While there may be a finite number of chances to be promoted or for career development where you work, there is never a shortage of opportunities to show off your own comfort level. If you can help engender a culture—even if in only your team—in which you are comfortable championing each other, it can change the way you show up for one another. A kind and powerful way to step out of your own way and let those around you shine is by saying something like, "You did a great job in that meeting" or "Min really killed it in that presentation, didn't she?"

And of course, it's just delightful for the colleague who feels your support. They will remember it and perhaps throw the light back on you at some time in the future. Many of my Google colleagues have since hired me back to coach at subsequent companies they've worked at, and it has been a humbling and beautiful thing to work again with people I love. I am certain none of us cheered one another on with any expectation of reciprocity; we just existed in a culture of championing one another's work.

Another, more public way to call out the success of others is to use what has come to be known as "amplification," famously popularized by President Obama in the White House, where two-thirds of his top aides were men when he first took office. Amplification is the idea that you can proactively call out someone's idea and attribute it to them if you see they've been spoken over or not credited for something they have said earlier. Specifically, "When a woman made a key point, other women would repeat it, giving credit to its author. This forced the men in the room to recognize the contribution—and denied them the chance to claim the idea as their own." If you find yourself able to notice an opportunity for amplification, you can say something like, "To Chetna's point earlier . . ." or "Just to reiterate what Florence was saying . . ." or "Erika—I'm not sure you had finished your idea earlier—do you want to pick that back up?" Amplification in these instances can let people actually be heard in a room. But you can also apply amplification to their success, as in, "I just want to shout out Josie's amazing job last week" or "Sarah did incredible work on that event on Monday"—bringing their achievement, which maybe had gone unnoticed, to the attention of the broader team.

While saying words of encouragement is helpful to others, part of feeling valued in a workplace is knowing that people are listening to you, so giving someone the space to speak when they might not feel able to take it for themselves is a true gift. Now I write this not to suggest that you should rely on or wait for others to amplify your words (although if they do, wonderful!) but so you can take opportunities to do this for other less senior folks around you. In turn, it may change the opinions of others who had previously dismissed the younger or less senior women in the room, and it may change their opinion of you, too. One note: it absolutely, 100 percent has to be a genuine endorsement of them and their work. People can smell sycophancy or ulterior motives a mile away, so if it's not genuine, it's better to say nothing at all.

> **Try this:** If there's someone around you, especially a woman or someone more junior to you, who has been doing great work, you might want to find an opportunity to call this out to a broader audience.

Take an Inventory of Your Assets That Turn Your Power Up (or Down)

I suspect one of the reasons you might be reading this book is because you, too, feel a tug in either direction of the powerful/ likeable binary. Maybe the quest for agreeableness hinders you, or maybe you've overcorrected and find yourself overly aggressive—whatever the situation, perhaps it's best summed up as "I just don't feel like myself"—a sentiment I've experienced before. I want to invite you to do an exercise with me. I'm a big believer in understanding our baselines before making any changes, and when it comes to communication, it's helpful to take an inventory of where you are right now.

When working with my clients, one of the first asks I have for them is to cast their minds to a time when they felt that their power was turned up, and you and I can do this together, too. What are the conditions that occur at work in which you feel in full flight, alive with possibility, and positive about your contributions? As you think about these moments, notice what is true in your body, how your voice sounds, and what room you're in. Consider how you're holding your breath, your voice, and your feet. What's true of this interaction? Are you alone or in a group? What other things are true about your surroundings?

On the other hand, what conditions occur for you when your power is down, when you might feel challenged, anxious, or frustrated? When you felt like you were made to feel small or when your message just didn't land the way you intended it to? Everyone will have different circumstances or preferences on their lists; there is not a right answer here. Determining what's on your personal list is a good way to begin to understand more fully what is energizing you at work and what might be taking a toll on your energy and presence, too.

For instance, property analyst Priyanka says when her boss delays a one-on-one meeting, she feels disregarded and overlooked, even when she knows it will happen eventually. "I know we're all busy, but it just feels like she doesn't respect my time or see my value, especially when she moves it at the last minute." Priyanka tells me her boss's actions can change the way she feels about her whole day.

On the other side of the energy curve is Annika, a junior lawyer, who says she feels "superhuman" when she can lead meetings and already knows all the participants well. She says, "There's something about having trust in the room before I even begin that makes me relax into what I'm talking about. I don't have to worry about making a first impression, which for me is the worst."

> **Try this:** You can start by taking an inventory of your last week. What were the moments in which you felt like your power was up high, like you were unstoppable, free, and in control? And conversely, what were the moments in which you felt stymied or frustrated by yourself or external conditions?

On the next page are some frequent examples I see on these lists when I coach leaders. They might give you some ideas when it comes to compiling your own list. I don't expect everything in these lists to resonate with you, and, in fact, some directly contradict others. I'm listing them to spark inspiration, rather than to exactly describe your situation.

My power is turned up high when . . .

I'm in rooms where I'm not the only woman.

I feel prepared.

I have the trust and respect of those around me.

My creativity is embraced.

My team can be productive together.

I have relevant expertise.

I'm in smaller, more intimate groups.

I can be empathetic and connected.

I feel like the conversation flows organically and isn't awkward.

My appearance is put together, and I'm not tired or disorganized.

There is a shared purpose.

I'm in a familiar space.

I'm in the spotlight in front of lots of people onstage.

I know I'm not being judged.

I've been able to do some exercise or listen to some music beforehand.

My power is turned down low when . . .

I hear unfamiliar terminology.

I am underskilled compared to others in the room.

There is time wasting and unnecessary chatter.

I feel everyone else is an expert and I'm not.

I'm stressed or tired.

I have to push back on things, especially a second or third time.

I know I have to follow up on the issue later.

I am the only woman present.

I am thrown under the bus (or someone else is).

I know my opinion isn't welcomed.

I don't feel invited to participate.

I am spoken over or not listened to.

I feel judged and uncertain.

I'm in an unfamiliar and uncomfortable location.

The stakes are high, which leads to feelings of pressure.

I'm working on a project that doesn't speak to my soul.

When it comes to writing your own list, you might also include certain sensory things, such as intense lighting, loud noises, uncomfortable chairs, or chilly rooms. These physical considerations can definitely contribute to you feeling powerful— or not—and we'll cover some of these in chapter 3 when we examine the body and speaking.

One of the things that these lists tell us is that the exact same situation can be liberating for some and deeply terrifying for others, as in "Hooray, I'm the only woman onstage!" or "Oh no, I'm the only woman onstage!" And that's the beauty of thinking about our own strengths and challenges. We are all as different in these ways as we are humans, so there is very much not a right or wrong list—it's just important that your list about yourself feels accurate to you.

Having a list like this is the first step toward being able to create or mitigate those conditions more regularly and even intentionally seeking out workplaces where we might feel our most powerful more often. One important note: when I do this exercise with groups of women, I often get a huge list of things that turn our power down, and it's invariably longer than the power-up list. Be gentle on yourself with these and aim for them to have an equal number, even if the power-up list takes you a bit longer to feel your way into.

Interestingly, these lists often shift as we change jobs or teams or simply grow in our careers. What challenged me in my mid-twenties is not the same as what challenges me now, and if you notice this too, that's great. We develop more muscles in different groups when we exercise them, so areas of growth are a result of working on that area.

> **Try this:** Write the top three scenarios from each list in a note on your phone or notebook and keep an eye out for when you notice these instances happening for you. Are there any other details you would like to add? We'll come back to these over the course of the book.

COMMUNICATIVE SELF-CARE

If you're at all online today, you've likely been aggressively pitched intelligent vitamins, red-light masks, fancy yoga pants, engineered lip balms, and more. It's clear that the self-care economy is alive and thriving. And don't get me wrong, I love panic-buying a good face mask as much as the next person. But one of the reasons I think the self-care movement has gained such easy traction is that self-care is seen as the antidote to the rampant culture of people-pleasing that we women are so often co-opted into.

If we really want to take care of ourselves, it's worth imagining what true self-care looks like when it comes to communication. How can we turn the insistent cultural drumbeat of "look after yourself" to the workplace, and how does it relate to our power and likeability? How can we remove some of the pressure we feel when it comes to being hyperagreeable and communicating more of our true selves? In short, what does *communicative* self-care look like, and how do we get there as powerfully likeable women operators and individuals?

Two major ideas for communicative self-care have to do with boundaries. Again, I think we hear a lot about boundaries in the culture, but I see fewer, more directly actionable ideas about what they mean in practice at work. So here I will talk through two very actionable self-care practices you can incorporate in the office as a counter to the pressure to be agreeable all the time.

Use Non-Goals as a Way to Lower Your Self-Expectations

The first idea, as we gently ease into powerful likeability, is to think about "non-goals." When I first heard the term in my early years in tech, I genuinely thought that I had misheard the speaker or perhaps that it was a joke. You mean, a to-don't list?! Why would you list out a non-goal? I learned it's actually a term commonly used in product management to mean a goal or requirement that is deliberately excluded from an upcoming project. What I love about this definition is the explicit component: you call out the non-goal as an overt thing so that everyone else can see and collectively agree *not* to do that thing. The very act of calling it out helps everyone to understand where they should be putting their energy, that is, specifically *not* toward a non-goal.

I've adopted non-goals like a long-lost cousin. I think about them all the time and use them in work (and non-work) scenarios to help define my parameters and to lessen the expectations I put on myself—and largely also because I think *non-goal* is a funny term. For instance, every week when writing out a to-do list for work and life, I have a non-goal column: it's usually for things that I know need to happen eventually (get in touch with a work contact, buy a new household appliance, wash the car), but they'll be named non-goals that week specifically to remind myself I have chosen not to prioritize them in a busy time. For me, this system helps alleviate any guilt or self-flagellation about not tackling them. It alleviates the pressure or mental gymnastics I'd do every time I thought about those tasks. Do I still have to do them at some stage? Yes, but knowing when I'm not doing them is almost as important.

Overtly talking about non-goals can be useful, neutral, and deeply clear language to use when we're communicating with others. When you're talking through what you will and won't undertake in, say, a group project, it's helpful to have a set of phrases or safe words that help you direct the conversation where you need it to go, and *non-goals* can be one of them. It's definitive and helpful to create the scope of the things you *are* working on and keep the focus there. Communications-wise, it can be a convenient phrase that helps you establish your swim lane and contribution as distinct from others on the project, and what you will (and won't) be collaborating on together. For instance, "I'm excited to jump in on this project—let's work through the goals and non-goals so we're all aligned as to how this next week will play out" is a proactive, clear, and helpful thing to say, and few people will resist your effort to bring more clarity to a project. In fact, many of my clients who have been self-confessed people pleasers find a lot of solace in the use of "non-goals." The clarity they invoke helps them decide what they want to spend time on and bring otherwise murky agreements ("No one said anything about organizing caterers for the event, so I guess I will?") to the fore, because you can point them out and allocate or delegate accordingly. Or plain just decide not to do them at all.

> **Try this:** What might be a non-goal worth calling out on a project you're currently working on? Who might benefit from you being overt about it?

Take Time: It's Not the Rush You Think It Is

The second foundational idea for communicative self-care is to take time. We will talk a lot about why we don't like to take up space and time in chapter 3, but for now I want to talk literally about taking longer than you might have otherwise.

After I started my communications strategy firm, I was offered an unusual job. Crisis communications isn't my favorite thing—it's where you have to assist a company in crisis to navigate their way out of it, helping to craft statements and strategy. I'm good at it, but I hate it—I find it stressful, emotional, and an adrenaline roller coaster. There are people who love exactly those parts of the work, and I'm so thankful they thrive in that environment. But this was in the early days of the business, when I irrationally believed if I didn't say yes to a client, I might never get another. (Don't ever think this. It just isn't true.)

Suffice to say, despite my hesitations, I said yes to the project, which, as discovered when I dug into the company, seemed to be covering up not only some unethical practices but maybe even some illegal ones, too. At 5:30 A.M. the next day—about twelve hours after I had initially accepted the work, I sent the founder a text saying I had to speak to him. I told him I couldn't do the engagement, telling him I felt uncomfortable representing the circumstances. Internally, I regretted not trusting my first instinct to say that this type of work wasn't a fit for me.

Time is something we often don't think we are entitled to—likely tied to our sense of wanting to get to a quick, satisfying answer. Say yes, put a bow on it, and move on. But trust the fit and feeling you have. Nothing is too late to change. I felt somewhat foolish for taking an extra day to think about it, as it looked inelegant, but I was anxious and had made a decision that wasn't aligned to my values or wishes. Oftentimes, we actually have a lot more time than we think we do. Maybe it's only an hour or a day, but even that can make a difference.

Taking time is also important to consider if we listen to our true desire underneath the concerns, whatever they may be: status, financial, and social pressures are just some of the many options. This is part of the agreeableness culture that so many of us have internalized. You might want to do more research before accepting an offer, talk with a trusted mentor for a gut check, or simply talk things over with a friend or family member. In the days when my children were very young, sometimes I would purposely try to take more time to reflect, as I found when I was deeply exhausted, I would trust myself a little less to make longer-term, robust decisions. Giving myself time meant that I could fully determine what felt good. Whatever the reason, taking time is a valid (and, I think, underused) approach to learning what you really want and then being able to communicate a full answer.

> **Try this:** Is there a work decision that you have felt rushed on recently? Is the time pressure real (an actual deadline) or perceived (you feel pushed to answer quickly)? Are you able to give yourself more time to decide on something, and would that feel better to you, if you could?

Now that we have a sense of our own baselines, inclinations, and areas we might want to focus on, the next chapter will delve into what happens when we overemphasize being agreeable and subsequently lose opportunity, status, and agency. Situated at the very intersection of power and likeability, it's Imposing Syndrome in action.

"It'll Only Take Two Seconds":

Why Imposing Syndrome Makes Us Play Small (and How to Beat It)

In which we learn who "Just Gina" is, remember to not play small and to take up space, identify that the real problem isn't imposter syndrome but Imposing Syndrome, consider why and when we use caveats (hint: a lot more than we should), and change our framing around being an imposition.

I want to introduce you to Gina, a successful chief financial officer of a large consumer hardware company. Whipsmart and many years into an impressive career, Gina blew me away with her deep thinking and strategic mind but would often relate stories to me in which she minimized herself. If you asked her, "Do you have the expertise for this role, or are you confident in your ability to do this job?" I'm sure she would answer a resounding (and justified) *yes*. But when she would interact with her colleagues, a different story would emerge.

Take this example: she explained that every day she had to call the CEO at noon to walk him through some financial metrics—it was a rough time for the company, and he had asked her for a daily update. Gina would begin the call by saying, "Hi, this will only take a second, it's just Gina." *Just* Gina. Just. Gina. Now, the CEO had *asked her* for a daily update: minimizing herself at the outset wasn't a requisite for that call. It subtly hints at her unimportance and her diminishment when there was no reason to do so. "Only take a second" also undermined the importance of the update itself, so this was a twofer. And what's most fascinating is that in this instance, she *wasn't imposing* on him, but rather she was giving him exactly what he'd asked for—the daily update at noon.

What is this disease, this aversion to taking up space? And it's not only Gina. You've probably seen it. I've done it for sure. It lurks in offices and boardrooms and colleges and doctors' offices. This creeping sense of shrinking down or metaphorically flattening oneself against a wall comes when we're out of our comfort zone. Sometimes it's a discomfort with taking up space. At other times, it's self-deprecation gone awry; we make ourselves small so as not to intimidate, threaten, or upset others. We stay small, obedient, and nice so that we won't hurt anyone (and so that they won't hurt us in the bargain, too).

When we minimize ourselves, we inadvertently declare our lack of importance—or at least that's what it can signal. I work with so many incredible women who unconsciously minimize themselves when they don't need to, as if neatly contorting themselves into a small cabin bag, ready to be stowed away for takeoff. But sometimes the plane just leaves them on the runway, because zipping ourselves up into a tiny space doesn't scream authority or confidence or importance.

Instead, it whispers, *I'm too mortified to share my idea—don't even look at me!* And all I can think when I see these impulses is that there is a lot of room between Dragon Lady and Doormat for a different, powerfully likeable way to show up.

DEATH TO IMPOSTER SYNDROME

I'm sure you're familiar with the term *imposter syndrome* when it comes to assuming various roles and responsibilities. It's the idea that one might feel like a fraud or doubt one's own self-worth or value in a given situation. First described by psychologists Pauline Rose Clance and Suzanne Imes in the late 1970s, imposter syndrome (or imposter phenomenon, as they initially named it) sometimes shows up in high achievers who are unable to internalize and accept their success. They ask themselves, "Do I have the right expertise, experience, age, gender, outfit [etc.] so that I won't be 'found out' by someone that I shouldn't be here?"

The feeling that we're not ready or experienced enough to be on a certain level of success or prestige can cause a lot of grief as we run through that slide deck for the hundredth time in preparation or—with more serious consequences—avoid putting ourselves up for promotion or taking on a new role, whether it's CEO or a junior account executive. As Ruchika Tulshyan and Jodi-Ann Burey argue in an article titled "Stop Telling Women They Have Imposter Syndrome," imposter syndrome also dangerously reframes a systemic workplace issue as individual responsibility. They write, "Imposter syndrome directs our view toward fixing women at work instead of fixing the places where women work."

My own view of imposter syndrome is simple: I choose not to believe in it. Imposters are trying to deceive others or impersonate somebody else. A true imposter is *intending* to be fraudulent. Instead, most of the time I hear two scenarios in which people tell me they experience imposter syndrome.

The first is a feeling of discomfort: "I don't feel comfortable at work—I'm an imposter." No, the work environment in which you find yourself is at best unwelcoming and at worst hostile and toxic. Assess whether you will be able to get more comfortable over time, or whether you should get out. This isn't being an imposter; it's rightly sensing threat or discomfort and being appropriately vigilant.

The second instance in which women relate their experience of imposter syndrome is when they tell me, "I haven't yet done The Thing—I'm an imposter!" No, you're a beautiful newborn chick ready to learn and grow. Don't confuse inexperience with imposter syndrome: that's a totally different and natural beast. We are all doing things all the time that are new and sometimes scary. On occasion, we don't know how to chart the path ahead of us, but again, this isn't imposter syndrome, it's just *learning*.

Pathologizing either discomfort or inexperience (turning it into a "syndrome") can make us feel even more stuck and more alone. I find myself reflecting that for every woman who tells me she has imposter syndrome, I meet three men who have never considered it as a possibility. The only thing wrong with imposter syndrome is that all the wrong people have it.

> **Try this:** The next time you hear imposter syndrome mentioned or feel as if you have it yourself, consider whether you are actually feeling a lack of experience instead. Reminding yourself that we all started from nowhere is important to knowing you can give yourself time and grace to learn.

IMPOSING SYNDROME AND WHAT IT MEANS FOR US

I also think something far more insidious beyond imposter syndrome is happening in the corporate context for women. And that's the recurring default to minimizing deference in the face of perceived power. I call this *Imposing Syndrome*: when our self-awareness of our own likeability limits our ability to exercise power or get what we want. Imposing Syndrome is the disease of playing small and not taking up space, and it often shows itself when we need to share an opinion, ask a question, take up someone's time, or even share our own accomplishments. And this is unsurprising, given a history of women being patronized, silenced, intimidated, belittled, and more. We fear being an imposition, and accordingly, we origami ourselves into the smallest possible size. We hope that if we're good enough, thin enough, small enough, fast enough, cute enough, maybe *that* will be the path to success. Maybe—we think—*not* imposing is the secret to maintaining our likeability: if we tread softly forever, no one will be put out or upset by our asks. Maybe, just maybe, if we silently submit and acquiesce and execute and keep our heads down, no one will even notice we're here.

Making an imposition is an enormous threat to traditional

notions of likeability. We're imposing ourselves or our needs on someone else, who may resist the ask or, worse, make us feel bad or guilty for having made it in the first place. This is not, we think, the way we can be at our most amenable and amiable. In a culture where much of the caring work is done by women (think primary parents or caring for aging parents), we often unconsciously embody and fetishize the notion that it is we women who remove the problems for others. We *solve* problems; we don't *make* them.

Incidentally, in a culture where executive assistants have traditionally overwhelmingly been female and even assistant AI voices today are by default voiced by an AI woman (think Siri, Alexa, and Google), it's unsurprising that there's a disconnect when a woman's voice *makes* a request or order, rather than receives one. We're literally training a generation of people to think of women in supporting roles rather than main roles. Indeed, according to a UNESCO report on the gendered biases in artificial intelligence, "Almost all voice assistants are given female names and voices and express a 'personality' that is engineered to be uniformly subservient."

The expectation that we should receive and act on inbound requests (but not make any ourselves) is obviously infuriating but underlies much of the tension when it comes to communicating our own needs. If we perceive making an ask as an imposition, it changes the way in which we take ownership of our work and contributions. It changes the help we receive and the perceived value of what we're working on, and it contributes to a reluctance to engage with those around us.

The idea that women fix problems and don't make more of them is also well in keeping with research pointing to women

taking on more "non-promotable work" in the workplace, defined as "the kind that is important to organizational func-
tioning, but unlikely to be rewarded or even recognized." You
know, that's organizing the cake and card for someone's birth-
day, putting up the holiday decorations, ordering food for the
off-site meeting, or any of a hundred other tasks that are often
overlooked but contribute to the enjoyment of the team. Of
course, there's also non-promotable work in family life, too:
completing thankless but obligation-heavy tasks like bringing a meal to a family gathering, cleaning up afterward, or
organizing logistics for a vacation is rarely rewarded or appre-
ciated in any meaningful way, yet often these concerns are left
to the domain of women to fix, solve, and organize.

In short, Imposing Syndrome can be dangerous precisely
because it wears many outfits, and we encounter it in such different ways. In this chapter, I explore several scenarios in
which we are faced with Imposing Syndrome and explain why
and how we can get more value from those interactions. Overcoming decades of training isn't easy, but we can start with
some basics to help us create a new mode through which to
show up—not minimized or squashed but just as we are.

Imposing Syndrome Scenario 1: Making Ourselves and Our Asks Small

Why do we squash ourselves into impossible time expectations? "I'll just take a second!" "It won't take long!" "I'll pop
by your desk!" or "Would you have just two minutes?" we say
brightly as we insist—nay, promise—that we will not be a
burden on anyone. It's only a sec! As my deeply literal nine-

year-old often reminds me, "Mum, nothing *actually* takes one second!"

Recently, I was on a call with a travel agent who was doing some itinerary planning for me, and we had agreed on a hard stop at 10:30 A.M. At 10:31 A.M., I had to gently interrupt her to remind her that I had to go but that we'd catch up the next day. It wasn't a big deal. I wasn't upset in any way, but she must have been embarrassed by not noticing the time, as she sent a follow-up text message in which she apologized for "quacking on." She had been explaining something technical and demonstrating excellent expertise; there was absolutely no *quacking* (and could you ever imagine a man using that verb?). I was sad to think that she would diminish herself and her value with a comment like that. Even if said as a joke, it felt like an unfair self-administered uppercut, and I wasn't going to stand for it!

Critically, it's helpful to think about what your minimizing might be costing you. Oftentimes, we soften and soothe to take the edge off, often demoting our abilities and capabilities in doing so. I'm going to make a radical suggestion: there's a big difference between a request or update and an *imposition*. It's okay that your update might take time; it's likely to be a reasonable query that needs attention or an issue with which you need help. That's literally the job of those around you to help you navigate—there is no need to kowtow with shame when asking.

Of course, the elephant in the room is that the wish to make ourselves small carries an echo of weight-loss language. It's not a long bow to draw to suggest that there is a connection between the industrial weight-loss machine insisting that there should be less of us and women internalizing the message to *be* less, to take up less space, less time, less energy, and fewer resources. To be clear, I'm not advocating a position here on the ideal weight or BMI, but I am pointing out that in a diet-obsessed, image-obsessed culture, it's extra sad that we extend minimization, which can cause all sorts of disordered eating, and restrictive, controlling rules to our very presence in the world. Consider the fact that it's entirely reasonable to take time and space to say what you've come to say.

I see minimization happen in other interesting ways, too. For instance, nice, considerate people who think about others often run into the problem at work that they don't want to be perceived as "stepping on other people's toes." And yes, I most commonly hear this from women. Stepping on someone else's toes is literally the fear of stepping outside or beyond your small circle of influence. It's scary because it implies overreach and spatial imposition. (And recall that glass ceiling, glass cliff, and glass wall—we're already hyperaware of our feminine "overreach.")

You might want to run a project that overlaps with someone else's areas of expertise or interest and fear the protectiveness or backlash that might ensue. A straightforward approach here is just to bring up the idea with them directly: "I'm energized by this idea of octopus habitat research, which I know you're deep into. I'd love to carve out a project here around individual octopus den design. Does that work for you, or is it something we could collaborate on?"

The projected toes that you fear stepping on in many cases don't actually exist; they're either imagined, or they're just not as sensitive as you predict. Often bringing up the idea lets the other party get a heads-up about your work, and you can both move on. Or maybe even both of you get excited about octopus habitats together! And you can stay in your own space with equilibrium and ease. Chances are if you're asking the question in the first place, it's an excellent indicator that you have communicative intelligence, because you're already wondering how your words or your ask might affect others. There's no reason to become small, as you might miss out on excellent opportunities by doing so.

Making our ideas small or short undermines the idea itself. I'm pretty sure that no one had a groundbreaking, world-shaking epiphany while also exclaiming it would take only "two seconds"—so whatever your idea or question is, it suddenly looks small, too, when you starve it of space and oxygen. This can work to undermine the very thing we're trying to draw attention to or present to others.

> **Try this:** Have you experienced the desire to minimize yourself or make yourself small at work? Take note of when and where this has happened and consider the triggers that make it happen. Be alert to those triggers when they come up next and decide on an alternative approach.

Imposing Syndrome Scenario 2: Caveating Yourself to Avoid Judgment

Imposing Syndrome is also noticeable when we're called on for an opinion. It's true that it's hard to feel powerful in a room that might judge us for a bad idea or poor preparation, so we overcompensate and play small by giving caveats. One of my clients, Aimee, says, "I usually begin with the phrase 'I'm sure you've already thought of this' like a stealthy beginning. I know it's bad, but I do this just so I don't annoy anyone at the table." Giving a caveat like this at the outset is such a fast way to lose credibility or diminish oneself. It's in a very similar genre to other caveats, such as "I'm not an expert, but . . ." or "I'm not an engineer, but . . ." or "This might be wrong, but . . ." Honey, I shrunk the executive.

These are classic Imposing Syndrome flags. When we make these comments, we sense a degree of impending judgment for an opinion or a feeling that our opinion might impose on the group to an unlikeable degree. Maybe we're pushing back against what everyone else thinks or expressing doubt about a plan, so we try to soften it by diminishing ourselves. Or maybe we're just genuinely unsure. Think of it this way: imagine if you went to see a mechanic and asked what was wrong with your smoking car, and they said, "Well, I'm not actually an expert in cars, but it might be, like, a blown gasket? Or the muffler? I'm not sure." It doesn't exactly engender confidence.

The worst part of this element of Imposing Syndrome is that many of the women I meet who say this *actually are* experts in their field. They are credentialed mechanics, to continue the metaphor, signaling that they don't *really* understand cars at all. They literally have degrees or deep experience in the area they're seeking to contribute to—so there is absolutely no need to undermine their own status in this way. And I'd suggest even if you're not Professor Doctor Expert Smarty-Pants, you should just cite the suggestion as what it is: a suggestion. Simple, straight to the point, and clear. And most important, by doing that, you are not falling on an invisible sword for the shame of making a suggestion or a perceived imposition. We must decouple competence from perfection. We're not always going to be right, but that doesn't mean we should never speak at all.

Imposing Syndrome can mess with our internal powerful/ likeable binary because it exists exactly at that pressure point— right at the painful intersection where we want to exert our power, but we also worry about being *that guy*. In these moments, Imposing Syndrome can show up uninvited and ready to party; its insistence is super loud and hard to wrangle with. While it might feel like hedges soften the blow or make it less strident, a caveat or disclaimer hints or warns others that we are on wobbly terrain and, in some deep sense, that we shouldn't be trusted. And I suspect we often give these caveats to seem approachable, humble, and kind. We're leaning in to the likeable side at the expense of having any power in the interaction.

> **Try this:** If caveats are your thing, note where and when you might be giving them. Does it happen with a particular person or in a particular situation? Spend the next week or so noticing if they come up again and decide if they feel appropriate or if you'd like to experiment with changing them.

Imposing Syndrome Scenario 3: Owning Our Accomplishments

Occasionally, I have a hard time telling people about my world ranking in debate, and not just because of the nerd credentials it invokes. A few years ago, I was interviewed for a podcast where the host tried to get me to mention it. I blushed and sort of meandered around the answer, like, "Oh yes, I've debated. To quite a high level." And of course, the real answer is that I won a world championship! When I listened to the interview later, I could almost hear the pretzel shape I had contorted myself into. There was awkwardness and reticence on my part to just say the damn thing. That made me realize I just had to *own* my accomplishment, especially in a forum where I was specifically asked to name what I had accomplished. Did I think I was going to hurt the host's feelings? Offend the listenership? It's just a factual part of my history, much like my place of birth or what my first CD single purchase was (Seal's "Kiss from a Rose," if you must know). Owning it more overtly would have meant that I had the opportunity to share what I know with the credibility that the accomplishment invokes—and also avoided the awkwardness that I created for both of us, too, which would have been a nice bonus.

You might have also run into Imposing Syndrome when it comes to owning your own accomplishments in your day-to-day life, too. I've met so many men who easily tell me they did their masters or PhDs at Harvard—and I've met their female classmates with the exact same credentials who "studied in Boston." Similarly, women often generalize saying they "teach" (when they're the school principal) or were "part of the team" (when they actually ran the group or did most of the work). Yes, this smells like Imposing Syndrome to me, too.

This under-the-radar self-presentation is interestingly related to the phenomenon of the "untitling" of women, where professional women who have a title such as "Doctor" are just referred to by their first names, whereas men are given their honorific. I get it. Sometimes it can be uncomfortable or seem boastful (or honestly, a bit weird) to wander around with your credential, as if you are saying "Behold! I've arrived!" But it remains important to *say the thing* if it comes up. Take the credit that you've worked hard for.

To illustrate this, let's meet one of my clients. Tarsha is the chief of staff at a large tech company. In our conversations, I noticed she would say things like, "The department grew, and I was so proud." Her use of the passive voice (it "grew"—all by itself!) was a pattern that recurred, and when I asked her about what had actually happened, she explained that under her leadership, she had redesigned the whole organization, increased the staff, managed a new budget, and fundamentally changed its purview, too. So . . . it *didn't* grow all by itself. I suggested this rewrite: "During my tenure, I grew the organization by 50 percent and increased staff and budget such that we were able to expand our mandate significantly." I asked Tarsha how that felt. She beamed; the relief was extremely evident on her face. It was a massive difference, and I could see the pride when she framed her contribution in this way. Speaking about your accomplishments truthfully is a way to own them *as yours*. They become a part of your narrative, and the more matter-of-fact you can be, the easier it is to say over time. And damn, a lot more impressive, too.

Here's one of the main reasons why I think we're tentative about calling out our own accomplishments. You've probably all had the experience of being around someone who tells you multiple times in the same conversation that they went to

Oxford or about that time they interned in Davos. And you think to yourself, *We get it! You went to Davos!* It seems like, in these situations, there is no real reason for them to tell you this information other than to brag or to impress, and if you're anything like me, it becomes burned on your brain never to name-drop unnecessary bona fides like this. And I'd agree that *throwing* around your accomplishments for no reason is probably not the quickest route to making friends or getting the respect of those around you.

But think about this reframe. What if you were to connect that accomplishment with something for the room? For example, you could say something like, "Many of the women I met at Oxford found the main challenge of being in academia was isolation—could we do a content campaign for our education platform encouraging community in the face of isolation?" Or what if you were to add to your résumé that you spoke six languages—would that be boasting or simply useful information that might open up opportunities for you? This way, you're demonstrating credibility but also swiftly turning to why that experience is *usefully informing your current project.* Coupling your accomplishment and experience with something that helps others is a way to move through any potential awkwardness of the name-drop or the self-consciousness of being able to bring up some relevant experience. If you've done work to get the accomplishment in the first instance, a far smaller step is getting comfortable with telling people about it in a way that feels right to you.

Calling out or naming your accomplishments can also be important to demonstrate your overt value to a team. A friend of mine, Sarah, is an investor at a venture capital firm, and she routinely finds herself in board meetings with men who are her seniors in terms of age and experience. She notes that in those rooms, she "naturally defers to the senior partners" and tells me that "when someone asks a question, I expect another senior man to answer first." To counter this hesitation, she says she chooses to add value "behind the scenes" by making introductions to useful people or texting the CEO practical information. The feedback from the CEO has been positive. He finds Sarah helpful, but no one else in that boardroom necessarily knows she is adding value. When your corporate love language is to be useful, it can be easy to think you're crushing it in Sarah's position; after all, she's providing smart, relevant, and timely help. But our job performance is also often rated on the optics. If no one in the boardroom knows you're adding value, you've found yourself, somewhat ironically, in a nonvaluable position for your own career. Instead, I suggested to Sarah to mention that help in the meeting when an organic opportunity arises. For instance, "Last week I connected Peter, our CEO, with Maria to help on hiring for that data science role—did anything come of that, Peter?" Finding the right moment for this shows the rest of the board that your participation is active, involved, and useful. This is showing your work, rather than hiding it.

> **Try this:** Is there an accomplishment you're reluctant to own? Have you played down your involvement in something? Challenge yourself to take the next natural opportunity and more proactively call it out and see if that feels more accurate and fair.

Imposing Syndrome Scenario 4: Adding "Does That Make Sense?" to the End of Your Perfectly Sensical Ideas

I have an especially negative response when people make a perfectly reasonable argument and then ask, "Does that make sense?" I hear it all the time—in conversations, podcasts, meetings—and I cringe every time. I don't know if I would be able to think of a faster way to undermine your credibility—and this happens at all levels of leadership, from new grads to seasoned executives. It is Imposing Syndrome in neon lights. The intention behind asking this is that the speaker is looking for consensus. They've said something that may be complex or disorganized, and they're asking whether the group is following.

If you're doubting me at this point, I'd like you to try to imagine your most persuasive mental role model make a point and then add, "Does that make sense?" at the end. Sounds weird, right? Not only can "Does that make sense?" make others feel like you've temporarily lost your faculties, but it also doesn't help you feel like you're giving the speech of a lifetime and engender any confidence in your own presence at that moment. Further, it can have the opposite intended effect and work to look patronizing, as in, are you capable of following my complex thought process, you puny-minded plebeian?! And yes, I think this can be a particularly gendered piece of softening language; women often use it to temper a strongly articulated position offered up earlier. While I understand the innate push to soften, we don't need to use minimizing, diminishing language.

Instead of doing that, you can ask, "Is everyone still with me? Does anyone have any questions?" But always take it for granted that you are making sense! Assume that you've made a good point. If someone doesn't understand you, they can always ask to clarify. You are likely the most expert person giving your thoughts on this subject. You've been employed to make sense and to share your credible information, so go for it.

One of the more interesting cases of this sense-making question came up with an incredibly articulate client who was generally precise in her word choices. Kristen is in her early forties and has a storied career in many household-name companies, finally reaching a vice president level with a large team and significant responsibilities. In short, I think she was where she had always hoped to be. But one element of our conversations stood out to me: Kristen would give me a pitch-perfect explanation of her team or a process, and almost as if sensing she was sounding too powerful or knowledgeable, she'd purposely end her sentence with a softening phrase like "if that makes sense" or "I could be wrong." When I pointed out that she'd used crutches like these four or five times in that one meeting, she knowingly said, "Oh, I know. I'm purposely just trying to soften myself so I sound more approachable."

As soon as she said it, she caught herself and immediately realized the implications of this. She explained, "I've been working so hard my whole career to get to this point, and honestly a lot of my success has come from ceding power at strategic moments." We had a fascinating discussion about why and when it's worth ceding that power, and she realized that softening the end of an eminently reasonable sentence or thought this way wasn't something she'd like to continue to do. But how to unlearn such softening tendencies?

I suggested she might want to try something like, "So the

projections for this quarter are four hundred, and the next quarter will be different because of tax reasons, so it'll be five hundred. If you have any questions, just let me know." Or if you are looking to foster collaboration, which is often what "Does that make sense?" is trying to do, you could say, "I'd love to open this discussion to the room and hear some other perspectives here."

I thought long and hard about including my objection to "Does that make sense?" in this book. Was it just a pet peeve of mine and mine alone? My coaching philosophy has always been to point out where and why something is having an effect, and of course, it's up to you to decide whether you're persuaded by my argument or not. So keep using it if you don't feel like this phrase diminishes your presence. But if you feel like it's an unnecessary softener and something you might want to experiment with getting rid of, I'd be interested to hear if you feel your authority changes in so doing.

Does that make sense?

> **Try this:** The framing language around your message can accidentally undermine the statement itself. Consider if you use any modifying end statements and whether you'd like to omit them or change them to something else. See if this feels different or more authoritative to you when you do so.

PUSHING BACK ON IMPOSING SYNDROME

Instead of falling prey to Imposing Syndrome in its many guises, how could we reimagine a powerfully likeable way to respond in these moments? Well, your idea is worth it, and so are you. And that same idea will be negatively perceived (and maybe you will, too) when it is squashed up and folded a hundred different ways. Let's look at three different actionable ways you can avoid Imposing Syndrome at work.

Stop Paying Attention to "How Things Are Usually Done"

I am a little embarrassed to say this, but I initially learned to avoid Imposing Syndrome by accident. I wish I could tell you this was some hard-won strategy, but it had a lot more to do with being Australian and not understanding the corporate American hierarchy. Back when I first immigrated to San Francisco, my role involved me working with a particular arm of the business helmed by a hardcore vice president who literally had his old *Top Gun* navy helmet in the corner of his office and lived for CrossFit. (You can probably tell how much we had in common, already.) While I was trying to get up to speed with the team and all the stakeholders, I figured it was only natural to have a regular meeting with this vice president to understand firsthand his preferences and goals for the team. I did not understand the hierarchy in place, which usually would have dictated that he have only a few recurring one-on-one meetings with his peers, so I went to his admin and asked for a recurring meeting to be placed on his calendar. I didn't even know enough to feel the bite of Imposing Syndrome—I was just trying to get my head around a lot of new things all at once.

I started meeting with him regularly to understand how his section of the business was working and what he needed. It wasn't long before I figured out that none of my peers were having one-on-one meetings with him. When they realized I was having them, they became almost deferential to me—and deeply confused. *"You* have a one-on-one with Tom?" was a question I heard a lot (and I couldn't help but think, *Why don't you?*). From that point on, they started treating me as more senior than I was. From my perspective, I had done the sensible thing. I had gotten direct access to the person I needed to help inform the work I was doing. And he didn't cancel these meetings, which I guess meant he saw value in downloading the latest information to me, too.

Unwittingly I had asserted a powerful move. By asking for the recurring meeting, I had shown that I was comfortable with directly talking to one of the most senior people in the organization at that time, and the optics of that move helped shape the way people perceived my role. It would have been equally easy for me to have sat at my desk and tried to intuit his wishes or read meaning into his company-wide presentations, but I wouldn't have been able to create the strategy I did without those firsthand interactions with him.

I was so delighted by this accidental leadership leap of mine that it made me reflect. If I hadn't had those meetings, I don't think I would or could have executed my role as well as I did. And if I had truly known what a big deal these meetings really were, I might never have initiated them in the first instance—what a huge lost opportunity that would have been!

My avoidance of Imposing Syndrome here happened because I had a mindset of "I have to learn what I need in this role." I got out of my own head, even if accidentally, and it was the best thing I could have done for my work and my team.

Don't be too concerned about what others might think your role looks like or how it's been done before. There's every chance your move might not work—maybe the vice president doesn't accept your meeting invite, for instance—but there's also every chance it will.

Try this: Consider what could happen if you didn't pay much mind to how things are usually run at work and what might really help you in your role if you had the ability to just make it happen. What might you do differently? How might you reframe certain situations or interactions?

Watch Your Language and Take Up Space

A useful reframing of your own language can be key. It might feel like you're only toying at the edges, but changing the way you speak about your own work can be powerful. Think about normal everyday moments when Imposing Syndrome might be creeping up on you. For instance, instead of stopping by someone's desk or texting with an ask that "will only take two seconds," consider booking some time with them more formally. Like this: "I've invited us to a thirty-minute meeting next week to talk through those numbers—would love your perspective" or "I've been thinking a lot about the tension between X and Y. Is that something we could consider embedding moving forward?"

This way, you're giving the idea (and, by inference, yourself) time and space, without making you or your idea small. If you're not yet convinced, consider this consequence: if we do ask for two seconds, we are then liable to feel rushed so that what comes out is not an orderly idea or concern but a hurried babble running against the clock. And whoever we're talking to actually *will* get restless if we do, in fact, take an otherwise reasonable five minutes. So, it's no good for either side of the conversation and likely doesn't set you up to be your most persuasive self, either.

The misguided intention to save time or space means that we also end up minimizing ourselves in the process of not imposing ourselves on others. You might remember the viral, meme-worthy moment from a House Committee hearing when Representative Maxine Waters (D-California) interrupted Treasury Secretary Steven Mnuchin with the phrase "reclaiming my time" every time he failed to answer her direct questions. The language comes from the House rules, whereby a congressional member can effectively pause their countdown clock when a witness is filibustering.

Part of why this was so newsworthy is that it was notable that a Black woman held the floor and, facing a Trump administration official, demanded that her time be restored. The reclamation of time is something we can all do, especially in small everyday situations (and not just when broadcast on television). Don't make yourself small. Normal size is great. Take the time and take the space you need.

> **Try this:** Take the space you need to learn what you're looking for. It's no judgment on you to take time and frame your asks accordingly.

Challenge Long-Held Assumptions

A helpful way to break through Imposing Syndrome is to question certain assumptions you or others might have. Whether it's making a request to use their paid leave days or asking for a raise, a common concession I hear is "Kate, I'd never be able to say *that* at work." And I say "concession," because it's usually accompanied by a strong sense of fait accompli—that we have come to believe that nothing will change or make it possible for us to change. For instance, a longtime employee at an insurance company, Megan, tells me that she could never broach the idea of taking on more responsibility with her manager. She said, "He would just hate me asking that" and "I'd be too embarrassed to ask." Megan's assumption is that she will, in fact, always be in her current role, because she always has been.

This is a great example of Imposing Syndrome being felt, viscerally. Sometimes it can feel as if you are frozen and cannot move to enact any change on your own behalf. It's not that the workplace is mandating any one particular way of doing things, but norms have cemented over time, making it feel more difficult to effect change. In Megan's case, her boss never overtly told her not to ask for more responsibility, but Megan just believed that to be true. So, what do you do if you're feeling similarly stuck or pigeonholed by Imposing Syndrome in a case like this? Consider being 1 or 2 percent different each day. Perhaps you start pushing back on certain things or speaking up a little more vocally in meetings. If you're left off a meeting invite, for example, that you would have liked to be in, send that person a short note that you'd like to be included in the next one. Some of my clients tell me, "Oh, but the other product managers don't do X" or "The normal marketing approach would be Y." You might not necessarily conform to the existing role or attitude, and it's helpful to think when or why you might step outside of that—and what doing so might offer you.

Try this: Think about the times you accidentally found yourself in the right place or accidentally doing the useful thing. What about this experience can you take into other areas of your work?

Advocate for Yourself

One of the most notable expressions of Imposing Syndrome is when it comes to asking for a raise or a promotion. I want to call this out specifically here, because it comes up so often in my coaching, and it's so important for us all to be pursuing advancement and more compensation when the time is right for us to do so. The powerful/likeable binary looms large when it comes to our own performance and, specifically, negotiating promotions, and it brings along some familiar tightropes, because the issue relates to money (greedy/generous), having to ask for it (aggressive/polite), and insisting that you have value (arrogant/humble). And of course, few people think, *Excellent! What our world needs is more self-promotion!* Self-promotion at work is tricky for most but, I'd argue, especially tricky for women. It positively reeks of imposition, no? And we know all the research here: women can incur social costs by advocating for themselves too strongly; they'll be seen as less likeable by those around them—including by other women. I once had a female manager literally laugh at me when I asked her whether she would advocate for me to be promoted—I didn't really see what was so funny.

Yet studies also show that women who don't advocate for themselves at all aren't seen as competent leaders. Leadership academics Herminia Ibarra, Robin Ely, and Deborah Kolb note that "accomplished, high-potential women who are evaluated as competent managers often fail the likability test, whereas competence and likability tend to go hand in hand for similarly accomplished men." Add to this the various cultural overlays in which women of color often come from families who taught different cultural codes, like not talking back, deferring to elders, or asking for what you want, and you get a perfect storm.

A study in the *Harvard Business Review* found that people choose their colleagues according to two criteria: likeability and competence. The study suggested that four archetypes of people emerge: the competent jerk (competent but unlikeable), the loveable fool (incompetent but likeable), the lovable star (competent and likeable), and the incompetent jerk (no real explanation needed here). Across a range of different organizations, the answer was the same: everyone wanted to work with the lovable star—and unsurprisingly, no one wanted to work with the incompetent jerk—weird, no? Interestingly for our purposes, the study found that personal feelings were so important that they worked as a "gating factor": if someone is strongly disliked by their colleagues, their competence is almost irrelevant, and people won't want to work with them anyway. By contrast, "if someone is liked, his colleagues will seek out every little bit of competence he has to offer."

So let me tell you a story. I had been working at a big tech company for two years in Sydney, Australia, and then was transferred to another team within the same company in San Francisco. The trouble was, I was up for promotion, but I was suddenly in a team where no one knew my value, and my lovely new boss couldn't speak to my achievements: I knew he liked me well enough, but naturally he wasn't familiar with my Australian work. I felt so downhearted. I knew I deserved the opportunity to be considered in that promotion cycle, but I was afraid he wouldn't know how to advocate for me.

I knew I didn't have it in me to sit him down and tell him how great I was (so mortifying, imposing on people like that!), so instead I wrote up a one-page document with a factual list of my accomplishments in my former role with data and metrics next to each of them. It wasn't bragging, it was just facts—at least, that's what I kept telling myself as I wrote it. I handed it to my new manager and told him, "I understand you won't necessarily know what I've been up to, so here's all the information in one place for the promotion meetings in case that's useful." Then I just let the situation play out. He later told me he took that piece of paper to the promotion committee and used it as a reference to argue and advocate for me, and I got the promotion. Yes, I love him, too.

A helpful way of combating Imposing Syndrome in a raise or promotion conversation can be to frame your accomplishments as facts, not as emotions. If I had told my new manager, "But I deserve this!" or "I'm overdue for this promotion!" (both of these felt true to me at the time, by the way), I'm not sure I would have gotten the same outcome. What I learned from this wasn't that a one-pager will solve all your problems—

if only!—but that most good people will fight for you if you make it easy for them to do so and if you base your argument on facts. Nothing was guaranteed, of course, but think of it from the manager's perspective: if he didn't have any facts at his disposal, I think it would have been easy for him to say, "Ah well, next time for Kate." But he became a fierce advocate for me, and I am still grateful to this day.

Now, this absolutely could have fallen under the Imposing Syndrome banner for me, and I might have sat mute and been passed over. But I was determined to be recognized for the work I had done and that I had believed in. Was this self-promotion? Absolutely—I *literally* wanted to get myself promoted. But it was more about making my accomplishments visible and then standing out of the way.

Finding your allies and making visible the work you're doing is an excellent way to think about answering the question of promotion itself. If you put the focus on the work and not the self, it's no longer about pushing yourself out into the limelight, which might feel cringey to you. Instead, you're simply taking your work out of hiding and letting it speak on your behalf. This takes some of the self-consciousness out of talking about yourself or feeling like you're being self-aggrandizing (and if you don't feel this, more power to you).

In my years of experience as a coach, far fewer women take ownership of their own mandate or accomplishments comfortably; instead, they often wait for an imagined criticism or backlash. When used in the right context, few people can argue with facts. You're not using the fact to ambush others or talk yourself up, you're just being true to the record. Even if it feels strange at first, if you're relaxed when you make the claim, others will probably be guided by your own mood and framing. If you're self-obsessed and affected, it'll come out that way. If you're warm and just reference it casually, it'll be taken in that way, too.

Try this: Think about factual, rational ways to explain your accomplishments and practice using them more. Especially when it comes to conversations about money, stick to the facts, know your worth, and go for it.

As we leave Imposing Syndrome behind us, it leads us nicely to the notion of delving deeper to reimagine the power we have within us, to reconceptualizing our bodies not as small, folded-up, and tentative but as true sites of authority.

THREE

Communicating Power and Authority
Through Our Voices and Physicality

In which we consider how authority lives in our bodies, ponder how our voices can hold power, investigate the perils of our fleshy oval, think about when and if we want to weaponize our smile, and discuss speaking in front of a crowd and presenting the best version of ourselves.

Powerful likeability demands that we find a place where we can both deliver information in a compelling way and feel like we're being ourselves, with no performances. In this chapter, I want to investigate how to amplify our presence and communicate authority through our bodies and our voices. There are as many ways to be authoritative and trusted as there are types of women in the world, and while there isn't a cookie-cutter template when it comes to finding a place of power that feels good to you, there are levers to turn up and down as you journey there.

It may appear that I'm about to be prescriptive about how you should show up. At the outset of this chapter, let me assure you that this is not going to be a chapter about *disciplining* your body or voice. This section will instead address many of the nervous questions I get from clients before a big meeting or presentation they're concerned about. You'll notice in this chapter that there isn't an absolute right or wrong. Rather, I'd like to share some helpful things you might like to know (such as wearing an outfit that can accommodate a microphone—something I annoyingly had to learn by trial and error).

There will be no invocations to deepen your voice, à la convicted fraudster and occasional baritone Elizabeth Holmes, or any recommendations to do power poses in the bathroom before you step on a stage. I would never suggest you do a radical one-eighty and change your fundamental self. Not only do we all have our own strengths, but we also operate in different cultural contexts, and it wouldn't be useful to tell all of you to adopt X or try Y. Further, it's hardly a good start to encourage women or anybody to betray *who they are* and try to embody someone else in the name of being more self-assured.

Instead, I want to encourage us to try to align our actual self with our work self, for the delta between these two should be as small as we can make it. I have long believed that we shouldn't embody an untrue self when we are at work—or anywhere else, for that matter. Sure, we might use corporate jargon like "low-hanging fruit" and "at the end of the day," but fundamentally we should be the same person at work as we are outside of it. The difference you might notice changing at work is your *energy* level, not your personality. When you're speaking on a stage, for instance, you're likely to be more physically animated (bigger smiles, expressions, gesticulations), louder, and generally have a "larger-than-life" presence. When you're in a conference room or on a video call, again, your personality is the same, but it's likely that your mannerisms will be more toned down by comparison. Trying to vary your energy rather than your core personality will likely help you feel more comfortable and happier with how you did than if you try to act like a corporate robot, directly imitating that one person you once saw run a meeting impressively.

But as you dig into the ways in which you can project presence and attract respect, you'll notice that some of the ways we show up are more or less *coded* for authority. So in that vein, I want to start with a framework to understand how we can inhabit more power within our bodies and make our voices strong in a way that feels right for our own unique situation, wherever we might start out.

HOW DOES AUTHORITY SHOW UP IN OUR BODIES?

One of the weird things about communication is that it starts before we even begin to talk. As linguistics professor Deborah Tannen notes, "Communication isn't as simple as saying what you mean. How you say what you mean is crucial, and differs from one person to the next, because using language is learned social behavior: How we talk and listen are deeply influenced by cultural experience." If we accept that we communicate with our whole bodies—our speech, our tone, and our body language—there are actually a lot of levers to consider and play with when it comes to finding a style that fits us well.

Consider that even in the second half of the twentieth century, much of our modern sensibility of performative, communicative authority came from a person we all saw every night in our living rooms: the anchorman. The person delivering the nightly news was usually an older, white, mellifluous gentleman with slow and deliberate movements and speech, and he imparted a sense of calm trustworthiness. Somewhere deep inside us all, we came to equate the slow, low voices of these men with power. They knew what we did not, and we passively received their explanations. These newscasters became early monocultural examples of typical male authority. It's not terribly surprising, then, that a male-dominated workforce would emulate a similar crinkly, slow power—and that women would find it hard to find a place within that system.

HOW CAN OUR VOICES HOLD POWER?

Women's voices are subject to oh-so-many penalties that men's voices are not, so this makes a good place for us to start. As feminist linguist Robin Lakoff points out, "With men, we listen for what they're saying, their point, their assertions. Which is what all of us want others to do when we speak. With women, we tend to listen to how they're talking, the words they use, what they emphasize, whether they smile." This certainly aligns with my own experience. When my words are baseline unremarkable, my voice and face are often commented on—and maybe yours have been, too. Remember that debate coach at the beginning of the book? My voice, rather than my content, was central in her critique, and I had to learn a lot about the power my voice really had.

We need only look to the world of radio and podcasts, where women presenters receive outsized negative feedback pertaining to their voices. Vocal fry, upward inflection—commonly known as "upspeak"—and higher pitch are some of the many reasons listening audiences complain vociferously. The same audiences, revealingly, rarely complain about men's voices. Ira Glass, host of the podcast and radio show *This American Life,* which has been on the air since 1995, notes, "I get criticized for a lot of things in the emails to the show. No one has ever pointed [my vocal fry] out." Of course, all these complaints are barely concealed sexism. There's nothing innately irritating about a woman's voice compared to a man's—it's just different. Instead of changing and performing monotone corporate robotspeak, I want to run through a list of tools when it comes to articulating yourself that you might think about adopting to help boost authority and power in your own words.

Volume

It can be hard to get cut-through in a conversation when a group of men or deeper-voiced people are speaking. Many women forget to project their voices forward or increase their volume, often being spoken over or not heard at all. Now I'm not talking about being willfully ignored; rather I mean in a literal sense that a person isn't heard in a discussion. Increasing our volume can be intimidating, and it may feel like I'm suggesting that you shout. On the contrary, I'm suggesting that you speak at the same volume as your counterparts, or *marginally* louder.

Vocal Projection: Speaking Up, Literally

I'm always reminded of *The Onion* article "Girl Finally Speaking Up Enough For People to Critique Her Speaking Voice" when I talk about speaking up. Hilarity aside, there are a number of practical fixes when it comes to actually being heard. For instance, sometimes, our voices aren't as loud because the way we sit might be squashing our diaphragm. Other times, it's because we're physically uncomfortable, so we end up speaking down into our laps. Or when we're shorter than men and happen to be standing, our words go into their chests and not their ears. If you sit back in your chair (instead of balancing at the front of it, squashing your volume), your voice will be naturally louder and project farther into the room. This body position is not aggressive—it's just *audible*. It's bad enough that our ideas are often not attributed to the right people, but we should be heard when we say them in the first instance.

Vocal Timbre

Importantly, a louder voice is not necessarily a deeper one. Unfortunately, there's a long history of deeper tones being understood as more authoritative. Historian Mary Beard references an ancient Roman treatise stating that a "low-pitched voice indicated mainly courage, [and] a high-pitched voice *cowardice.*" Given this, perhaps I shouldn't be so surprised that I've been asked this question multiple times: "Should I try to lower my voice when I speak?" Apart from thinking that it must feel incredibly uncomfortable and inauthentic to *perform* a different tone, my answer is a resounding (yet fairly medium-sounding) "No!"

Deep vocal timbre is not superior to other tones on the scale; what is being asked here is, should I literally masculinize to gain authority? And this question doesn't come out of nowhere. For instance, research on Hillary Clinton's linguistic style over twenty years showed that over time, her vocal tone grew increasingly masculine. But the more we get used to hearing varied women's voices in public, the more we understand a new standard. You're doing no one—especially future generations of women—a service by imitating masculinity. Plus, it's going to give you a sore throat and won't be the panacea you're looking for. Keep your words clear and audible and at whatever pitch feels normal to you. Your content can have depth, but your voice need not.

> **Try this:** If you've been masking your true voice, consider speaking in the same tone and pitch you do in your ordinary, non-work life. Does this feel more comfortable? More authentic? Find the voice that feels the most like yourself and try using that in work contexts, too, if you weren't already doing so.

Speed

A lot of male CEOs emulate a version of power that echoes the male news anchor, even though they're not necessarily on television. They sit relatively still, don't move their head or hands much, and often speak with unhurried, unflappable ease. This absolutely isn't to say we *want* to present exactly like an old anchorman (*non merci*) but more that if our cultural understanding of authority centers around slow, authoritative, and deliberate speech, we can use that to our advantage.

In fact, what I'd suggest here is that we subconsciously equate a slow deliberateness with *seniority*. If you are a woman who is sometimes prone to speaking like a hurried, harried junior, you'd do especially well to think about holding firm and grounding your voice a little slower, with a sense of deliberateness, an unsaid sense of "yes, this is the plan" and "this is what we're doing."

Showing control over the speed of your voice, for example, is a great way to nod to the authority of the anchorman and give yourself more thinking time to get a point across. Speaking slightly slower is especially helpful when you are asked a hard question. Instead of having to keep the same faster pace you might otherwise have had, you can take your time in answering. In this way, you will not look as if you've been caught off guard, because your pace won't change considerably. Anything that provides you with more cover and time to answer a question or look less conspicuous in that moment can be a game changer. And it's worth noting this is the same advice I give to men: it's universally a sign of authority, outside of gender.

One of my clients, Katelin, is a natural fast-talker. I often call this a "smart person problem"—her brain is fast, and her mouth is just doing its best to catch up. When she is in conversation, I have observed that she will think of five interesting ways to answer a question and will want to say them all as quickly as she can. I could imagine that this can leave an audience a little windswept. They can tell she's smart, but the speed at which she speaks doesn't allow for any of her points to land. She came to me frustrated by the feedback that she needed to slow down: "Why can't everyone just get on board with the fact that I'm a fast-talker?" she asked. Oh, if it were only that easy!

Fast-talking isn't a crime. But it can work against your attempt to lend a sense of profundity to your arguments because you don't let them breathe and you don't let the full impact of what you're saying sink in. Further, if you're a naturally fast talker and you get wrong-footed by a question and take a long pause, it's extra noticeable that you've stopped. It looks out of the ordinary. If you tend to speed up when nervous, you may think, *How might I slow down or be more deliberate in my speech to help make that less obvious?* You might want to generally slow your roll so that if you do stop to answer or consider a question, it will look more like your normal speed and less like a deer in headlights.

Try this: Experiment with changing your pace and see what sort of positive or negative changes you notice. Does it feel good in your body to give yourself some space and time? Do you feel inauthentic, as if you're acting? Find the space—and speed—that feels like you.

Vocal Variance

Another skill you can employ is to control and vary your tone. I acknowledge that this is hard to do because we're usually focused on remembering the content of what we're presenting or trying to regulate emotion or for a ton of other reasons, too. But it is a powerful way to connect and find vocal authority.

When I was deep in the debate world, I knew I could create solid, logical arguments, but they meant little if I couldn't connect and build a rapport with my audience. What do I mean by that? When we listen to someone speak, we often quickly normalize their manner so that any quirks they might have (a repetitive gesture, a verbal crutch, not making eye contact) quickly become unnoticeable. What *is* noticeable, however, is where there is a *variation or change to that baseline*. For instance, if someone speaks too quickly, we'll mentally adjust to that speed (or try to), but we double-take if they stop or slow down. This idea is a helpful one, and we can use it to our own advantage if we're trying to create points of emphasis or memorable snippets by using contrast. We might speak at a normal speed and then stop short to emphasize a major point, which is a great way to verbally underline a point. And you can do that with writing, too. See? Just like this.

Of course, this can also work in the inverse, too, and vocal variance can reveal areas where you're not comfortable at all. Here's a story that places us right in the thick of it with negative vocal variance. One of the executives I coach, Lise, is a brilliant woman at a large tech company. I noticed Lise would present calmly and clearly when she knew the topic, but her tone would change dramatically when she was less sure. She'd switch to upspeak (when you go up? at the end? of every phrase?). Now, a lot has been written on upspeak, and I think the criticism pointed toward it is unfairly gendered. But when upspeak is used in *contrast to* otherwise clear and normally inflected speech, it definitely transmits a significant red flag of tonal *uncertainty*. This is because it's often the case that we go up at the end of a sentence when asking a question, so when you're *not* actually asking a question, but still inflecting upward, you can signify a sense of questioning to whatever you're saying. When Lise hit a point she wasn't sure about, her sudden upward inflection would communicate the loudest—her answers would feel wobbly, tentative, and unsure.

Lise and I worked together to keep her vocal register more consistently like her normal mode even when she got a difficult question. Over time, it became more difficult to *hear* when she was uncertain. It's not to say she always had the right or perfect answer, but her vocal tone held its authority, which gave the impression that she wasn't rattled by the question in the first instance, an incredibly useful skill to have.

Similarly, if you notice you have a different "tell"—playing with your hair, fiddling with something, looking away, or looking down—it is important to be aware of that tell if you're trying to appear certain and authoritative. This doesn't mean that any of these behaviors are bad per se or that you should avoid them at all costs but rather that they're coded a particular way, and it's helpful to know that at the outset. In fact, it's worth calling out that any contrast that feels like a negative one is going to be like a billboard advertising to your audience that you're losing authority or feeling uncertain about what you're saying.

Understanding tone and its impact can also help build rapport and make you a more interesting and memorable person to listen to. Think about how you might speak to a baby versus how you'd speak to your partner or close friend and, then again, to your boss. We are, in fact, used to changing the tone of our voice a lot—even if we've never thought about it intentionally. We change volume, pitch, register, tone, speed, and energy—all are so important in helping us land our message in the right way.

> **Try this:** Pay attention to your voice's speed, volume, and energy—anything that changes it up. Consider how you can vary—or keep consistent—each aspect to create an authoritative connection between you and your audience.

WHAT YOUR FACE IS SAYING (OR THE PERILS OF NOT BEING ABLE TO CONTROL YOUR FLESHY OVAL)

If our voices are places of likeability and power angst, they've got nothing on the body. And specifically the face. Imagine. We carry around this weird, fleshy oval with eyes, a nose, and a mouth, from which we communicate an enormous amount of information to the person or people we're talking with. Our faces give visceral import to what we're saying and help shape the response of the person receiving it. Their fleshy ovals, in turn, communicate the same volume of information back to us.

Faces recur in many different metaphors that relate to coming to knowledge: facing the music, facing the facts, taking things at face value, being in someone's face. And we even import the word *face* to other inanimate objects from which we can read information, like the face of a watch or the face of a die. The face is the public image a person presents or wants to present: we can lose face or save face, our face can fall, and so much more.

Faces are the reason why it can be easier (or, for others,

paradoxically harder) to have conversations over the phone: some people find the lack of facial data transmission easier because they can focus more on the words, and others struggle without facial context clues to properly understand what's being said. This is especially true if you're talking on the phone in a language other than your first; without bodily context clues and facial expressions, it can be a lot more challenging. And of course (you might have guessed this by now), women's faces are far more critically read and judged than men's, with women receiving snap diagnoses of resting bitch face or persistently exhorted to "smile more." And by the way, that there is no male equivalent of a resting bitch face should tell you just as much as there not being a female equivalent of mansplaining.

Many women I work with express frustration about their faces and the pressure to "perform" a specific face. In fact, women often face (ha) huge penalties for giving the *wrong* face, with female world leaders and their facial expressions becoming the hotly debated subject of front-page tabloids. One of my friends was told by a former boss (who incidentally sounds like a psychopath) that she had "angry eyebrows." This extraordinary comment is a perfect metaphor for many of these issues: that many of these critiques are directed at things we cannot control, like having . . . eyebrows?!

So, what's a woman with a face to do? First, I think it's crucial to say that I don't coach anyone to change their face— mainly because that would be weird. As you might guess, this is super gendered, too, because the men I work with are extremely unlikely even to think about their facial expressions, which is a whole other dissertation on the male gaze, enculturated femininity, gender performance, and who knows what else. If you have resting concentration face, as I do— usually a sign that I'm deeply interested or trying to grapple with what you're saying—it might not always read as such in conversation. And if you have heard feedback about your facial expressions or you want to create deeper connections with the people around you, there are a few non-facial ideas you could try.

Adding More Verbal Expressions

You could add a verbal expression, like "Hmm, that's a great question" or "Let me think about that some more" or another signifier to show you're engaged and paying attention. I tend to add a few nods or say "Hmm" to assure the other person I'm alive and interested—if, in fact, I am. The other thing you could try is more open body language. If you are stony-faced with crossed arms, for instance, you will present as much more closed off than you might intend. Relaxing your body more— shoulders back and loose arms, for example—can help you get away with fewer facial expressions if that's your style. Resting concentration face is also especially common for some neurodiverse folks who might have a bigger gap between their facial expression and their true feelings and opinions.

> **Try this:** Take note of what you might add—gestures, expressions, phrases—if you feel you need to supplement your facial expression for a stronger connection.

USING YOUR SMILE TO DISARM

One of the fascinating things about faces is that our own face can affect other faces in the room around us. Don't believe me? Before you begin to speak to someone, assume a smile or a frown and notice how before you've spoken, their face will likely mirror the same expression back to you. This is known as the chameleon effect—the unconscious mimicry of facial expressions, when our brains react to visual and verbal cues. The chameleon effect is especially interesting because it's another tool you can use to influence people in a conversation or a presentation. Unfortunately, I learned this the hard way.

As a young debater, I had a poker face as I prepared for my speech, concentrating deeply on the arguments and how I was going to refute my opposition. I regret to inform you that when I took the floor to begin my own speech, I wore a steely expression, showing little emotion other than grim determination. That was a bad strategy for two reasons. First, I didn't use the full spectrum of my own expressions to reel in my audience and the judges. I'm charming, dammit, and yet I wasn't showing anyone I had that capability. And second, when I would stand in front of a room looking intense and stone-faced, I would invariably be met with . . . a room full of intense and stone-faced people! Yes, the chameleon effect was hard at work; the audience took cues from my own face and literally mirrored it back to me. And I will tell you, when you're feeling nervous already, there's almost nothing worse than fifty or so stern faces looking back at you in silence. So what is a simple way to avoid this? Smiling.

Oh, I know, smiles are more than a little divisive when it

comes to communicating while female. Like me, you've probably been told to smile more on many an occasion, and like me, you've probably bristled every time. My favorite response to (not) smiling while being female is from eleven-time Olympic medalist Simone Biles on the TV show *Dancing with the Stars.* When she was asked why she didn't smile at the judges' positive comments, she replied, "Smiling doesn't win you gold medals." I'm hyper-aware of the anti-feminist implications of telling anyone to smile: I've lived that life, and I strongly believe women and young girls are acculturated to smile in order to hide emotions that might otherwise be difficult or confronting for adults in their lives. In particular circumstances, smiling can feel like acquiescence, approval-seeking behavior, deference, and so many more problematic things.

Yet despite all that, smiling at the beginning of a presentation can be an extremely strategic and helpful move to make. Whether on men or women, stricken, unsmiling faces often look nervous, and smiling faces look more self-assured. When I used this technique in debate, I was consistently met with an audience of warm, smiling people. Even the opposition was confused and sometimes even intimidated: *Why does she look so . . . happy? Oh God, she must be about to unleash some really good material!*

If you walk into a big room wanting a crowd to be on your side, smiling can help win them over, and suddenly you'll have a much friendlier-looking audience. Which, in turn, can help you relax and become more self-assured in the moment. Further, smiling means you have to move your facial muscles, which makes speaking physically easier. If you have a rigid, nervous jaw posture for ages before you speak, it can feel literally harder to open your mouth, as it can feel like your face is frozen. A smile can be a nice on-ramp to warm up your face to begin to speak. I like to think even my forced smile tells my body and brain that I'm not under threat, and sometimes I think smiling works to calm me down, too.

Of course, there are plenty of scenarios where you *don't* want to smile and, interestingly for this discussion, scenarios where you actually *want* your audience to be nervous or on edge. If, for example, you're negotiating a difficult deal or want to show that your company won't budge on something, you can use a serious facial expression to underscore the point you're making. Learning to sit with that non-smile can be extremely confrontational for women, many of whom have been told to smile in the name of making other people feel comfortable.

> **Try this:** Understand that your smile—whether you choose to give it or not—carries weight and power. Deploy it (or don't) when you choose, and experiment with the outcomes.

PRESENTING IN FRONT OF OTHERS

Moving from the face to the body itself, I know it can be very intimidating to stand up in front of a crowd. I somewhat compulsively click on those periodic studies saying people fear public speaking more than spiders or, literally, death. Death! But I hear you. Speaking in public can absolutely be a triggering exercise. It puts our thoughts and bodies under a spotlight in which we might not feel comfortable, making us doubt every part of our bodies, faces, and selves. (Does my self-esteem look big in this?)

Presenting requires specific skills and demands from us that we might not have ever shown anyone else or have practiced before. Many of my clients come to me at a moment when they need to assume a space on a big stage for a company-wide presentation or a big conference with thousands of people. It can feel extremely overwhelming, especially if you've never done it before. Not all of us have a TED Talk inside us just waiting to come out, and that is absolutely okay.

Practice, Practice

If you've ever felt dread or anxiety before giving a speech, I'm talking directly to you now. The first thing I can tell you is that practicing your talk is your best chance at overcoming these nerves. Gently run through it a few times so that you know the flow and can get a sense of what happens in which section. But the second thing I'll follow up with might feel counterintuitive: don't practice that one same speech too much. I can spot an over-practiced speech a mile away. (We'll discuss this more in chapter 8.) Over-practicing is like over-mixing a cake batter: you've beaten out all the air and jokes and fun of the delivery, and now you're left with a flat, boring pancake of a speech. Instead, think about every time you're in front of anyone as an opportunity to practice speaking. Not giving them the speech, you understand, but using everyday conversations and meetings you have to really observe how you're presenting yourself. *Live* your speech, if you like. Notice, for example, if your breathing is calm and regulated. Ask yourself if you can push yourself to be more articulate and clear. Try for a little more polish each time you speak, and over time, you'll see that flexing your presentation muscles a few times a week can make that *big speech* feel less of an anomaly and more of an extension of an everyday habit.

I should say that I still feel adrenaline before I get up to speak, even though I have done it so many times. But honestly, I'm not afraid of that feeling anymore. I think of it as though my body is letting me know it's on high alert and ready to perform in the moment. The energy pushes me out to the lectern, and I can begin.

Find Your Talisman

One of the ways I coach people to overcome anxiety when presenting is to find a talisman or lucky charm. This is a physical, visual, sensory, or verbal artifact that you return to that helps you envision yourself as the aspirational speaker you wish to be. Think of a talisman as something that you can carry, hold, or invoke to make you channel a certain mode of being. You might carry a paper clip when you're giving a talk (I do this sometimes), rub your fingertips together softly, smile, listen to a hype song, wear a piece of clothing or jewelry—the possibilities are constrained only by your imagination and what's practical to, you know, bring to work.

Sometimes a talisman can be a physical reminder that you're safe and not under threat; other times it can be a call for you to summon a persona that you want to bring to the fore—your best negotiating self or your most forthright public speaker.

Whatever it might be, a symbol can sometimes be useful when switching to a different gear to remind your mind and body that you're here to focus and bring calm along with you.

Talismans can take many different forms. I once saw an actor in an interview saying she wore different perfumes in each role she played, so that she could viscerally feel the difference of stepping out of her own reality into that of her character, and this is much the same sort of idea. What sort of trigger will help you stand in the right position for the task at hand? For sure, different things work for different people. An ex-Olympian once told me that she liked to say, "I shine when the lights are bright" before she stepped out to play volleyball, which I've always thought sounded magical. A line of poetry, a song lyric, or a special phrase can be a beautiful talisman, too.

Mainly, a talisman is an overt cue we can give our body and mind that we're safe and ready to play. One of my clients had trouble finding her talisman—nothing felt right, but eventually, we worked out a verbal cue that would be useful in difficult situations. She says to herself, "I'm really looking forward to this conversation," and she finds it relaxes her body into the meeting and opens a nice, generative space between herself and her interlocutor. It's not an especially fancy-sounding phrase, but it's a secret just for her—which is exactly what a talisman could be for you, too.

> **Try this:** Think of a phrase, an object, or a gesture that might remind you of who you'd like to be in the moment. Either carry it with you or think of it before you get up to speak. Notice if you can associate this talisman with moments of success over time.

Eye Contact and Why We Care About It

When we think about facial expressions and connecting with the room around us, it's natural that we also think about eye contact. Eyes may be the window to the soul, but eye contact also signifies whether someone is paying attention. (If you've ever caught someone looking at their watch or their phone while you are talking to them, you know exactly what I'm talking about.) Looking at someone directly in the eyes can be confronting for some. It can be unexpectedly intimate, intimidating, or just plain intense. I have a close friend who finds eye contact almost painful, so she often looks at another part of the face, so she's still communicating her attention in that person's direction, but the lack of direct eye contact is less draining for her. So, what does giving (or not giving) eye contact mean in our interactions? While it's common in a one-on-one conversation to look away on occasion (when you are thinking of a word, reflecting on the topic, or just need a change of scene), this isn't the case when you're trying to connect with a room full of people.

The best advice I can give you is to look around the audience to find three or four different people, in different spots, whose faces appear receptive to you—maybe you know them already, maybe they're smiling, or maybe they just have a good vibe. Pick these individuals as your "audience friends": they might not know it, but when you look up and connect with the audience, they're going to be your portals, where you'll focus your energy. I've heard lots of coaches suggest looking to the back of the room or just over the audience's heads, and there's always the old chestnut of imagining everyone naked, and honestly, those have never worked for me, and I don't think they're especially helpful suggestions. For an audience member, it's obvious if the speaker isn't generally looking your way, and it can make you disengage quickly. *If the speaker isn't giving me their attention,* we think, *why should I give them mine?*

If you were watching me present this chapter onstage instead of reading it, this is how you'd see me: I'd be making eye contact with everyone the stage lights would let me see, moving my concentration and energy around the room. And if I spotted someone who wasn't paying attention or who looked in some way unconvinced, I might focus on them for a while, waiting to see if I could win them over or get a sign that they're getting the message I'm trying to send. Usually, I can tell this if I get a smile or if they release their crossed arms into their lap, for instance. This is something I've honed over a long time of speaking to big groups. I somewhat sadistically seek out the person who seems the most unconvinced by me and try to win them over, my logic being that if I can win over the hardest person in the room, I'm probably going to be doing well with everyone else, too. You don't have to be this intense about it, but try to move your attention around the room so that everyone has a chance of feeling like you're connecting with them.

> **Try this:** If you're speaking to a crowd, remember to find your audience ally or allies—the people who look at least a little open or friendly at the outset—and deliver to them if everyone else looks hostile. Once you feel like you're up and running with one person, you can move your attention to more of the room.

PRESENTING TO A DISCONNECTED AUDIENCE

We've all been there: that awkward moment when you're presenting your point and looking for an encouraging nod or even an *aha!* face, and instead you ramble on because you haven't received a reaction, and oh God just keep talking because maybe you'll get a reaction and then you're melting, melting into the ground. Just me? Sometimes we keep going on those interminable sentences because we expect a change or a facial signifier from someone in our audience.

Audience Non-Engagement

Many of my clients tell me this is true for them, and I hear variations of "I never know what he's thinking," "I always think I'm about to be fired," or "I'm sure she hates me" about people at work they have to interact with. There may be a lot of reasons for these expressionless, terrifying faces: some folks have a good poker face; for others, it may be a clinical flat affect due to a range of different diagnoses. Regardless as to why, it's a special kind of pain when you have a boss or colleague whose facial expressions show no emotion. When I dig in with my clients and ask them about this faceless nemesis, it's usually that he (yes, often a he) likes the work they're doing and, in some cases, has even promoted them—but his face never reflects positive expressions, like smiles, nods, or eye contact.

The best thing I can tell you when dealing with someone like this is to concede at the outset that you may not get a smile, nod, or any facial encouragement. Tell yourself before the interaction that from the moment it starts until the moment it ends, you should not be on the lookout for one and you should not try to lighten the mood with jokes or small talk—it's likely not going to change the situation. Instead, if you present what you need and keep it short and sharp, they'll likely tell you if there's an issue. It is not incumbent on you to change this person or to elicit a response—that's their prerogative, and yours is just to do your job.

In my practice, I often work with these non-smilers, and they're surprised to hear that people read into their lack of expression: "I'm just concentrating!" they say—entirely perplexed that anyone would think ill of them. So that may provide you with some comfort: many people aren't aware of their face—especially men who have not been conditioned to smile, as women have—and they often mean absolutely nothing by it.

Of course, there are also reasons to take hostile-looking faces seriously. Many years ago, I used to participate in a weekly meeting that my colleagues and I secretly nicknamed "public shaming" (there's your first red flag, honestly). Each week, the CEO seemed arbitrarily to pick on one of us senior leaders and excoriate us in front of the others, seemingly just for kicks. Super fun times! In this case it wasn't about a "good person with a flat affect"; it was extremely toxic and, at its worst, became a litmus test as to whether I wanted to stay at the company or leave. You might find affectless faces hard to manage, which is very reasonable, but I also think knowing something about their existence might even be relieving for you.

> **Try this:** If you are waiting for facial engagement like a smile from a colleague and it's not forthcoming, consider that it may have more to do with them than with you. Proceed as if you had received the validation (and smile) you were looking for, and take it from there. Over time, you may learn more about their reactions (or lack thereof) and may be able to better anticipate what they mean and how you can respond accordingly.

Few people wish to have a tricky audience to present to, but sometimes that's exactly what you get. Sometimes it's because they're tired, hungry, bored—really, any number of reasons that might have little to do with you. Many of those reasons are out of our control as speakers. After many years of practicing speaking to big audiences, some of which were not especially engaged, I have a few tricks of my own.

What Is Helpful to My Audience?

I always like to think about how I can be helpful to my specific audience: What can I tell them in my allotted time that might resonate with them and be useful in their everyday lives? This means I try to do as much research as I can on who will be in the room, whether it's a small meeting or a big address. I talk to the organizers and ask specifically who will be there. Not their names, you understand, but what sorts of jobs they have, their level of seniority, and their reason for attending the event or conference in the first place. You'll find that getting this type of information will help inform the way you construct your speech, what sorts of examples you include and how you can "speak" with the audience.

For instance, one of my clients, Katherine, struggled with speaking to big audiences because it felt "sales-y"—something she found to be distasteful. After asking her what sorts of communication she did respect and resonate with, she mentioned her parents' presentation style and how they are both academics, who present with clear, logical frameworks. Katherine and I worked together on adapting an "educator" mindset, so that when she spoke, she'd remember she was in the service of helping through educating her audience, rather than selling a product. Importantly, the *content* of her presentation stayed much the same, but the *mindset* through which she approached it was completely different, and it helped liberate her to feel more useful and relevant almost immediately.

> **Try this:** Think about a mode in which you feel useful or helpful to someone. Can you position yourself as being of service to an audience? Does that feel better and more like yourself, instead of selling a product or selling yourself?

BUT I'VE GOT NOTHING TO WEAR: MAKING OUR BODIES FEEL COMFORTABLE WHEN PRESENTING

It would be remiss of me to talk about the body and not talk about what to wear when we speak. Clothes are supposed to be frivolous, but they are also part of telling the world something about ourselves—communicating, if you will. And besides, I like clothes, so please indulge me for a moment. While I have absolutely no "do and don't" list of what to wear, there are a few things I've found extremely useful over the years.

Plan Ahead

I always suggest that you should decide what to wear to a pre-sentation or event in advance so that you can stop worrying about it and concentrate more fully on your preparation. Also, deciding in advance means you can practice in your chosen outfit, if you want to. I recently went to a rehearsal for a speech in a 1,500-person capacity room and happened to be wearing sneakers. Upon getting on the stage, I realized that the stage floor was very loud wood and that the heels I had planned to wear the following day would have been extremely *clompy*. So, I changed plans and wore the same sneakers the next day so that I could move around stealthily, and it was great. For the same reason, I often take a spare pair of shoes with me—just in case the ones I had originally chosen aren't the right fit for whatever reason.

Go Toward Comfort

Wear what makes you feel comfortable. If COVID revealed anything about fashion, it was that much of our in-person office attire is so damn constricting. Years of pandemic athleisure wear proved that maybe those high heels were actually unwalkable or those trousers actually too small (or maybe that one's just me). This discovery opens up an intriguing thought: maybe wearing clothing that doesn't cut, grab, and hurt us might help us show up more comfortably, too. So much time is spent talking about the "appropriateness" of clothing, like are your tattoos exposed or is too much cleavage showing, but there's not enough emphasis on questions like, Are you comfortable? Are you worried about your top riding up or getting a hole in your stockings? If you need to bend and move a lot, would choosing flowy clothing allow for more flexibility?

Anticipate the "Dress Code"

Knowing your audience will help inform your decision on your clothing. Understanding the general dress code for an event is a useful way to determine what you might feel good to be dressed in, too. Whether it's a leather jacket, a hoodie, or a suit, you have to find the thing you know will feel comfortable *that connects with* your audience and that you will enjoy wearing and can feel proud of. I've seen executives wear full suits to tech conferences, and I've also spotted them worriedly taking off their ties and rolling up their shirt sleeves in a last-ditch effort to look more casual in front of a room of branded T-shirts. If you're someone who thrives on standing out, this will be less important for you, but many of us find some relief in knowing we're largely within the dress code. You might decide to avoid clothing that restricts your movement; you want to be able to, say, raise your arms or point or gesture or bend down, and physically constricting clothing can exacerbate the feeling you might already have of being pinned to the spot, which is a horrible feeling generally and especially in front of a crowd.

Solving these sorts of concerns will make you feel much more authoritative in your own space; much more important than the choice of clothing is your own comfort in it. The key part of you being comfortable is that whatever you choose must feel right *to you*—and that will look different for all of us.

I once asked a makeup artist to refrain from applying lipstick or lip gloss because I didn't want to get it on my teeth or worry about it smudging. She ended up putting a thick gloss on my lips anyway, with the comment that none of her other clients had any trouble with it. Predictably, I spent the Q&A portion of my speech trying to unstick my lips from each other! I should have wiped it off before I started. Trust your gut and go with what is comfortable for you.

It's worth saying that this type of bodily comfort isn't just for special occasions and events when you're speaking in front of a live audience. It can be in any type of work environment when you have to communicate even to only one other person at a time.

Embrace Creature Comforts

It's worth investigating if any physical constraints might be bothering you, too. For me, this process started at least ten years ago as I began to think about the small creature comforts that made working—the action itself—more palatable. A small thermos near my computer with hot water so I could easily have a warm drink in winter. Noise-canceling headphones to wear when I commuted on the super-loud BART train into San Francisco. A blanket for my lap in a freezing cold office. A bigger computer monitor so that I wasn't hunched over for video calls at my desk.

All these things made the labor of work—the micro-environment in which I participated—more comfortable and gentler and, therefore, an easier place in which to find my composure when things got stressful. This is not to say that a cup of even the best tea or the fanciest headphones will fix a toxic workplace; I can personally vouch that they cannot. But it's deeply important to think about what you can do to your physical surroundings to engender a feeling of belonging, safety, and calm. This might feel especially resonant to you if you're very sensitive to sensory information: noisy fluorescent lights that hum, the brightness of a monitor, the smells of lunch wafting through the office, a cold draft behind you. Taking comfort seriously and listening to your needs on an animal, primal level will directly lead you to a place where you're lowering your anxiety response and you're able to communicate more effectively.

Finally, two practical notes. A former manager of mine who was a former TV reporter gave me the invaluable advice to wear "jewel tones" on TV: highly saturated colors like royal blue, deep red, and bright green, which tend to make you look more animated than, say, black or dark gray. And it works! Color is always compelling to an audience when you're presenting (whether on-screen or in person), as it tends to make you look more alive. You don't need to wear a red pantsuit everywhere, clearly, but don't be afraid of embracing something bright, especially if you're in front of people. Further, if you need to wear a headset microphone or one pinned on your lapel, consider a jacket and pants or skirt so that the microphone has a lapel to pin onto and a waistband for the bodypack to be tucked into at the small of your back. (A dress with a belt can work, too.) You might want to avoid heavy or noisy jewelry—the small noises they make can be picked up by microphones and distract the audience from how amazing you're being.

Try this: Worry less about what you "should" wear and think more about what feels comfortable and happy-making for you when you speak. Your whole presence will be freed up and amplified by clothing that makes you feel good and like yourself when you wear it.

EXAGGERATE TO PROJECT YOUR ENERGY

Now that we have our body dressed and onstage, it can be hard to know how to hold our own once we're out there. A lot of my clients ask me, "How do I know if I'm projecting my voice and my energy appropriately in the room?" And this is such a great question. If you've ever seen a play or musical and then happened to see actors after the show with their makeup still on, you might have noticed that it looks heavier and darker than you'd expect—sometimes outright overdone. It's like an online contouring tutorial gone wrong. But when the actors were onstage, their faces looked in perfect proportion. So what's going on? Under the bright lights of the stage and for patrons all the way at the back of the theater, stage makeup is doing a lot of heavy lifting to highlight the features of the actors and help them communicate their performance with even greater impact. As we move farther away from the actors, the exaggerated stage makeup helps us connect with them and shows their faces in the most impactful way possible.

This metaphor of stage makeup can be useful when you find yourself on a bigger stage, whether it's a literal speech or a panel interview. Your energy, assuredness, and animation need to increase beyond what it would be in a more ordinary one-on-one situation to project in that space. It's going to feel a little foreign or over-the-top as you start, but trust that you need to take up more space in those situations—you might want to incorporate bigger gestures, more vocal variations, a bigger smile, a louder voice—all of which would be overwhelming in a small room but absolutely *need* to happen in a big one.

Remember to use your metaphorical stage makeup. Your exaggerated actions might feel like too-big shoes to you, but they work well for a crowd. This is especially important if you're on a phone call with others or where you have *only* your voice to play with. Too often, people make the mistake of saying, "Great, my camera is off; this will be much easier," but because you have *only* your voice at your disposal, you counterintuitively need to put a lot more energy into it to show emotion and connectedness. I've given executives a lot of feedback over the years when they show up to a radio or telephone interview with a hangover or are under the weather and they sound half-dead; as you might imagine, the recording sounds even less energetic and engaged than normal.

> **Try this:** What might be the ways you could augment your energy through your voice? Your body? Your gestures? Remember, like stage makeup, it will all feel a little clownish at first, but it makes sense when delivering to a bigger group.

RECOVERY MODE AFTER A BIG PRESENTATION

Another element to consider when you give a big presentation is your preferred recovery mode. Some people I know thrive on giving presentations and come off the stage wanting to talk longer and keep that energy going. For me, I expend an enormous amount of energy onstage. It's my biggest energy expense and probably one of my biggest joys, too. I can almost guarantee that after a long presentation I will need a quiet room and some snacks to recover. It's worth thinking through your introvert/extrovert tendencies here, too. If you are someone like me who needs some downtime in between, make sure you try to schedule that time so your energy can stay high when needed.

Once, I ran a two-day workshop in Singapore in which I delivered eight sessions over two days. (I know.) Now, for me, that is a lot of energy being given to a room. But the mistake I made was not having anywhere to retire to in the breaks. Instead, amazing women would approach me during the "breaks," wanting to talk about the sessions. Their interest obviously warmed my heart so much, and I didn't want to miss out on the discussion, either, but by the end of two days I could hardly stand up straight—quite literally. I adored the experience, but my energy and I would have been better served if I could have retired to a quiet room for even thirty minutes during the days.

It's not always possible to leave the party for some quiet time. But to the extent you can, think about how you're planning the day around your big moment. If you need rest, like me, try to schedule even ten minutes beforehand so that you can get some quiet, or have a less intense meeting afterward. Conversely, if you know you need a warm-up before, make sure you schedule some time in which you can get your engine running—maybe phoning a friend, working out, listening to some music—so by the time it comes to speak, your energy is high and ready to go. Dehydration is a real thing in these sorts of situations, too—make sure to remind yourself to drink or pack some electrolytes so you won't end up like a dry, exhausted husk, either.

For all the negativity around our voices, faces, and bodies in the media (and over the past several centuries), I find nothing more thrilling than standing up and saying my piece. Whether it's onstage, in a workshop, or in a one-on-one conversation, I find it incredibly gratifying to take the floor. I marvel at the generational speed at which things can change: my mother and grandmother never had this opportunity, and here I am, reveling in my own type of power and authority— one in which I can share warmth, collaboration, and connection with the room and can include others in my space without fear of competition or collapse. I am unafraid. I no longer fear difficult questions; I welcome them. I no longer hurry through; I speak with calm assurance.

Having explored the different ways in which we can find power and authority in our bodies and voices, I want to discuss the real confidence-killer: telling ourselves to "be more confident." Who knew that such an innocuous phrase could have such a disastrous impact?

FOUR

Kill Your Confidence:

Find Your Power

In which we discover that focusing on confidence prevents us from connecting with those around us, understand why focusing on "executive presence" is a true bummer, find that expertise can be forever out of reach unless we choose otherwise, reveal that seeking out ambivalence is an undervalued way of gaining power, and reimagine new ways of presenting ourselves to find powerful likeability.

Scenario #1: Three candidates walk into a job interview. This is not a joke, but I wish it was. Instead, it's a story my friend relayed to me that happened at her company. Two of the candidates are men and do an excellent job of talking up why they would be a great fit for the role—they are articulate and clear, and the hiring committee is getting the feeling that they'd be in safe hands. The third candidate is a woman. Her ideas are far more audacious and creative, but she presents poorly. "I just wish she had been more confident," my friend tells me afterward. She does not get the job.

Scenario #2: Maggie is a young woman in her late twenties who comes to see me with a very specific problem. A capable and smart junior lawyer, she tells me quietly that she wants to "become more confident." And then she corrects herself: "Well, I've been *told* I need to work on my confidence." Sound familiar?

I'm certain that there is nothing worse than telling someone who is trying to succeed that they need to be more confident. Few things can make a person question their own confidence, value, and self-worth as much as this simple phrase. And these scenarios might seem quite familiar to you or those you work with. The potentially well-meaning encouragement of "just be more confident" almost automatically and definitionally destroys any sense of even burgeoning self-assurance one might have had. In many of my clients I see an insistent accompanying sense of shame that they're not "there" yet—wherever "there" may be. Take Maggie, for instance. In her early career, being told to be more confident was something she agreed with, at least in theory—she thought she could show up more powerfully. But the feedback ended up making her, in her words, "paranoid" about her confidence. Maggie questioned many of her interactions and found herself becoming so self-conscious of her contributions that she said much less in meetings after that.

Why does this particular piece of feedback work this way? Part of the reason is that confidence is an *outcome*. Sure, it's a positive one, but it's the destination and not the journey. Giving someone feedback that they should "be more confident" is like saying "be healthier"; it's an output that depends on a lot of variables that are particular to you and where you are right now. Using confidence as a metric or prescription in the first instance is a big mistake: it's not a pathway that instructs you how to get there. Another way to say it? It's just not *actionable*. Even well-intentioned people like Maggie will want to act on the suggestion but be at pains to know exactly how, thus triggering a painful infinite loop of throwing spaghetti at the confidence wall and hoping some of it sticks.

OVER-INDEXING ON CONFIDENCE PREVENTS YOU FROM CONNECTING, LISTENING, AND BEING PRESENT

No one says, "Thanks so much for that confident meeting!" That's because while we might expect confidence as a baseline, we don't prize it above everything else or congratulate you for being confident as an end in itself. You might have experienced disconnection and alienation from trying to be confident at work. In fact, entering a conversation or meeting with the aim of "being confident" is often a one-way ticket to isolation and self-consciousness. So focused are you on appearing one way that you can often lose track of your content, your connections, and frankly, yourself. In this way, confidence is ultimately selfish. It makes you get into your own head and can prevent you from listening to and connecting with your audience.

Further, the pursuit of confidence for confidence's sake encourages inauthenticity. One of the pieces of advice I constantly see is "Just fake it 'til you make it." I'd like to go on the record here and say that this is terrible, horrible, no good, very bad advice. I have so many bones to pick with this phrase. The biggest problem is that this phrase endorses inauthenticity as a premise; it encourages you to pretend to be something for an indeterminate amount of time until someone—you? an invisible other?—judges you have "made it," which, trust me, no one ever believes they have. I work with countless C-level executives who have huge responsibilities, and many still privately wonder if they have "made it." Having someone tell you to fake being confident—not be your genuine self—is a real bummer. Finding confidence is not a quick fix. It cannot be found in listicles—trust me, I've looked!—but in an ongoing, loving experiment to see where your influence, persuasion, and stability lie.

> **Try this:** Have you ever wished you could "be more confident"? Instead, consider thinking about how you can connect, listen, and be present in your interactions. Using these actions as guiding lights will give you much stronger relational currency than any amorphous "confidence currency" will.

THE CONFIDENCE COMBINATION: REIMAGINING A NEW WAY OF PRESENTING YOURSELF

Part of what makes confidence difficult to jump to as an end point is the way we think about it in extremes. We have images of corporate confidence that stick in our minds and are also often quite masculine. This can prevent us women from wanting to inhabit that space (and even hamstring men who aren't comfortable adopting an extreme archetype, either). Subconsciously, we code confidence as masculine, with deep voices, wide stances, big opinions, and firm handshakes. I believe this is why a lot of women I work with feel *outside* of confidence—not invited to the confidence party, as it were. But of course, we know both men and women can be confident—and we know it when we see it.

The problems can arise when we as women embrace masculine-coded language or attributes. Diversity and inclusion expert Pragya Agarwal says women are "traditionally expected to be caring, warm, deferential, emotional, sensitive . . . and men are expected to be assertive, rational, competent and objective." So when we talk about authority being *coded* masculine, we mean that we're more habituated to seeing men in positions of authority, and it's hard to recode what that looks like for a woman.

On the communications side, we associate things like speaking in a low register and a calm and self-assured manner with authority (remember our nightly anchorman?). We'll also discuss other attributes that are coded masculine authoritative later in the book, like shouting, which is a *totally* normal thing emotional men sometimes do at work. We're overly familiar with the social penalties women pay when they seek to inhabit these spaces. When women attempt to enter the authority arenas, they often face a high degree of scrutiny, questions of likeability, generalizations, and double standards.

How, then, can we reimagine what confidence looks like so that it's actionable and usable in our everyday work lives? And how can we unlock a new space in which to show up, be seen, and escape the powerful/likeable binary? As we practice seeing who we are and who we want to be, confidence-wise, we can think about new combinations or modes to experiment and play with. I call this exercise the Confidence Combination, and it's designed to help you find a more nuanced positioning of how you'd like to show up and communicate yourself to others. As a start, let's consider the following two lists, which aren't exhaustive, but rather present example attributes.

A	B
Assertive	Open-minded
Rational	Emotional
Objective	Compassionate
Fact-based	Sensitive
Competitive	Collaborative
Driven	Empowering
Ambitious	Loyal
Self-oriented	Communal
Independent	Warm

You can think of the first column as "masculine" and the second as "feminine" attributes, if only because they've traditionally been encoded that way. I'm interested in the deeply productive, generative, and interesting combinations we can make on these lists by *connecting* one from the first column with one from the second.

Imagine inhabiting "rationally compassionate," "ambitiously communal," or "assertively empowering" behavior in your communication. And unlike deeply limiting archetypes or personality test categories, the possibilities here are not limited by anything. They don't live in a textbook; they exist to be dreamed up and imagined by you. These combinations look like significantly different versions of what we'd traditionally categorize as "confidence," but they allow so much more nuance and flexibility as we think about showing up in a way that aligns with who we think we are as well as who we want to be.

When I showed the Confidence Combination exercise to one of my clients, a nonprofit campaigner named Maddy, she lit up and began excitedly talking out options that suited her; she felt that "a driven warmth" summed up how she showed up as a contributor on her broader team—and more important, it was how she wanted to show up in the future. She told me, "I always thought 'driven' was so bro-coded, like it meant you didn't care about anything else. But I am really driven. I'm really ambitious, but I care a lot about all my team doing really well, too—and being their manager in a kind way." I asked Maddy how she felt after we had this descriptor for her style. She thought for a moment and said, "I feel a massive sense of relief. Like it's okay to be me." I was moved by her honesty and have seen her draw on this idea of "driven warmth" while doing everything from giving a speech to meeting new clients. That phrase helped her shape her sense of herself in those interactions.

Another client, Hana, who runs operations at a high-growth start-up, told me that she has always felt like the odd one out whenever she expresses her competitiveness. "I'm the sort of person who has to win the pub trivia quiz even when there is no prize for doing so—I just get really competitive about everything." She looked at the Confidence Combination lists and immediately picked "competitive collaborative" as her combination. I asked her to tell me more about the combination, and she said, "I'm really competitive, in that I want to win and do the best, but I also want our company to do that, and I always jump in to help anyone I can succeed in their roles. I bring a strong sense of 'let's do this' to all the other teams I work with, and I think that's when I feel like the best of me is coming through."

The "best of me" is really a beautiful way to think about the Confidence Combination. Indeed, I presented this idea at a conference recently, and afterward a man came up to me and said, "Thanks for your rationally warm presentation" and I have to tell you, I've rarely felt so seen! The promise of powerful likeability is that we don't have to be beholden to one archetype or way of being but can dismantle the binaries of masculine and feminine coded behaviors and find a space that combines both to feel truer to the person we can be: the excellent communicator we all have inside.

Try this: Are there any attributes on these lists that jumped out to you as meaningful or aspirational? Play with mixing two traditionally oppositional attributes and see if you can find a mode that suits your own behavior and communication style.

There is an untapped opportunity for us to combine emotive, sensitive attributes with the more traditionally transactional, logical ones. And of course, the specific recipe and weighting is up to you: you may well already skew one way or another in your communication, and that may serve you well. Instead of chasing after the white whale of confidence, which has so many downsides and land mines, you'll find a much more dependable, reliable sense of yourself if you try this combination exercise. You might just find a more interesting and powerful way to show up for your colleagues, your team, and yourself. Kill your confidence and find your true power.

EXECUTIVE PRESENCE AND PRESENCE DYSMORPHIA

You may have also been in a position where you have received the feedback that you needed to work on your "executive presence." This happened to me repeatedly early in my career, and I was often frustrated that I never knew exactly what that meant or how to practice the skill. Executive presence is a weirdly specific brand of confidence: it usually means how well you can demonstrate confidence to your boss, peers, and team so that they see you as capable and reliable—as "safe hands." So often, "executive presence" is used as an annoyingly vague catchall in reviews or feedback, and in my experience, it is more frequently cited as lacking in women rather than in men.

> "I've been told I need to work on my executive partnership skills."
> "They liked my proposal, but he said my presence was lacking."
> "She said before I can manage people, I need to develop more executive presence."

My clients have mentioned these refrains to me in the last month alone: it's clear that the landscape hasn't changed much since I was told this fifteen or so years ago. What is most common in my clients is what I term "presence dysmorphia." By this I mean we don't fully grasp or perhaps incorrectly understand the extent of our own presence and struggle to know how to fix it—while simultaneously fixating on it.

Let me explain. My own version of presence dysmorphia

used to show up when I'd say to a colleague, "I'm sure she/he doesn't remember me," as if I were so small and insignificant as to be entirely forgettable. It was usually when I felt intimidated by the person—in this case, a terse vice president who had low EQ—so I'd smile and laugh nervously, hating myself for doing so instead of just having a normal conversation. A close friend of mine called me out on it one day. She asked me, "Why do you always say, 'I'm sure they don't remember me'? They obviously do!"

I hadn't even noticed I was doing it. It's important to say here that when this was happening, I was the head of the department, and this person had met me multiple times and clearly had to know who I was. What was I thinking?

One of the most familiar patterns of presence dysmorphia is a widespread and chronic underestimation of our own abilities. When we're just starting our careers, it's common to feel on the back foot on day one. But even when we have a fancy degree or a big title or great potential, many of us still don't feel empowered or important; we still feel like we have a long way to go. In fact, we often look at anything we already know or have achieved and discount it immediately. *Oh, that? It's just my master's degree—what I need to know in this role are other things. Oh, this? My time at a law firm? Aw, that's nothing.* It's as if the credential or experience that we earned suddenly becomes worthless *by virtue of us owning it.* Weird, no? (And how deeply surprising that we get feedback to be more confident . . .)

When we underestimate our own credentials and experience, we tend not to remember how competent (or even excellent) we might be in that area—and importantly, we don't give ourselves a chance to communicate our confidence related to that expertise. So, one of the statements I find myself constantly prompting brilliant women with is "Tell me honestly about your role, responsibilities, and background." And I invariably get a slew of impressive expertise that is hard-won and extremely valuable. It's almost as if telling me helps reanimate its importance in their minds.

And then there are the surprises. One of my clients, Stella, introduced herself to me with language that was so down on herself that I was genuinely taken aback. Was this the same person I had been emailing with? Her descriptions of her own career were laden with strong judgment, shame, and disappointment. It was thoroughly surprising for someone as interesting and credentialed as she was. For instance, Stella mentioned a stint where she co-founded a startup, and almost as if through clenched teeth, she explained it hadn't worked out, and she had returned to be an investor at a venture capital fund.

She was telling me a largely incredible career trajectory story, but her communication of the story was at odds with how impressive it was. As she spoke, her shoulders curved in and her head dipped low; she overwhelmingly undercut and undervalued her expertise, further communicating to me a strong sense of sadness and regret. It was hard to reconcile the woman in front of me with the career milestones and reputation I had read about online. Now first, you must know that in tech, this is an all-too-familiar story: most start-ups don't succeed, and stories of trying and starting over are well-trodden terrain. Second, the fund she returned to is one of the best in the world: it was hardly an embarrassing tail-between-

my-legs disappearance and instead could have easily been por-
trayed as an exuberant homecoming.

Stella and I worked together for some months on what
amounted to reckoning with her sense of self: How did she
conceptualize herself now and into the future? Was her judgment of herself *accurate*? Over time, she came to see that while
she still harbored some disappointment relating to her start-
up's closure, it wasn't representative of her whole story; it was
a single page in a much larger book of achievements. Hiding
the rest of her expertise, especially when meeting people for
the first time, was undercutting her value. Moreover, each
time she'd tell the story and relive that part of her journey so
painfully, it became exhausting, too.

> **Try this:** Do you identify with presence dysmorphia? Is there
> some value of yours that you aren't seeing or communicating ac-
> curately? Take stock and consider positioning it differently and
> more positively the next time it comes up in conversation.

See Yourself Through the Eyes of Your Best Friend

One of the questions I asked Stella when we were working on
owning her expertise to build her confidence was "How might
you tell the story of a close friend's career?" Usually when I ask
clients this, they immediately light up, telling me with great
authority how incredible this person is and proudly listing out
her accomplishments. And then I ask semi-seriously, "Are you
lying? Is this woman *really* that good?" And they always insis-
tently cry, "Oh, *absolutely*!"

For instance, Amelia, who works in sales, says of her friend Jaya, "She's one of the most hardworking people I know; she always has a work-around when something goes wrong. She also graduated from college cum laude—she's super smart."

Product marketing manager Lani says of her "work-wife," Akiko, that she feels lucky to work so closely with someone who is "so brilliant." She talks up Akiko's various external accreditations she's been taking online (while working full-time) as well as her recent promotion on their team.

A senior vice president in engineering, Emily, tells me that she's never learned more from someone than from her current manager; that watching this woman work up close has been the "privilege of a lifetime." Emily tells me, "She manages a team of 150 people, and still, she seems always to know exactly what everyone's working on. It's mind-blowing."

To which I say, you have an internal voice of confidence that can accurately see the best in someone else—their skills and their achievements—and you need to turn that voice of assurance to *yourself*. If you try describing yourself with that same voice and speak of yourself with esteem and respect, you'll see there's no room for disappointment or shame when you're telling a stranger about yourself. If you feel in doubt or in any way shaky, channel that mental best friend. Her voice is likely both kinder and more accurate—she sees you and understands how to champion you and what you've achieved.

Take my friend who pointed out my presence dysmorphia in front of executives all those years ago. I was so grateful she told me, as it caused me to think about what was going on and how I could move beyond it. In those instances, I realized I was honestly a little in awe of the other person. I began to reframe those moments, and when I'd find myself feeling small or overawed, I would say to myself, "We are peers. There's no reason she has forgotten who I am. Go in and assume she knows exactly who you are, and if she doesn't, at this point that's on her!" In this way, I was able to pivot myself to a more realistic appraisal of my presence in that interaction, and I could move forward with so much less worry and concern.

The point of this exercise in owning your expertise is not how long or short that list of achievements is but your *attitude* toward how you communicate it to others. When I worked with Stella, the process involved slowly getting her to recognize that her list of genuine accomplishments was impressive and hard-won. This changed the way she introduced herself dramatically. The emotional weight was lifted, and she could show up just as she was.

> **Try this:** Channel the best friend voice if you're in doubt. How would she describe you? What would she point out as exceptional or impressive? She sees you for you. Use that as a mental compass to see your accomplishments more accurately and begin to build faith in your own presence.

How to Value Our Own Expertise

When we talk about claiming our authority, an interesting word that often comes up in my work is *expert*. Many of the women I work with often talk about their peers as "experts" but never seem to give that label to themselves. Often this is true of extraordinarily credentialed women: they have degrees and experience, they manage teams, and yet they still refer to others as being the "experts." I often find myself prompting clients with the question "What is 'an expert' to you?" And then I ask, "When do you think you would be able to call yourself an expert?" The way we think about defining expertise at the outset is interesting, too. Some use the time they've been in a role; others the numbers or types of degrees. Oftentimes the answer I get is a variation of "I might be an expert in five to ten years," which is faulty logic. I'll bet in five to ten years they would give me the exact same answer!

If we keep moving arbitrary goalposts for ourselves, we'll definitionally never reach the goal we're setting out for. In fact, if you always think that being an expert will happen "in five years" or "when you have a graduate degree" or "when you've been here longer than anyone else," you're effectively postponing the event, sometimes indefinitely. Few people expect you to be the one and only expert on a topic, but it can be grounding and even confidence-building to think about being "an" expert—even one of many is better than not one at all. When we can reposition our expertise in this way, we can relax into it more and feel a sense of readiness. We don't have to be *the expert* (who really decides that, anyway?), but we can certainly be *an expert.* We all have valuable expertise to share and that's liberating and empowering to remember.

Try this: Consider how you define *an expert*. What implications does this definition have for your own trajectory and ability to fulfill the role of expert one day?

What Were You Hired For? Assuming Appropriate Responsibility

Let's take another one of my clients—Cheryl, a business development vice president at a large tech company. She works on negotiating big deals with external stakeholders and runs the strategy and business operations side of the house, and her counterparts are overwhelmingly male engineers. While she has a background in computer science, she is usually the least technical person in the room. Cheryl told me she gets anxious when she receives a technical question at a company town hall meeting because she might not know the best way to answer it.

Not only do we underestimate our achievements, but when we devalue our skills, we effectively experience failure because we don't know *everything*. Here's the question I offered Cheryl: "What were you hired for?" If you were hired to be the vice president of engineering, getting a technical question is in your wheelhouse, and you should have the right answer. But Cheryl was hired as the vice president of business development, so a deeply technical question isn't exactly in her role. In that situation, she could use the opportunity to educate the broader team on the scope of her role (and hopefully train folks to understand which questions should be directed to her in the future).

In a town hall meeting, Cheryl would say something like, "Thanks for the question. To answer that from my business development team's perspective, what I can tell you is . . . and to speak to the more technical engineering side of things, I'd point you to XYZ person." When she pivots to her own area of expertise—her home turf—she'll likely feel much more comfortable.

It's not her job to be more technical than the most technical person, any more than it's her job to be more comfortable with sales than the most senior salesperson. It's her job to do, well, her job.

It's true that we need a degree of familiarity with the other parts of the business over time, but you don't need to be the ultimate expert about everything—that's literally no one's job. We'd never counsel an engineer to know everything about a non-technical role or an HR manager to know everything about product management. So release yourselves from the burden of feeling self-conscious about not knowing absolutely *everything*. It's okay and indeed preferable to point people to the right resources without any sense of shame or guilt. This trains your audience on your areas of expertise and reminds us that we don't have to have the answers to everything—we only need to oversee our own domain.

Try this: If you experience feelings of "Argh, I can't believe I don't know everything" about an area, consider if that is within your mandate in the first instance. Is there instead someone you could ask? What are the implications if you ask for an explanation?

Be Your Own Detective

Have you ever been in a situation where you feel a rising sense of disquiet or resistance in the people you're talking to? It can be tempting to ignore it and stick to what you've prepared and barrel forth, oftentimes losing energy as you go. Some-times, we don't know where that ambivalence is coming from—Do they hate *me*? Do they hate the *proposal*?—and other times, it's hard to know how to pivot to something else when we've only prepared one thing. It can be difficult to concentrate when these reactions occur, because you feel the slow slide of confidence leaving your body. This is when my best advice is to be a detective. What I mean by this is that it can be your role to seek out the answers as to what might be happening instead of feeling passive and sitting back, hoping that everything will be okay. Just as a detective might, lean in to the problem and try to understand more in order to work out your next move.

I was recently coaching a client named Matt, and I explained that he needed to simplify his explanations. His preference was to answer questions in an extremely thorough but long and complex manner, such that sometimes you'd forget what you had asked him in the first instance. So, I suggested he do an exercise with me involving a templated structure where he could make his arguments but pick out a relevant headline, an example, and so on to see if he could become more concise and digestible for his team and clients. As I was explaining what I felt was a useful but ultimately low-stakes exercise, I could see Matt change. He crossed his arms, his mouth became a flat line, and he leaned away from me. Earlier in my career, when this happened, I'd think something along the lines of "He'll come around and like this soon!" and valiantly carry on with my explanations.

But now in such instances, my most common strategy is to pretend to be a detective: I lean in to the disquiet I'm feeling and, if it feels appropriate, try to get to the bottom of it together through questions and conversation. In this instance, I decided our relationship was strong enough that I could call out the ambivalence or tension that I had seen in Matt directly. I asked him, "Matt, I'm sensing some resistance in you when I'm suggesting this exercise; would it be helpful to take a moment and dig into what's going on here?" He looked relieved and honestly a little surprised and explained that he didn't like the notion of simplifying his ideas. He prided himself, he said, on complicated thinking and intellectualism. Aha! I knew this about him, but understanding that my exercise had triggered a special kind of resistance was very helpful. I was able to focus the rest of the conversation on how I conceptualized simplicity of communication as not being "dumbed down" ideas but complex ideas, simply put.

Once he understood the distinction, he was game to carry on with the work and saw significant improvement in his connection with his clients. The act of calling out the resistance is such a powerful one because it's validating to the other person. If they haven't felt able to tell you something in words, their body language often tells you first. For me, too, my own faith in my process was restored: I could happily pick up where we were, without distraction. For Matt, I'm not even sure if he had thought about what he wanted to tell me yet, but he was intuitively recoiling from the exercise. Getting his explanation gave me valuable data about what was happening for him and helped me to course-correct and get us to a more productive place together.

I would have loved the lens of being a detective earlier in my career: a noncombative tool or mental reframe to salvage interactions that had gone sideways or where I could sense something was wrong but wasn't sure how to fix it in the moment.

When I recall other instances with colleagues or clients when I haven't done this, I reflect that I lost out on so many opportunities to call out or uncover what was going on in our interaction—and that was to the detriment of us both. In part this happened because it may have felt scary or presumptuous to call it out, or maybe I felt too junior. Or perhaps I was afraid of what they would say. And all these answers may occasionally resonate for you, too. But what I'd tell myself if I could travel back to those conversations would be that there is great power, compassion, and wisdom in understanding the nuances of your working relationships more closely. And if handled with care, it can result in deeper, more productive, and ultimately less guarded working relationships, too.

> **Try this:** You can adopt the mindset of a detective if you feel you're searching for a connection with someone or feeling a sense of ambivalence and want to know more about it. It can be a helpful tool to uncover what's going on when something doesn't feel quite right.

Embrace Hesitation

One of the fastest ways to feel like you're losing confidence is when you feel yourself hesitating. If you can learn to treat hesitation like a gift, you can become a lot more open to receiving what it's trying to tell you. The underlying reason(s) for hesitation can often reveal the direction you need to take or the real issue at hand. Listen carefully and learn more about the problem. Let's see this in action.

Some years ago, my friend Deborah came to me with a dilemma. She was working at an inspiring nonprofit and had been offered a big donation of $1.2 million from a company going through a bad run of publicity on the condition of doing joint press about the donation. The donation—the biggest her organization had ever been offered—would mean life-changing things, but she was worried that the donor's negative PR crisis might rub off onto them if she accepted it. She wanted to keep the relationship on a good footing, but felt she was losing confidence in her decision-making.

The first question I asked was "Can you get the money elsewhere?" This is the "best alternative to a negotiated agreement" theory: that it's always worth looking at when you're considering taking or not taking what's on the table. Her answer here was "No, we've never been able to secure a donation this big, so it's unlikely we can easily get it from someone else quickly." Then I asked, "What's the worst thing that could happen?" We played out all the scenarios that could ensue from this gift and concluded that the worst-case scenario would be a bad headline that might come from taking the gift—which she decided she could accept.

Finally, I asked, "Why are you still hesitating?" She considered the question and answered, "Well, I just think that they need us right now a lot more than we need them." Aha! The golden phrase. The idea that one party needs the other more is excellent leverage, and the fact that they wanted to close the deal quickly was even better news. My friend ended up going back to the besieged company and asking whether the company could up their contribution to $2 million because it would achieve a better outcome for both parties, and the company agreed to the terms. This is an example of a great win: my friend's organization was well compensated by the big company, they were able to do the press they wanted, and everyone was happy with their outcome.

This story of the donation is illustrative because it brings into focus how hesitation might feel like you're on shaky ground but it can actually be the missing piece of a puzzle. Once Deborah understood that the company "needed" the deal more, she was able to persuade them to invest more: their motivation and emotion (in this case, urgency) were integral to the deal coming together.

Hesitation can be something many of us are hard on ourselves for doing, especially if it makes us feel unsteady. "I should be more decisive" or "I should know this already" are sentences I hear over and over again in my work—and many folks also report getting that feedback from managers or peers (or their partners at home!). And there's some truth to frustration with hesitation—it stops forward motion, which is something we're all after. But in the case of communicating, it's one of those excellent tells that can reveal so much if you just listen to what's beneath it.

> **Try this:** Don't despair if you're feeling hesitation. It's often a great way of understanding more about the issue or your own feelings toward communicating it. Hesitation can tell you so much, if you only listen.

Trying for confidence is a surefire way to find disappointment, frustration, and often, anticlimax. If you're wavering before a difficult interaction, think about connection and presence instead. Ask yourself, *How can I show up in a way that helps the room or that allows the work to be done more easily? How can I say my piece and allow the work to flow through me?* These are questions that will anchor you in a much stronger, more truly confident position.

FIVE

Asking Great Questions and Giving Great Answers

In which we remember that not everyone around us knows what we know, explain how to manage some of the "ew" of self-promotion, tackle the perennial "I could never say that" blocker, see what happens when we present people with too much information, walk through some best practices for feedback, and talk about sushi more than you were expecting in a book like this.

Early in my career I worked at YouTube headquarters in California, the tech company that is home of trillions of videos about almost anything you could imagine. At the time, it was shifting from dogs on skateboards to a more serious video platform, empowering creators to earn a livelihood from their passions. I learned about creators, monetization, the challenges of curating vast swaths of content, and so much more. Some years later, I ran global communications at another platform company in San Francisco that hosted user-generated written content, and I kept observing the interesting overlaps between the two platforms. So many of the same lessons I had learned at YouTube applied to this new company, yet no one asked for my opinion on what I saw as deeply obvious similarities. My new colleagues all knew I had YouTube on my résumé. Why didn't they want to know what I had learned there? I sat in meeting after meeting, my overflowing ideas hungry for an escape route, frustrated at not having a venue in which to explain what I had learned and why it might help us. *Why*, I thought, *isn't anyone asking me about this?*

Why isn't anyone asking us, indeed. Many women worry about getting a tough question or being put on the spot, but interestingly, we worry equally, too, about not being asked to contribute at all! This anxiety around the asking and answering of questions is paradoxical, and it makes us anticipate the worst outcome for both, which will make us likely to undersell our own contributions and capabilities. Of course, this is a powerfully likeable classic hit: we want to look authoritative without being alienating; we want to be helpful but not bossy, informative but not imperious.

Negotiation and leadership academics Carol Frohlinger and Deborah Kolb coined the phrase "tiara syndrome," referring to the idea that women often think if they just put their heads down and do excellent work, someone will recognize that and crown their achievements. And of course, this often happens in vain. But this tiara hit different. I wasn't waiting for rewards; I just wanted someone to ask me my thoughts and opinions, to solicit my feedback. I was passively waiting for an invitation that never came.

One day, it struck me that I was actually waiting for other people to read my mind and shortchanging myself in the process. It was liberating to realize I didn't have to wait for anyone or anything: I could just . . . begin. I wrote up a long memo about the similarities between the two platforms and posted it internally and then delighted in having various meetings afterward in which I felt like I could offer the genuinely useful ideas I had learned. That memo helped me unlock my experience to share with others and begin a much more connected chapter at that workplace, and I'm very grateful for that.

In hindsight, what an obvious and eminently solvable roadblock I had put in my own path. I hear similar stories from people I coach all the time. We are often waiting for a tiara that might never come. Hannah, an experienced start-up operator, says, "I'd rather wait until I'm called on, in case others aren't ready for another idea in that meeting." Devi, who works in HR, says, "I guess I don't like the feeling that I might be distracting if I change the subject, even if what is being discussed isn't that relevant." And Christina from a fast-moving legal team says, "Sometimes I sit, really hoping someone will ask me because I know I have something useful to say, but I just don't know when to interrupt to bring it up."

Recognize a pattern here? There's a pernicious cycle happening where we want to contribute but often don't know how to make the on-ramp to begin the conversation. In this chapter, I want to cover some starting points to help in these stuck moments when it feels impossible to breach the city walls of the conversations that are happening around you. It's one thing if colleagues aren't listening; it's quite another if they never heard you in the first place.

One of the most challenging parts of communicating is that we're required to do it live, often with no rehearsal. Sure, you might have a big presentation onstage on occasion, but for the most part, we're participating in fast-moving, impromptu conversations. It's one of the reasons you might have a mental "Cool Comebacks I Should Have Said in That Moment but Never Got to Use" list—I know I do. A helpful way to think about this is to consider how to focus our communication so that we're attuned to the right thing at the right time.

THE POWER OF ASKING QUESTIONS

I often see the feeling of dread on people's faces when they want to ask a question in a group but are terrified to do so. You know the feeling: you're afraid it's an obvious question, that it might take time away from important stuff and will prove you to be the idiot you always suspected you were. Yep, I get it. I distinctly remember being in a meeting where I tried to discreetly google something under the table. It turns out there's not a discreet way to google anything, especially under a table.

But as my career progressed, I noticed something. I started to ask the question. I started to say things like "Would you mind talking me through what that acronym means?" and "Could you let me know where that 78 percent is coming from?" and "I'm keen to get up to speed quickly here; what's the measurement ratio we're using?" I was stunned to learn that . . . no one cared. I would ask in a way that suggested I was interested and engaged and trying to move us all forward toward the answer, and I'm delighted to inform you that no one dropped dead of shock and no ceiling caved in. In one particularly memorable meeting, no one else knew the answer, either, which was deeply validating and kind of funny, now that I think back on it.

In meeting scenarios, we can be icebergs. In that much of what we have to contribute can—like mine did—stay below the surface. But what if your idea could help change the trajectory of a project for the better? What if your question clarified something that everyone else was unsure of? What if standing up for a value helped everyone else feel freer to do the same? The voices of self-doubt can be so loud, but usually if you're paying attention, the thing you want to say is likely really valuable to others. Next time, think about how speaking up might benefit the team, the project, or yourself.

Check Your Credit

The first thing about asking questions is to check your credit. When asking questions, it's crucial to have done your homework and to have been listening carefully. If so, there's a chance that if you don't understand something, others won't either. Certainly, if you pipe up with "So what's this meeting about, again?" after it's nearly over, your query is decidedly certain not to dazzle. I'd be remiss if I told you to just show up and start asking random questions and expect your co-workers to think you're a wizard! But often just asking for clarification can help everyone get on the same page. If you don't know something, calling it out without drama saves everyone a lot of time and stress. Questions can be powerful and help you navigate through the morass of imposing feelings—they don't require you to fall on your sword or decry your ineptitude;

they just mean you're eager to get your head around the new thing and to keep moving forward.

One of the interesting things about question-asking is that questions can be a powerful tool to help reinforce your *own* power. I know, it feels counterintuitive. *But, Kate, how can I be persuasive if I'm asking a question? Isn't that a deferential position by definition?* We often fear asking the dumb question because it makes us look uneducated or underprepared.

Shaping the Conversation with Questions

One of my debating teammates years ago used to have a slick way of asking for help before we'd get up to speak. Instead of saying, "Uh-oh, I don't know anything about decriminalizing drugs," he'd say, "Talk me through banning drugs" in this super casual and very relaxed way. It took quite a long time for it to dawn on me that this was code for "Yikes, I'm lost." It was so elegant, and it allowed for a really productive sharing of information between us. I remember realizing his tactic one day and marveling at how powerful the phrase was. His un-rattled calm and anchored manner gave no clue as to his own cluelessness on a subject. I was amazed.

So it can be helpful to think about questions as being a device to help *shape* a conversation. For instance, powerful questions can be useful when you want to get a group back on track ("What are we solving for here? Can we take a moment to recap our goals and non-goals?") or when you want to demonstrate your understanding ("Am I right in thinking you're primarily concerned about X and want to make sure we can protect Y?"). Instead of looking deferential, the powerful question can give you more information and therefore more ability to get up to speed—fast. And of course, questions help demonstrate that we're actively listening and following along. This sounds obvious (Listening in a meeting? Groundbreaking!) but sometimes it's helpful to signal to the group that you're listening by *speaking*.

Interestingly, the powerful question will occasionally reveal an answer that was different from what you expected, so listen and wait for it. Alice, a client of mine, is a vice president in sales, and says she has learned to listen to her customers differently and to ask more questions. They might come to a meeting saying that they want help with shipping their products faster, for example, but after a few questions it could emerge that they were actually looking for more reliable communication about the shipping—speed might not be the real issue. These subtleties can get brushed over easily, so listening and probing gently with questions can give you a lot of helpful information. A clarifying question here isn't an imposition; it's critical data to inform your decision-making. Other times, the concern they raise from your questions might be something you didn't even think of.

Watch Out for "Why" Questions

One thing to note about questions: be judicious about using "why" questions. They can sometimes come off as looking defensive or interrogatory when you're actually just trying to get to the root of the problem. Consider "Why are we spending budget on that?" and "Why is that group involved in the sales campaign when they're not trained in sales?" It sounds a little like you're putting someone on the spot, and this might not be the place for your *"J'accuse!"* moment. You likely don't want to purposely wrong-foot someone or catch them off guard (unless that's your intention, to which I say, well played, and please email me the details). To get the same outcome, you could instead try saying, "I'd love to get a better sense of how we're allocating resources here. Could you talk me through the budget allocation?" Collecting good data points often comes from asking good questions and listening carefully to the answers. The quicker you can get the information you need, the quicker you can turn around whatever you're working on.

Ask a Powerful Question of Yourself

There's another special, secret type of question-asking: when you can ask a powerful question of yourself. (Plot twist!) Sometimes it's easy to feel dread about asking questions when people around you are using insane amounts of acronyms or jargon, which can be hard to understand. Oh, you're not aware of the GTM strategy for the i18n launch event in Q1 with the x-fn team?* You'd be forgiven for wondering if some of those sentences were math equations. (Hey, in some places, maybe they *are* math equations!) In highly specialized fields, it can be intimidating if you're not in on particular verbiage or subject matter. Terminology or jargon can be exclusionary, and usu-

---

* This is not intended to make you panic. Translated, this means: "the go-to-market strategy for the internationalization launch event in Q1 (January–March) with the cross-functional team."

ally not on purpose—it's just quicker to use the industry terms and abbreviate things to move quickly.

If you're new to some information being discussed, one of the best things to do is to ask *yourself* questions and think it through from first principles: *What is logically being asked here? Is this person asking for my help? For permission? Are they informing me of something I need to do or just giving me an update?* Looking at the issue with fresh, unadulterated eyes can be extremely helpful to the team, because they've been scuba diving down deep among the details, and sometimes it's the fact that you might not know all the minutiae that can offer a fresh perspective. Use your being different to provide value and a point of view to your team. Obviously, there's rarely a useful black-and-white rule of "always use Y" or "never use X," so you'll be the best judge of how and when to deploy powerful questions. My hope is that you find it useful and powerful to have a question up your sleeve and feel like it gives you more control, rather than taking it away.

Many of us worry about the moment when someone *does* ask us a question. And many of us worry when we are not even asked in the first place at all. A conundrum, indeed! In fact, I coach a lot of women who tell me they feel insecure or self-conscious when they don't immediately know the answer to a question, especially when it feels like they've been put on the spot in public. This feels like a pretty reasonable response at first glance; no one wants to feel like they're being shown up or judged on what they do or don't know, especially in front of an audience. But let's dig into this a little more. The women I have the pleasure of working with are not women who don't understand their respective assignments, but rather they are incredibly credentialed and experienced, and I would be surprised if they absolutely had no idea when it came to a question that related to their team or function. I know this because I usually pepper them with tons of questions in our work, and they're quick to answer with deliberate, thoughtful insights about their job. So, what's going on here? Why is there such a big, lived disconnect between the reality of the questions they're telling me about and how they feel about them?

> **Try this:** Next time you find yourself wanting to ask a question, consider what's holding you back and whether you need the information you're seeking. Chances are, you do: thinking through a way to ask that feels comfortable might break the back of the fear, and then you can be more involved in the discussion that ensues.

Managing Up

Managing up is a term that I've always found really gross. It implies that I'm trying to manage or manipulate someone above me. But really, managing up is effectively communicating to your peers or seniors and keeping them up-to-date with how your work is progressing. This sounds like a simple ask or an obvious thing to do, but it's shocking how many problems result when this particular train goes off the tracks. I think about the communications (and miscommunications) between different parties a lot, and it's amazing how many universal truths we can recognize, whether it's between a founder and a peer, a big boss and a middle manager, or even, counterintuitively, a lawyer and a judge. For instance, my lawyer friend Edward says this of his court appearances: "The best thing I can try to aim for is simply to give the judge the right information in the right order . . . and then showing them (rather than just telling) where that information can be found in objective places, like in evidence or cases." This statement has so many gems in it, I think it's worth unbundling it as there are some best communication "managing up" practices hiding in plain sight.

First, give the right information. Too often we're coming to a manager with our own list of worries, or some tangential thing rather than thinking, *What do they need of me right now? What can I do to specifically answer a question they have or fix an urgent problem?* We think we're aligned, but oftentimes we can diverge from each other quickly, so think about whether the focus of your meeting and time with them is most usefully allocated and flex accordingly.

Second, give the information in the right order. This idea doesn't get nearly enough airtime. Think carefully about the logical and strategic benefits to the order in which you present your ideas or agenda items. For example, don't start with the least-urgent idea first. Or do, but because you know it's easier to get a yes early in the meeting. For instance, if you always run out of time with this person, then think about what your must-have item of discussion will be and put that first. Similarly, if your ask needs context, put that up top and then signpost where you're going so your interlocutor can be ready for what's ahead.

Third, show, don't tell. Evidence, data, case studies—whatever it's called in your work—it's the key to excellent persuasion and helps anchor your argument rather than flailing about. When used in the right context, few people can argue with facts. You're not using the fact to ambush them or talk yourself up, you're just being true to the record.

Also remember that managers are just like us! They have their own worries, fears, and pressures from their higher-ups, so leading with compassion here can help a lot.

Try this: Remember that giving the right information in the right order with the right evidence is a skill that should not be underestimated. Try it in your next one-on-one meeting.

DEFENDING AN IDEA WITHOUT BEING DEFENSIVE

Sometimes we're called to defend a position but not *be* defensive about it. That may feel like a semantic quibble, but the distinction is critical. Defending an idea or a position is a fundamental communication tactic, but *being* defensive is not. Put another way, defensiveness is a surefire way to alienate the person you're trying to persuade—they might feel like you're antagonistic or avoidant, which isn't a great emotional state to evoke in someone you're trying to coax to your way of thinking. Instead, think about ways in which you can hold your line, while also connecting as a human.

One of my clients, Mariko, told me about a frustrating situation at work. As an engineer, Mariko was more specialized in her area than her manager was and felt irritated when he requested the same ask for a second or a third time. Each time, he asked her to look longer to find a piece of data she believed just wasn't there, and she didn't know how to express that without sounding like she was being defensive.

When she relayed this story to me, I wondered if he knew how long she had worked on the problem—maybe he thought she had only fleetingly looked?—so I told her about my Getting on the Same Side framework. Think about it like this: *What is our area of common interest, or what is a common goal we share? And how can I demonstrate that I'm on the same side as the other person?* For example, Mariko could say, "Absolutely— I know we both want to find that data. Can I give you a summary of where I've looked so far, and you can let me know if there's anywhere else I should be searching? I want to make sure we're both on the same page here so that I'm being efficient." This way, she is showing the work that's already done (a seemingly thorough job) but also asking for more information that might be useful for them both and, importantly, positioning them on the same team. Any frustration he might have felt would be mitigated by the messaging that she's on his side. She's not trying to be oppositional.

You could also use this framework in a situation where you need to de-escalate a conversation or interaction. If you're feeling animosity or aggression from someone, a clear way of redrawing your engagement is to remember you're both on the same side. So, you could emphasize your shared goal and say something like, "I know it's really critical for both our teams to get a final launch date confirmed. From what it sounds like, if you can get signoff from legal and I can confirm with engineering, we might be able to confirm this by tomorrow."

The powerful/likeable binary is loud here. I could almost feel the way Mariko wanted to assert her belief that the data wasn't there but also maintain a professional relationship with her manager. Sometimes, using the Getting on the Same Side framework can help make overt what you're looking for or what help you need; sharing information is a helpful way of looking open and offers a stepping stone *to* persuasion. If Mariko's manager was, in fact, unable to suggest any further places to search, it helps solidify Mariko's own position and she can move on from that task.

For what it's worth, I think this framework is widely applicable in life. I use it with my own boys on the mornings I take them to school. Sometimes they might be grouchy and I don't want to micromanage them, but I also want to get out the door on time without incident. The Getting on the Same Side framework in this situation looks like this:

"I know we all don't want a stressful morning."
[*Shared goal*]

"I've laid out your school clothes. If you put them on, I'll make sure your bags are packed."
[*Evidence of past work and a request for specific action*]

"If we finish early, we can play piano/you can use the computer before we leave on time."
[*Emphasizing the shared goal and a wish to move forward*]

This framework alleviates the need to be defensive or push uncomfortably; rather, it allows you to find an area of common ground and common goal and keep the focus there. One of the main areas where clients tell me they experience feeling defensive or even outright being told they're being defensive is in the process of giving or receiving feedback—something we'll move to now.

> **Try this:** Has your frustration ever led to communicating defensiveness? Or are you feeling irritation with a team member or close colleague? Try isolating your shared goal or interest and using that framework to approach the issue with them.

THE PAIN OF GIVING (OR RECEIVING) FEEDBACK

"Thanks for your feedback!" is something I once yelled back at an angry driver who honked and hollered at me that I had parked too close to another car. (Reader, I would never.) Many of us crave good feedback—we want to know we're on the right track, doing good work, and we want our enormous efforts to be validated by someone else. Good feedback is a delight to receive, while "constructive" feedback can be a real kick in the teeth. The (overused) saying is that "feedback is a gift," but sometimes it's a gift we'd prefer to return. So how, then, to embed a culture of useful feedback into your working relationships?

To some extent, it depends on where you work: some organizations, such as the investment firm Bridgewater or Netflix, are extremely overt with the giving and receiving of feedback, building it directly into their core values and principles. But I consciously use the phrase "working relationships" as distinct from your workplace, because you can still seek and give feedback even if you're working in a place that doesn't regularly do that.

First, you must start by modeling openness to feedback yourself. Begin by soliciting feedback easily ("I'm open to your feedback" or "I'd love feedback for how you think that went"). And then whether you've invited feedback or not, the ideal tactic is—to the best of your ability—to receive that feedback openly and calmly, thanking the other person for their insight. You don't have to—and often shouldn't—respond or deny it right away. Go away, reflect on it, and if it still doesn't sit right with you, perhaps you can bring it up with that person at a later time. But taking the time to reflect is critical, as sometimes it might take time for it to hit home. I have had someone on my team many years later reach out to me about some feedback I gave, saying, "I didn't hear it back then, but now, looking back, it makes a lot of sense, and I'm grateful for it." We all hear things in our own time.

Ideally, feedback that you communicate to others should be timely, relevant, and actionable. It should provide examples of when that behavior has occurred and how it impacted you or the broader team, if you're in a management role. For me, I'm also a big believer in sharing good feedback. I love passing on a compliment ("Oh, Mary said she loved your presentation yesterday!") and giving my own ("I love the way you split up those sections, it was a really smart take") because I believe in anchoring compliments to reality.

Katie, a friend of mine, works for a truculent manager who rarely says one nice thing about her work. And Katie spends a lot of her energy wondering when that compliment will come (or continually working harder and harder to try and outdo her previous contributions). Sometimes the smartest thing to do in these situations is to accept that that compliment is just not coming. It is not that manager's style, and your being in that role and, in some cases, simply not being fired is the only reflection you will get of that manager's approval. Similarly, if you hear "I'm open to feedback" from your manager or your direct report and then that person *isn't* open when you try to give it, it can be disorienting and cause you to wonder how to get new information across to them.

Getting comfortable with soliciting feedback and actively finding out what people are thinking about you and your work might feel like your worst nightmare. Why would I want to go and find out why that person doesn't like me? And I get it: it sounds counterintuitive. But sometimes it's excellent data that can dispel any disquiet you've had working with each other and point to a more generative way forward together.

> **Try this:** Are you getting the right amount of feedback to truly understand where you can improve your value to your team and organization? Are you giving an appropriate amount and sharing compliments and areas of improvement? If not, consider soliciting more from your manager and peers or giving more to those around you.

LESS CAN BE MORE: DON'T MAKE PEOPLE EAT A 1,400-POUND TUNA

I often performed my worst debates when I knew the most about the topic. I know, it's mean. I have given stellar speeches when I knew very little about a topic area, and I have given terrible speeches when I knew too much. In one memorable instance where I knew a lot about commercial surrogacy, I essentially wrote my teammates' notes, and they gave excellent speeches that were smart, articulate, and driving right at the issue. Mine turned out to be long-winded, a little confused, and overly in the weeds.

As I stood at the lectern, I saw the adjudicator lose interest in me and my speech in real time as I meandered through my arguments. I had edited my work badly. I was too enmeshed in the details and forgot to do a bird's-eye view and zoom out—and I was also way over time, a big no-no. We've discussed a lot of the pitfalls of *not* wanting to speak or ask questions, but what about giving *too much* context? Being concise in your communications is a superpower that can imbue us with a ton of authority and make everything easier for those around us, too.

One of the key ways of communicating persuasively is to say *less,* which feels counterintuitive. Brevity may be harder to come by, but it's oh-so-important. Often, we think that in order to justify our decisions or to look persuasive, we must show every piece of information we have ever amassed about the topic. Saying a lot feels thorough, thoughtful, rigorous, and transparent. Here is all the thinking I've ever done on the subject—I'm not hiding a thing! Surely that's what our colleagues or bosses or friends expect of us, right? Well, yes and no. What we want to be offering is *digestible* amounts of information.

Are you trying to get people to eat a 1,400-pound tuna? When we know a lot about a subject, sometimes we metaphorically deposit a huge fish in front of an audience when they're expecting a neat little fillet. We think, *Behold! My gigantic fish! My beloved topic area of interest that I've spent years obsessing and learning about!* And they think, *How the heck am I going to eat* that? Not every audience is ready for the whole fish. Some are going to require some deft cutting (read: editing) to make your message more, ahem, digestible. So, always think about the audience you're presenting to and what they need to know: *What's the most valuable contribution I can make to the conversation, meeting, or presentation?* A piece of sushi, message-wise, is much easier to interact with, understand, and consume. And if tasty, a lot more memorable.

Using Sushi Train Logic to Structure Your Arguments Persuasively

In fact, speaking of sushi, have you ever been to a sushi train restaurant? I often get weird looks when I ask this—it's either bafflement or immediate joy—but they're one of my favorite dining experiences. Imagine sitting at a counter in front of a small conveyor belt, upon which small plates of sushi underneath little plastic domes glide past you. Each small dish comes with a plate (usually color-coded to indicate price), the sushi itself, and a little protective lid. As customers, we're used to seeing each plate emerge and deciding which ones we'll choose to eat. The math of the sushi train is simple: plate plus fish plus lid equals deliciousness.

I'm always impressed by the logic of this transaction and how smooth it is: it's a simple and elegant structure, and it seems to translate across language and culture with ease. I've been to these restaurants in multiple different countries, and without words, the whole system automatically makes sense. But now I want you to imagine the dismay if something were to upset this structure, such as an empty plate with no sushi or, worse, a piece of sushi on the conveyor belt, plateless and lonely. It would immediately stand out as aberrant and wrong. I suspect few people would choose the plateless sushi if it emerged from the kitchen.

You might be wondering, *Why is Kate talking about sushi?* Well, this is a convenient metaphor I like to use when explaining how to structure your arguments. In part because it's delicious, but also, people rarely forget it. I learned similar structures while debating when I had limited time and had to make maximum impact. I had to prune and edit everything fairly ferociously in order to be left with only the important pieces. Once you see arguments this way, it's easier both to structure your own arguments persuasively and to pick holes in everyone else's. Think about the underlying argument as the plate, the sushi as the example that brings it to life, and the lid as wrapping it all together neatly. Let's try it!

Argument: "It's time for us to hire a head of communications; we can't wait any longer."
[*Plate*]

Example: "We've recently had extensive bad press such as the hit job on one of our executives, which was personal and in bad faith. That could have been ameliorated by some strategy and better handling of the reporter."
[*Sushi*]

What's next: "I'm going to work on a job description and circulate for your feedback."
[*Lid*]

This is a good template if you're looking for an easy-to-remember way to compose your arguments, especially if you're under pressure. Using a structure like this—especially with the "what's next" component—helps propel you and your idea forward rather than just being stuck in the "so . . . anyway" trail-off, which, let's be honest, is never your friend in persuading anybody of anything.

Consider if I'm trying to teach you about a historical event that happened ten years ago. I'm unlikely to begin with the dawn of time and work my way forward. Sometimes we think, "Let me tell you the twenty-seven steps I took in order to make this happen," because it feels like we're covering all our bases. But saying less often makes for a much more effective communication vehicle than we credit it. (Ironically, when people say little, it has the double effect of hiding the fact we might not know everything, anyway.)

It's helpful to think about what I need you to know: what's the topline, most important thing. Busy people don't want to be overwhelmed with looking at what amounts to a double page of *Where's Waldo?*—they just want to know you've found him. Giving a topline, architectural explanation can also enforce a lot of authority. You'll sound decisive and clear, which in turn gives others faith in you and your plan. Again, if others want to understand or know more details, they'll ask, and you can go deeper. Less, it turns out, is actually more.

Sushi Train Logic enables us as your audience to understand your position clearly, build trust with you and your process, and dig in on the details if we need to (without being overwhelmed at the outset). You've all received that email that takes an eternity to get to the ask—sometimes you might even wonder if there was an ask in the first instance. Don't be that guy! While I think giving too much context is somewhat gendered, what's more revealing is this is also *level*-specific. Giving too much context is an immediate signal of non-seniority. Senior folks don't give long contextual overviews—they are biased toward short updates, in part because they're time-poor and in part because they have honed this skill over time. If you're eager to assume authority, mirroring modes of shorter, sharper comms is a quick way to help you get your correspondent the information they need and help you look authoritative at the same time. Short and brilliant. Five stars.

> **Try this:** When you next have to write an email or present an idea to someone, consider breaking it down with Sushi Train Logic. What is the argument, the example, and what's next? Try presenting it in this order and see if it streamlines the way your message lands.

The paradox of the modern workplace for many of us is that we often dread being asked the question, and we simultaneously want to be the one who is asked in the first place. The first answer to this quandary is to stop fearing the questions. There is power in asking and answering them, if you have the right framework to do so.

Locating Our Powerful Likeability
When Our Batteries Are Low

In which we learn some frameworks to lean on when we're not at our best, laugh at a corporate workshop moment, understand why generosity is so critical, and become acquainted with the virtues of signposting (very meta, because I'm doing that right now!).

Many years ago, I was at a corporate offsite in Seoul, where my team and I had to endure a number of painful group sessions. I say "painful" because we were jet-lagged and had so much work to do while we were there that many of us were resentful to have to spend time on pithy exercises that weren't actionable or related to our work. (It's possible I was just projecting.) An overly cheerful facilitator had a large group of us write "six-word career memoirs" as part of a bonding session. I was not, as the kids say, feeling it, so I wrote something down that made me smile, and of course the facilitator must have sensed it. He came over to me with his microphone and asked me to read it out to the group.

"No, thank you, I'm fine not to share."

"Oh, go on!" he goaded. "I know you've finished—share it with us!"

"No, truly. I'd rather not."

He started trying to get a chant going in the room of "Share it! Share it!" The rest of the room joined in only half-heartedly.

"Fine," I said. "My six-word career memoir is 'High-functioning introvert; hates group exercises.'"

There was a palpable silence and some muffled laughter, and it was noticeable that he didn't ask me to contribute anything after that. Yes, it was harsh, but to be fair, I honestly wrote it thinking that I would not have to share it with anyone else.

While I stand by my memoir—truer words about myself have never been spoken—I think it highlights almost in haiku-form the challenges of powerful likeability when we're tired, disinterested, jet-lagged, or just plain not in the zone. Given that many of us have those days (or even weeks) at work, I wanted to dedicate a chapter to frameworks and ways we can rethink how we show up in times when our batteries might be running on low.

I know using the word *energy* puts me at risk of sounding a lot more woo-woo than I am but think of the attitude you bring to an interaction as your energy. You might start a meeting feeling tired, hungover, bored, resentful, distracted—any number of negative emotions that will affect your mood and energy. If those are communicated to others, you'll find your own message getting lost, and what's left is a negative feeling in the room. This is not to say we shouldn't experience negative feelings—of course, avoiding that is impossible. But the better you're able to regulate those emotions, the better you can help regulate others' emotions, too. A true gift to a working group is the use of your energy to positively affect theirs.

If good communicators can impart their knowledge with impact, truly gifted communicators can fundamentally change the room they're in. I once worked with a colleague who was outwardly unrattled by almost everything. He famously once jumped into an ambulance with a pregnant colleague who had gone into labor and waited with her in the delivery room until her partner could get to the hospital. His gift to his team was his ability to manage his emotions in service of the group's needs. When a crisis hit, he was able to be calm, solid, and stoic, looking to the next steps and helping others follow a clear path. In effect, his energy was so confidently expressed that it was contagious to others. They sensed from him a groundedness, an "I've got this" mentality, that suffused their work together. While this was him channeling calm, which we'll discuss in chapter 9, it also often read as self-assuredness to others. I want to cover two main ways we can structure our communication when we're tired so that we can lend some positive energy, clarity, and groundedness to our colleagues.

COMMUNICATIVE INCLUSION AND SHARING THE ENERGY LOAD

The first way to help when your batteries are low is to be as generous as you can to those around you and solicit their involvement. When our batteries are low, we can become naturally less verbose or even terse. Our irritation can pique faster, and maybe we let that show more, too. One of my clients, Mary, says of her boss, "When she's tired, she is extra blunt and she can sound impatient with the team." This is, of course, deeply human. I don't have a direct antidote to this, except maybe taking a nap if you're able or, even better, a vacation.

What I do have is the idea of communicating your inclusion, which can be a powerful lever to make everyone in the team feel closer to you and to their goals. This takes little effort but has big rewards, which is excellent when your batteries are already low. I don't mean diversity initiatives (which are brilliant and necessary). I mean more of a *communicative* inclusion—literally working to make sure everyone in every interaction is made to feel welcome to speak.

I first thought deeply about this idea when I was a teacher's aide at college during my own PhD candidacy years. In tutorials, each student could earn about 20 percent of their final mark by participating in class conversation. Over time, I realized that many students didn't participate much at all, missing out on a valuable section of their final mark. Sure, there were some students who hadn't read the book or who didn't turn up to class, but of the others, I could usually tell who had engaged with the text that week but were just shy or intimidated by the room. I tried lots of different ways to engage the class and here's the one that succeeded.

Instead of always calling on the few folks who were quick to put their hands up to answer questions, I started saying things such as, "Would anyone who hasn't spoken yet like to share something with the group?" A question like this accomplished two things: first, it was a gentle invitation to those who hadn't volunteered an answer to feel as though they had overt permission to speak up. And second, it reminded the folks who had their hands up—often the more extroverted ones—to be mindful of the rest of the room and the atmosphere that we were cultivating together.

Crucially, when you hear your own voice in a room once, it becomes a little bit easier to contribute a second time—and I still see this played out when I run programs at companies today. There's a fine line between putting someone on the spot and causing potential embarrassment and actively, inclusively helping them to find their voice. This is a kind and gentle way of getting those who may have felt unwelcome to speak to do so: but it also doesn't put the spotlight on them by calling them out by name, which will make a lot of people feel pressure or panic.

At work, if you spot moments where another colleague might have been spoken over or had credit taken away for an idea, you can call attention to their contributions by saying, "I think Heidi had that idea earlier" or "Shilpa, did you want to finish what you were saying before?" Inclusive communication is so key in getting everyone to feel comfortable and as if their ideas are important (they are) and worth listening to (ditto). Once you make a working group, team, or cross-functional group more inclusive, everyone will feel more comfortable contributing and appreciate your leadership for allowing them to be heard.

A side effect of communicative inclusion is that it can also help shift the energy deficit you might be feeling and shine a light on others who might be able to take up the reins. If you're feeling exhausted, for instance, name someone else to run a meeting in your stead or to do something visible with good energy—this is why we have teams. We're not all robots and not all able to communicate at the exact same level of natural enthusiasm at the same time. Two co-founders who work together who also happen to be brothers tell me this is a strategy they have used, often. When pitching investors, they often let the brother who is more fired up that day lead the meeting, while the other takes the proverbial back seat. Endearingly, when the younger brother had children and was often sleep-deprived, the older brother stepped in and carried some of the energetic load in those pitch meetings. Leveraging the energy and skills of those around you when you might not be in the best shape isn't a cop-out; it's smart, human leadership that recognizes we all have our good days and bad.

> **Try this:** Consider how many people around you might not be speaking up. Include them openly and overtly when you can, especially if your own energy is low.

BE CLEAR AND SPECIFIC TO OPTIMIZE FOR GENEROSITY

When you are time-poor or just plain tired, it can be even more exhausting to filter through all the asks you get in a given day. I work with many leaders who have many people or departments asking for their time and energy, and it can become a strain to figure out which ones need attention, which ones can be delegated, and which ones can be ignored.

Of course, some of those asks are coming from people who have worked up the courage to make an ask, so having it be interpreted as noise and not receive a proper answer is a shame. So, it's worth thinking through, if you're the one making the ask, how to make it so the person receiving it will find value in it, too. Entirely one-sided asks can be easy for busy people to ignore. For instance, many of the executives I work with get lots of requests to "pick their brain." This is a deeply frustrating ask to get because it's vague, it's viscerally gross—maybe that's just me—and it implies I have to do the work to unpick my brain for your benefit. In particular, the vagueness of the ask makes it hard to know how to answer in a timely way. *What do they want to know? How would I even prepare for that meeting? Do they want to know about my specific role now or something from my past?*

When you're approaching someone who might be more senior than you with an ask such as this—which is, by the way, a very reasonable thing to do—think about the framing of the ask itself. For instance, be *specific* as to what you're looking for—what sort of job opportunities they might know about or their opinion on a particular issue—and then that saves the recipient a lot of cognitive load. Further, here's a helpful test. If you wouldn't ask a dentist or lawyer for an hour where you could "pick their brain," don't ask another professional. Just because everyone doesn't charge in six-minute billable increments doesn't mean their time isn't equally valuable—so treat it as such. The same goes for asking someone for a favor or attempting to get them to become your mentor.

> **Try this:** When making an ask of someone else, assume they are tired and overwhelmed. What is the easiest thing for them to say yes to? Be specific in the ask so they can make a fast, informed decision as to whether or how to help you.

SIGNPOSTING TO OTHERS (AND TO YOURSELF)

Tell me if this feels familiar. You're rushing from meeting to meeting, and you might even be nervous about an upcoming moment when you know you must be persuasive. Maybe you're pitching a product, interviewing for a job, or seeking stakeholder buy-in. And when the moment comes—and you know it because your heart is beating wildly—you jump straight in the middle and start paddling fast. For your audience, this can be like walking into a movie halfway through. I've been on the receiving end of so many pitches from companies or individuals, and it always surprises me that I often must interrupt and ask, "Sorry, who are you? What do you do?" All the basics can get lost when the stakes are high and our adrenaline is, too.

It's helpful when we want to be authoritative to think about having some frameworks for presenting in our pocket, ready to go. When we want to be our most persuasive, the best advice I can give is to simplify and make clear what our argument is, at the very beginning. That can often mean starting at the beginning: covering all the basics as to the who, what, how, and where of what you're discussing—recap so that any new folks will be caught up before you begin and make your case. No one is persuaded by something gnarly and scary; they're open and receptive when it feels neat, doable, and knowable. It's often tough to make your own issues—naturally complicated and interesting to you—simple to others. We spend so much time thinking about our ideas that when we go to explain them to others, they can be hard to follow. Not everyone has spent the hours we have deep in the weeds, and so maybe you've found your manager or a colleague or partner to be a little confused about the path you're trying to trace when you present back to them a series of ideas that may or may not be clearly connected.

Enter your new BFF: the signpost. Just as you're used to seeing signposts when you're traveling (LAKE TAHOE, 20 MILES, for instance), it can be useful to have conversational signposts in your communication. They can help your persuasion style and give you structure and sense. There's an often-used idea that you must—sticking with the Tahoe theme—tell your audience you're going to Tahoe, go to Tahoe, and then tell them you went to Tahoe. I think this can be fairly overused, but it's worth bearing in mind for some things you might want to communicate that are highly technical or difficult to get across quickly. In these instances, you might start at the beginning of a meeting explaining your intention, cover the subject material, and then explain you've done so in a summary form.

Here's a useful signposting template I've used for years:

1. Explain What You're Doing

I know, this feels obvious, no? But it's amazing how many people forget to do so and barrel forward without context, which is confusing and can be hard to follow. Try using the following statements:

> "I'm here to walk through the latest sales figures and give some next steps."

"Thanks for your time. I'm going to be conducting an informational interview today."

"Thanks for meeting with me. I'm here to talk about my son's recent test results."

2. Foreground Your Work

You can think about breaking this up into two or three sections, too, if it's a bit unwieldy. For example, "I'm going to talk through three things today: (1) the sales figures from Q1, (2) comparisons with Q4, and (3) some projections for the year ahead."

3. Codify What's Next

A simple way of persuading here is to say what's going to happen next. For instance, "I'm going to take these projections and connect with the marketing team. In the meantime, I'd like your input specifically on X and Y before we begin that review." Or similarly, "I'll put a meeting in for next week and share notes before then."

Another key benefit of signposting is that it gives you a natural beginning, middle, and end, which is helpful if you're someone who might be prone to rambling, especially when you're nervous. We ramble when we don't know what we're talking about: it's a curious reflex that when we know only a little, we tend to want to say a lot. It's like Mark Twain's line, "I didn't have time to write you a short letter, so I wrote you a long one"—except in this case, the letter is an interminable sentence. Giving yourself a structure of sorts, as in "I'm going to run through three main ideas we've had," automatically gives you a gate to run toward and then finish at the third idea; it's expected, everyone including you knows it's happening, and you get a natural feeling of completion.

Signposting is automatically a signifier of persuasion and authority because it gives you structure and explains your process clearly. If others in the meeting have concerns, you're preemptively answering them by telling them you'll be getting to that point later. People generally feel more relaxed because they see and experience your structure, rather than that remaining in your head. You can have the best-laid plans in mind, but if they're not communicated, they can't make an impression on those around you. And this helps your persuasion because the clarity is what others take away in that moment: you've presented a clean and clear offering, so it makes saying yes or accepting it all the easier.

Importantly, I can't leave this section without explaining that the other interesting thing about signposting is that you can signpost . . . yourself. Bear with me here. I often hear from early-career folks that sometimes they're brought in to take over a project or as an associate on a project, so they never lead the meeting but are always present. It's hard in these instances to have any authority with your client, especially if you've been brought in by a more senior member of your broader team. A simple way to signpost yourself up front is to introduce yourself and explain your presence. (Sometimes the more senior person forgets to do this. If you're a senior person, please always give a generous intro to your junior colleagues!)

You could say something like, "Hi, I'm Samira. I'm going

to be joining these meetings going forward. I'll be listening and context-gathering for today, but I'm excited to get up to speed on this account." That way you're not signing yourself up to contribute immediately if that's a concern, and you're also allowing yourself to get used to the cadence and rhythm of that relationship before you take it over (if that is a possibility). This sets you up to be persuasive later and saves face a little in the moment when you might be feeling like a hapless junior (we've all been there, and it sucks). You could even signpost yourself in a new role, where you might feel anxious to make a good impression quickly or to start actively working on things. You could offer something like, "Hi, I'm Apoorva, I'm new to the team leading content marketing. I will spend the next two weeks listening and learning and will present my initial findings in our one-on-one meeting with a plan to go forward from there." The signpost can make the work you're doing obvious and alleviate other people's questions before they arise. Persuasive, neat, and authoritative.

> **Try this:** An easy way to cut through the noise is through great signposting. Consider adopting signposting in an upcoming meeting or interaction to simplify your own flow and to get clarity in your message.

SENSING IRRATIONAL DISTRUST OR DISLIKE FROM ANOTHER

Hoo boy, this section is a doozy. Have you ever been in a situation at work where you can sense someone just plain doesn't like you? Where you're getting not-so-subtle (or even extremely aggressive) cues that you're not really welcome in their space? There are few things that can drain a person's batteries faster than the incessant spinning rainbow wheel of speculating whether it's your workmanship, your personality, or your new perfume that has them fuming—it can be an exhausting carousel.

Now it's obviously important to work out whether there is a real problem hiding here: are they anxious, do they feel slighted, are they being disenfranchised, and so on are all good things to look into and, if you can, have an overt conversation about together. It's especially important to clear the air and ensure, if not a perfect working relationship going forward, at least a workable one. You could suggest going for a walk or having a conversation where you can simply call it out. Saying something like, "I've been sensing some pushback from you recently" or "I wanted to talk to you to see if there's something between us that I should know more about, as I really want to work closely and well with you." It can be a hard conversation, for sure, but sometimes it can be really rewarding. At the very least, it shows fearlessness on your part—that you're happy to call out behavior that makes you uncomfortable and that you'd like to see change.

But there's another category here that I think is also worth calling out, and that is when someone is just plain threatened by you. Maybe you got the promotion they wanted, maybe you're younger than they are or more credentialed—anything can be a trigger point. And on this one, if you've exhausted all the real issues that could be coming between you, it can be immensely toxic to exist alongside this person in close work proximity.

My best wisdom in these situations is that in my experience, I've found that when excellence enters the room, mediocrity becomes furious. If you happen to be the trigger point for someone else's insecurities, it's unlikely that a conversation will be able to remedy that. At that stage, it's up to you to determine whether that level of work-fury is tolerable (Can you laugh it off to yourself? Distract yourself?) or whether you need to remove yourself from their orbit by ignoring the behavior, changing roles, or perhaps in more extreme circumstances, changing companies. Few people will admit that they are triggered by you or your expertise, but at least you might get a better sense of how seriously to take their concern and how you want to mentally position it to yourself.

I come from Australia, where tall poppy syndrome was born—and variations of it exist around the world in other guises, too. Tall poppy syndrome refers to successful people being criticized or denigrated when they are deemed to have become "too" successful (whatever that means). It's criticism *because* of the success, and the too-tall poppy must be cut down, so to speak, to be in line with all the others. While tall poppy syndrome is a largely Australian phenomenon, a Canadian survey on the subject of tall poppy syndrome was conducted in 2023, with 4,710 respondents across 103 countries. It found that 86.8 percent of respondents "indicated that at some point in their career, either past or present, they have experienced hostility or have been penalized and/or ostracized because of their success or achievements." Even if you haven't put a name to this phenomenon before, you may have felt this in your life and career at some point, and if you've decided—even on a subliminal level—to correlate success with criticism, the implication is that you can also correlate failure with likeability.

Try this: If you are sensing what feels like irrational hostility from someone in your workplace, set yourself to have a conversation with them that overtly calls out the behavior to see if you can get closer to identifying the problem.

Given the variables that life often throws our way, it's not surprising that all days won't look the same and that some days have a higher energy deficit than others. Rather than being frustrated by that or trying to act the part, it's helpful to think of ways to streamline your communication when the going gets tough, as well as try to use those around you to help boost your own presence and energy.

SEVEN

Recasting Difference as Strength

In which we experience an embarrassing plane trip, rethink difference and what it means for our communication, learn the uses of difference, understand why embracing our weird is critical, find that difference can open up new opportunities for us, and discover warmth as a beautiful antidote to deference.

"Get out of that seat!" The flight attendant rushed over to me, looking extremely annoyed. "You!" she called, pointing at me. My cheeks flamed red, and my heart thrummed fast as I rustled through my bag, trying to find my boarding pass. "Stand up! And get *out* of that seat," she insisted. By now, the whole section of the plane was looking at me. "That seat"—she almost hissed while looking at me with loathing—"is for Dr. Mason!"

Ah, here we are again. Meekly, I suggested that I was indeed he—"Dr. Mason" in this case was a twenty-eight-year-old woman. It was the first time I had flown since being awarded my doctorate a month earlier, and it was the first time I'd ever chosen "Dr." from the dropdown list when I made my booking. After five long (*loooong*) years of writing my thesis, it was such a novelty and delight to do so: a secret joy, just for me. But in this moment, with a flood of blank, judgy faces looking at me from the surrounding seats, that private moment of joy had turned into public embarrassment. The attendant triple-checked her list and my boarding pass and, without a murmur of apology, left me alone—and deeply sad.

I want to be clear. This anecdote isn't about "Boo hoo, no one recognized that I'm a doctor," because, well, that would be crazy. But it is about difference. My difference, in fact, from what that flight attendant had imagined. What does it mean that it *didn't even cross your mind* that I could be the person listed on your manifest? I felt small and ridiculous and guilty, as if I had done something wrong, and I felt myself blink fast so the tears pricking at my eyes wouldn't fall. Mainly, I just felt enormous disappointment.

What happens when you become something and yet remain invisible to the culture despite standing in row 13? And how do we treat the disease of difference, underestimation, and bias that so often swirls around us? If only a doctor had been on the plane, we might have actually gotten a diagnosis.

Academics Amy Diehl and Leanne Dzubinski call the flight attendant's mistake an example of "role incredulity," a pattern in which women are "mistakenly assumed to be in a support or stereotypically female role." In this instance, the stereotype she picked was that a "Dr." was a distinguished-looking older male, and the younger woman in front of her didn't match the picture in her head. What was it about my body that others read so differently? On some psychic level, do we have to carry the dated physical designations of male power and authority (think briefcases or ties) to prove our bona fides?

In fact, when people talk about developing one's "executive presence," they are actually asking, "Can you exude leadership and authority through your *physical* presence?" What does it mean to "look the part"? And what part are we looking like, exactly, if we're not tall white men?

Difference can feel as though it might threaten or diminish our power, but it can also offer us opportunities to step into a more powerful or authoritative position. We know diverse teams are better teams—all the research points to that being the case—but of course, that feels trickier when you're the one who is "diverse." Think about the times when you have had a strong sense of being different in a room. Where was it? What made you feel that way? Whether it's a fancy boardroom, facing down a receptionist at a doctor's office, or visiting a mechanic, difference is one of those things that triggers the powerful/likeable binary in full force. I've spent much of my career being one of a few women in meetings and for almost my entire debating career I was the only woman on the team.

And maybe it's not always gender. Elements such as our race, background, zip code, age, and experience level can all make us recognize our difference. And often these differences make us doubt ourselves or feel more keenly obvious and small in the room. In fact, feeling different in a room can often feel like a force that's powering your impact and presence *down*. It lies heavily on our shoulders and quiets our sense of self. It can feel harder to get your voice across—often literally, with deeper, louder male voices dominating a room. It can feel as though you don't have a friend with whom to exchange a knowing look or back up a point you've made. That we have to do our actual jobs while also grappling with the disconnect between ourselves and where we work weighing heavily on us as an insistent and gnawing sense of disquiet and alienation.

The Upsides of Difference

Sometimes the culture around us feels immutable, as if it will never expand to encompass our difference and new definitions of power. Or even the mundane act of taking your seat on a plane. And it can be reasonable to think that when we still see outdated practices or bias in place, which unavoidably makes us think that attitudes have been frozen in amber. This is where I want to focus, because it's a space of potential and usually has less to do with trying to implement wholesale changes across a company or organization and more to do with implementing a change to suit you and your team.

Let's face it, there are lots of things to fear at work. One of the most common concerns I hear is anxiety about our differences. *What if they think that's weird? Should I hide my tattoos? Will they accept my neurodiversity?* Being different can elicit a deep fear-based reaction: we intuitively feel unsafe and ready to be judged harshly without "our people" around us. And when we feel alone, we may as well place the target on our own backs. In many instances, the rest of the group might not even be conscious of how you, the only woman or the only person of color, for example, might be feeling out of place. And it's not always a one-way street, either. You can be the most powerful person in an objective sense yet still be cognizant of difference and its strangeness.

Even someone who, from the outside, looks powerful and in control might still be keenly aware that they do not fit in with the larger status quo. One of my clients, Amanda, a vice president at a large media company, said she's struggling now in her mid-forties, and as a new mom. Most of her direct reports are in their twenties, and she feels self-conscious that she must occasionally leave early to pick up her child. She worries her team might question her commitment or see her as out of touch, despite being a brilliantly capable individual and leader. I felt similarly self-conscious as a new mother in a San Francisco start-up environment; many of my peers were coders in their early twenties who arrived at work by noon and stayed until midnight. There was even a weekly Tuesday night 7 to 10 P.M. all-hands work session—something I could never attend, because I wanted to be at home for bedtime with my son before logging back online.

We're less likely to be anxious about our difference if we are part of a supportive, close, connected group. But being the odd one out makes us feel like an unenviable spotlight is being pointed straight toward us, waiting to show up any misstep we make. As we think through difference, I want to offer some thoughts about reframing difference as our ally and not something to fear. This is not to say that difference is always easy, but that it can have its upsides.

Leveraging our difference as a strength can be deeply satisfying. At the beginning of my career, I struggled with my difference. I felt deeply aware that I had to ask many clarifying questions about how a particular technology worked or how a launch would happen. Even though I knew that being an engineer wasn't my job description, some people occasionally treated non-technical folks as mere support staff, which didn't feel good.

But one day I had the joy of realizing the differences my team and I had were precisely what was going to make a project work. I wasn't looking at the minutiae of the code— I knew how to message the launch to the press and make sure they understood how it worked on a consumer level. My strong humanities background (and my ability to write a killer FAQ document) meant I could protect my technical teams with the right preparation and even help them articulate the intricacies of the project to a less technical audience. I felt like I was the team's defender: I was protecting their time and their reputations when aggressive reporters would have loved to attack both. That difference can be a liberating or relieving advantage is something I've never forgotten: my problem-solving, my ability to see what others cannot were real gifts. It is helpful to think of that to remind myself to ask people who are different from me what their perspective is, too, so that I can grow from the interaction. In this way, embracing my difference enabled a mode for me that allows me to show up as myself with my particular skill set more fully. More broadly, difference can allow us to express what we need and want in a comfortable way that speaks to who we are.

Embracing the Weird

Your differences can also be memorable and make for a more powerful connection with others. When I first moved to the United States in 2012, I had a ton of difficulty getting people to understand my Australian accent. (One time, a shop assistant asked me to wait while she went to get her colleague to talk with me . . . in Spanish! *No bueno.*) I wondered whether I should somehow Americanize my accent and use different words, such as *sidewalk* instead of *footpath* or *trash can* instead of *garbage bin.* After a deeply awkward period of flip-flopping between the two, I ended up realizing that my difference was useful because it made me memorable. I worked with lots of reporters in my first job in the United States, and many would remember me quickly when they'd take my call and found me more charming than maybe they should have.

While difference can be memorable, it can also help us create an in-joke, bond, or deeper connection more quickly. People invariably asking me about kangaroos or Steve Irwin or Crocodile Dundee (unfortunately) was a fun way to make a mark and move past any initial awkwardness together. Did my difference make me more successful than my peers? Absolutely not—we were all still judged on merit. But you can use being memorable to your advantage rather than necessarily feeling self-conscious and strange about something you can't change anyway.

Positive difference can be a beautiful and powerful lever to use: it's an enormous lost opportunity to ignore or paper over your difference. Take, for example, Melanie, who works in a sales organization and says her superpower is that she is "Midwestern, earnest, and [her]self" in her interactions. She tells me, "All the men around me are like 'I'm going to put on my sales hat and use overused sales pitches and not care about you as a person' and I'm like, 'Hey, how's your cat? And kids? How can I help?'" Embracing her difference in her male-dominated office has been core to her success; she credits her own differences as helping her to be "one of the most successful sales reps in my company." Some differences—disabilities, ethnicities, cultural practices, for instance—are often much harder divides to bridge, and I don't diminish them with this point. Each difference will need its own thoughtful approach, but I think the larger idea of deciding to be up-front about one's difference and proceed to own it and keeping it as part of oneself shouldn't be underestimated.

> **Try this:** Do you have a difference of which you feel very aware at work? How could you reframe this as a superpower or a feeling of strength instead? What does it give you that no one else has?

LET YOUR DIFFERENCES OPEN THE DOOR TO OPPORTUNITIES

One of the big cross-functional projects I was involved in many years ago was an especially high-stakes event for a tech company. We had a kick-off meeting for the event with the executive leadership in which I didn't say a word. I remember feeling intimidated by the leadership team, and feeling noticeably young and new in a room full of tenured execs. I also didn't want to repeat anything that had already been said and thought my peers had done a great job explaining the parameters of the project.

Later, when the project wrapped up successfully, the CMO gave me a glowing review and told my manager, "I didn't know Kate had it in her—she didn't say a word in that kick-off meeting." I was so surprised that she had linked not speaking in that meeting with a wholesale judgment of my capacity, but people only join the dots on the information they have—and I didn't furnish her with anything in that meeting. And it drove an important point home for me: if people are waiting to get a sense of who you are or how you're thinking about something—especially in something like a kick-off meeting—it's an opportunity for you to speak, show your engagement early, and impress upon them that you do, in fact, have it in you. Had I said something earlier, I think she would have never had the chance to doubt me, which is a shame because I probably had to do even more to prove my worth. In this case, my difference was that I was one of the least senior people in that room—and I didn't use it to my advantage, which was a lost opportunity on my part.

Differences can be a good excuse to speak up and show engagement. Many of the women I coach often feel as though they're excluded from a group when they're the only woman, for example, and no one has made them feel included in the conversation. Sasha, who works at a venture capital firm with not many other women, recently told me, "I become quieter in meetings when I'm not given overt cues to act." I thought this idea of "overt cues" was so interesting: as if in a sea of male colleagues, her difference dictated to her that she must be invited to join, as if she were outside the arena, despite working directly in it. Speaking up in a meeting or spurring an interaction is an excellent way to increase your visibility and show that you're engaged and paying attention, even when you feel more junior, for example, than others.

DIFFERENCE CAN LEAD TO DEFERENCE: OUR PAINFUL
TENDENCY TO APOLOGIZE AND HEDGE

I'm sitting at a fancy restaurant in San Francisco waiting for my new client, Julie, to arrive. White linen tablecloths and polished silverware shine brightly on an unusually sunny day, and Julie comes to the table, apologizing for being late (she isn't), and then within moments apologizes for not having decided on her order yet (she just sat down), then tells me we should get whatever I want (that's nice, but I want her to choose her own food), and then apologizes again for the service being slow (that's not her job). This is a woman I greatly admire and whose professional accomplishments are extraordinary, yet I sensed she felt out of place. This restaurant, she explains, isn't somewhere she's eaten before, and she feels nervous and uncomfortable. Her feeling of difference is palpable to me.

Have you noticed in yourself that when your difference feels acute, you're more likely to become deferential? You might apologize unnecessarily or refuse an opportunity to make a choice—anything that will, you hope, take the spotlight of difference off you. We've arrived here at a particularly important part of communication, and I want to be crystal clear: deference is a big red flag that you're in a power deficit. While communicative power can be subtle, it can also sing the goddamned national anthem. The most common types of deference I tend to see in my work are unnecessary apologies and hedges, and I wanted to address both before going on to what we can do in their place.

Back in the restaurant, I told Julie that she didn't have to apologize to me—especially as often as she was doing—as she hadn't done anything wrong. Her response was to apologize to me for . . . saying sorry. We laughed about it after, but it's deep juju we're working with here, acculturated by many decades of normative deference and obedience. Unnecessary apologizing can often give the impression that we are somehow subordinate because it echoes and references, even indirectly, the servant or newbie. That inference can be especially undermining, particularly if you're already in a disempowered position, such as being the youngest person present, the only woman in the room, or both.

Of course, I have strong opinions on unnecessary apologies, as I am a recovering apologizer. I used to do it all the time—when I walked into a room and someone else was there, when someone else's video call audio didn't work properly, when I walked into a table, or when a room didn't have whiteboard markers. You get the point. I said "sorry" far too often and with way too much assumption of guilt. Maybe this will feel familiar to you or you have noticed it in others.

Think carefully about when you might want to use an apology and when it might be redundant: you might be surprised at the tally. Linguistics professor Deborah Tannen calls these "ritual apologies," which are a "learned element of conversational style that girls often use to establish rapport." Sometimes, they do establish rapport; at other times, they plainly put us back down on the very first rung of the hierarchical ladder. You don't need to take on the social cost or awkwardness that you're apologizing for; instead, you can just sit there in silence, and you don't have to own it. It's literally a quiet revelation. When I say this in workshops, I can see women drop their shoulders and exhale, so I'll say it again: you don't have to pick up the extra labor with an apology when it's not required. The awkward contortions of women apologizing at work also has to stop. If nothing else, it's plain exhausting and leads to an unnecessary lack of authority, which I'm passionate about correcting in any way I can.

I'm deeply politically aware of the pitfalls associated with becoming another voice telling women what to do and what not to do. Cindy Gallop, activist and all-round hero, writes, "The world would be a much better place, and the workplace a great deal happier, if instead of telling women to say sorry less, we told men to say sorry a whole lot more. The truth is, we need to worry less about editing women, and more about editing incompetent and inappropriate men." I certainly agree with the emphasis on editing incompetent and inappropriate men (and women, for that matter), but I do think that the internalized deference in an apology makes for an uneven playground for women from the outset.

I should say here that I think it's important to apologize when you are, in fact, wrong. "Sorry I'm late," "Sorry I missed your email," "Sorry I interrupted you earlier"—all of these are excellent and important parts of being human, and I'm a big advocate for apologizing as soon as you've realized you're at fault. But I think it's equally important to *stop* apologizing when you are not at fault or if the error is something outside of your control, like whether it's raining. "Sorry" should only apply in particular circumstances: when you've made a mistake or as an expression of consolation for someone's misfortune or grief. (Grief is the one exception where you can apologize for something you didn't do. Unless, of course, you did kill their loved one, in which case you've got bigger fish to fry.) If you're still saying sorry for anything else, well, I'm sorry, but you're just plain wrong.

> **Try this:** Apology can undermine even the strongest argument. When do you say sorry, and is it appropriate when you do so? Might you consider changing if not?

I once received an email from a colleague asking me for a favor. I pulled it up on my phone and saw large chunks of text and wondered if everything was okay. Scrolling down, I eventually figured out that she needed me to move a meeting, but the email itself was four paragraphs long! She had probably spent ages writing what she thought was a polite and unassuming email. It was filled with every hedge you can imagine, and many of the old chestnuts, including, "If you can't that's okay," "Totally fine if not," "No worries if not!" and many more in the same family.

The real issue here of course was that she actually *did* need me to move the meeting. But she buried that ask in such a long blanket of text, which made her aim a bit confusing. Speaking for her (a genuinely lovely person), I think her intention here was to couch the ask in softer language, to show a gentleness so she wouldn't be perceived as aggressive, harsh, or demanding. And I understand and resonate with this impulse: it's core to feeling the burden of likeability or niceness.

So let's talk about another form of apology: the hedge. Hedging is when we don't make a straightforward ask. Or we do ask, and we sort of hover over retracting it out of embarrassment or a lack of confidence as we sense the impending imposition. You'll recognize this if you've ever said, "Feel free to disregard this" or "It's probably a stupid idea" or "I'm sure you've already thought of this" or any variations on the theme.

In fact, when I was writing my PhD, my supervisor used to read draft after draft of my thesis, encouraging me to get to my point earlier. (Hi Liz! Promise I'm getting there!) She'd say, "Kate—you're backing into your point: you take a whole paragraph to get to your main argument." And time and again I'd rewrite my draft, hedging, tentatively meandering toward my point. One day—I think both to be provocative and because nothing else had gotten through to me—she said, "Why don't you try to write like a man?" And I went home and wrote the best draft of my life—much of it even made the final copy. And I wondered afterward why that worked so well. Why was such a provocative statement the thing that pushed me over the edge into an authoritative, definitive draft?

The exhortation to "write like a man" was, maybe to anyone reading, an insult. But I suspect Liz knew it would rile me up and get rid of the hedging I was doing. There's a ton of research about how women and girls categorically perform worse in multiple-choice exams. We look at all the options with nuance and deliberate over them, often to our own detriment. *Well, it could be A, but if you took the bicycle into account, it's probably B. But you know, it could also be C . . .* Writing a draft is a lot like presenting or speaking anywhere else: putting our big argument first is not a traditionally gentle attribute. It's brash! It says, *Look at me!*

I looked at that draft and went and grabbed the lede (which I had buried midway through each paragraph) and put it at the beginning, where it should have rightfully been. I did a scrub of any "probably," "possibly," "maybe," "could," and "almost" hedges and started to get comfortable with more definitive statements, like "I argue that the implication is" and "My research conclusively demonstrates," and started to believe *myself* in the process. When I'd get anxious about my ability to speak on my own thesis topic, Liz would say, "Well, it's your PhD—you're the expert on this now." And I'd remember, *Huh, it is, and I am.*

Another familiar hedge is the use of "kind of," not as a thinking crutch (like we might use "um" or "you know" when we're trying to think of the right word), but when we want to downplay or make casual our use of a big word or concept. Fearing sounding too earnest or too intellectual, we might say, for instance, "It's really kind of paradoxical" instead of just saying "it's paradoxical." The "kind of" here is both a hedge and a softener. It signals to our counterpart that we're still cool, still casual, and that they should not judge our eloquence too harshly. Which of course can be strategic in the moment, but be careful if you think this is becoming imposing or limiting behavior. Sometimes it's just cool to use the big word and move on.

> **Try this:** Consider what your speech or writing would look like if you omitted any hedges you might be using. Does it feel less weighty? More authentically like you? Find a balance that feels more like yourself.

CHANNELING WARMTH AS AN ALTERNATIVE MODE

One of the women I coach, Sara, told me she got some feedback on her email writing saying that it was too brusque and officious. "I was only trying to be efficient," she said, which sounds entirely reasonable. Another client, Clara, apologized for a short email she sent me, saying, "Sorry I was terse before—I was in action mode!" If you feel the shift toward deference in your communication—or feel like your pendulum has swung too far in the other direction and you're now blunter and that doesn't feel right either—the best reframing I can give is to move toward *warmth*.

Warmth is an admittedly amorphous thing to quantify, and it's going to look different for all of us, but it's a great way to help you get out of deferential modes. Let's assume the ask you wanted to make in the first instance was important, in which case it deserves not to be undercut by any deference. So let's play it out. Say you need someone to send you an article, and your first draft looks like this:

> *Hey Nina, sorry to bother you! Wondered if it was possible to get that article to send soon? No worries if you can't! Thanks!*

If I were seeing this email in the wild, I'd guess the person sending isn't very senior—and crucially, I'd also think that there wasn't any urgency in her getting the article. If you do need them to send you that article, adding on the casual "No worries if you can't!" isn't really appropriate, because there *is* a worry if you don't get it. So let's try again:

Could you please send me the article asap?

While there is nothing incorrect about this email at all, a lot of women I work with say, "Oh no, it's too abrupt or harsh—I could never send an email like that." This type of email might be a good fit for you—it equally might be a little abrasive-feeling or feel like you've overcorrected from super deferential to super non-emotive. For what it's worth, I quite like action mode, but I appreciate this is sparse and doesn't give a lot of opportunity for connection. So, let's try yet again:

Hi Nina, So lovely seeing you earlier today. Are you able to send me the article we mentioned by EOD as I need to share the notes with Carrie tonight. Thanks so much—have a great week!

You'll see here a balance of explaining what's needed (the article) and when (by the end of the day) and a reason, too, which can help justify or reinforce the ask, as we'll discuss later in the chapter. Now you needn't copy anything verbatim, but I think it's helpful to look at these three examples and see how you can up the warmth and still hold what's important about the ask.

Try this: Do you have a bias toward deference in your communication? Take note over the next week of whether this is happening and see what other ways you might try to approach that interaction. Alternately, are you biased toward being more terse? If that isn't serving you, think about aiming for warmth to engender a sense of connection in your communication. Again, take note and see how that feels after a week or so.

REASONING YOUR PRESENCE

A helpful mental framework to adopt when you might feel pressure to be small is to rely on reason. And in this case, I mean actually giving reasons. You'll notice in the third email example from the last exercise, I called out the reason that I needed the article: "I need to share the notes with Carrie tonight." Most fair-minded people understand a reason and usually take the request seriously and act on it. In fact, there's a ton of research that points to the word *because* as a key to influencing. If you can say you need something with a reason, you're a lot more likely to receive help.

One of my favorite studies in this area is the copy machine experiment that was conducted in the late 1970s by psychologist Ellen Langer and her research team at Harvard. It took place in a library where people were lining up to make photocopies—I like to imagine some groovy bell-bottoms and long hair to set the scene. The researchers attempted to cut in the middle of the line, each time using different language to do so:

- "Excuse me, I have 5 pages, may I use the photocopier?"
  (*Request*)
- "Excuse me, I have 5 pages, may I use the photocopier because I am in a rush?"
  (*Request and a fair reason*)
- "Excuse me, I have 5 pages, may I use the photocopier because I need to make copies?"
  (*Request and a terrible reason*)

They calculated the success rate of these no doubt annoying interventions and came to a surprising conclusion. With the request alone, about 60 percent of people allowed the researcher to cut in front of them. But the request with a fair reason scored 94 percent *and* the request with a terrible reason scored 93 percent! Which just goes to show that the quality of the reason didn't matter as much as having any reason at all. Weird, I know, but I think it's a useful thing to remember when making an ask. Add on the "because" and, ideally, a fair reason and you'll likely have more success—no apologies needed.

There are, of course, appropriate places for deference, such as when you're meeting someone extremely important or an older person or it's a somber occasion. There are many places where we would use deference appropriately. The problem isn't necessarily deference itself, but that we pick it up as a first option when there are so many other tools in the box.

> **Try this:** If you have a tendency toward deference and find yourself apologizing or hedging, giving a reason may be an excellent way to work yourself out of that pattern and into a more authoritative and less draining one.

NEGOTIATING WHILE FEMALE

Negotiating is an activity in which our difference can most acutely be felt. In fact, when I mention the word *negotiation* in my coaching practice, some women instinctively cross their arms and lean back away from me with an "absolutely no, not today, no thank you" kind of energy. As if I've uttered a dirty word or had the audacity to curse at the dinner table. And I get it.

When you search for images of the word *negotiation* online, you get multitudes of men in suits shaking hands, usually across the table from one another. Right at the outset and deep in our collective psyche, negotiation is coded as male, adversarial, and outcome-focused, rather than as a process or a conversation. It's straight-up coded as a different space in which we shouldn't be.

In fact, as academics Suzanne de Janasz and Beth Cabrera write, "When selecting metaphors for the process of negotiation, men pick 'winning a ballgame,' while women pick 'going to the dentist.'" Talk about an entirely different conceptualization of an activity! One is super fun and the other a dreaded obligation. (Apologies to my own delightful dentist, Dr. Dominic.)

The single most helpful way to think about negotiation is that it's just another manifestation of a persuasive conversation, something I think women naturally excel at. While I also tend to hate sports metaphors (and actually, a lot of sports, too), there is natural back-and-forth like in negotiation that can feel like a ballgame. And like sports, it's not all painful, either. In fact, it can even be fun.

More critically, the ballgame metaphor gives a sense of competitive joy —the fun is not only in the playing but in the winning, too. Contrast that with the dentist, which for the patient is often painful, scary, and passive.

When we invoke the word *negotiation,* we remember that we exist in a world where we consistently read statistics about how women negotiate less than men and that for women, sometimes it does "hurt to ask." In fact, most of the literature on negotiation bears out the idea that women don't like to negotiate, because they're worried if they do, they'll be less likeable (and they lose hundreds of thousands of dollars over their lifetimes because of it).

But here's the fascinating insight. In a 2017 paper looking at differences between same-sex groups negotiating, researchers found that women in groups of their friends negotiate *as well as men*. They found that "women negotiate better outcomes when negotiating on behalf of others whom they care about. Men do not exhibit a difference in this respect. What's important for women is the sense of fighting for others, for their friends, for something bigger than themselves." One of the reasons for this could be that the women felt more freedom to negotiate assertively, with less fear of being judged, when advocating for another person. They can be powerful—and likeable!—because their own sense of ambition or strength isn't at play. Rather, it's used for communal or collective benefit.

The findings suggest that women may be able to improve their own outcomes by linking their results to those of others. This is such a fascinating revelation to me: it proves to me that it's not that we're incapable of negotiating but that we're so often hamstrung by invisible, expensive cultural norms, most notably power and likeability. And let's think about traditionally coded feminine traits such as community, cooperativeness, empathy, and sensitivity. If we're thinking of the group around us, the "something bigger than ourselves," then we're some of the best negotiators out there. Yet when we negotiate on behalf of ourselves, we often overexplain or justify or we simply don't do it in the first place. The eagerness to lift up others is difference operating at its most powerful: our expertise and deftness when it comes to negotiation on behalf of others is something only we have. Which begs the question, If we can negotiate so well for others, why don't we translate that skill set and use it on behalf of ourselves, too?

If indeed we think of our difference in negotiation as an act of conversational *persuasion,* a whole different frame appears for us. After all, if we can fight for others, let's show ourselves that same grace and skill, and get what we deserve, too. Perhaps switching out the going-to-the-dentist mindset for the winning-a-ballgame one might be a useful mental frame as you think through your own position on negotiating persuasively.

Specifically, conversations or negotiations about money always dig into the powerful/likeable binary for us: we want to preserve and maintain relationships, but we also want to get paid. Of course, we want to get what we deserve, but God forbid anyone think of us as greedy. Given the feminine traits of providing comfort and communality and keeping everyone on an even keel, it's perhaps not surprising that women are somewhat used to putting others' needs above their own. Even perceived greediness goes directly against this because it's asking for something for oneself. (And to be clear, quoting a price isn't greedy; it's a normal business practice!) I often notice freelancers or contractors—who by definition aren't pricing their services through a bigger company and must quote directly—expend anxiety on communicating their pricing structure.

Consider treating any money talk like any other transaction. Be up-front and clear, and it's then up to the other
person if they want to bargain or to ask for a discount—but
it's not incumbent on you to offer that first. I've coached some
clients to artificially inflate their prices and then discount
them down, so they get a feeling of being kind by offering
something to the prospective client, but don't lose out finan-
cially. Use whatever will work for you, but don't undersell
yourself before you've actually sold your client on working
with you.

Just in case you're thinking, *Well, that's all good in theory,
Kate, but how might it work in the real world?* I want to tell you
a story. Some years ago, a good friend of mine was a senior
director at a large Silicon Valley start-up. The vice president
above her left the company, and she was put in charge of all his
teams and now reported directly to the CEO, effectively doing
everything he was doing in his role, plus her own, too. She told
me about this, and I was thrilled for her. I knew she wanted
the vice president role, and here it was! Oh no, she told me.
They haven't given me a promotion; I just didn't want to have
that conversation, she said.

The conversation to which she's referring (aka the job negotiation) is one of the most feared negotiations, especially
when you're already inside the company, because it feels like
you have so little leverage. So here was my friend, doing all
the same parts of her original job, plus all of her former manager's job, with no title or salary bump to acknowledge the
difference. This is referred to as a "dry promotion"—when you
do all the same responsibilities and more, sometimes with a
new title but not a raise.

So how could she summon her difference and change the outcome? There is no exact right answer, but there are many possibilities that you could ask for in any situation like this. Often, we assume that everything is immovable and unchangeable: *They won't be able to pay me more,* or *They won't accept my request to work four days a week.* And we come to these conclusions often before we've even listed out all the options we could play with. If you can play with all the variables, you might find a more creative outcome that could be interesting to the other party. There are myriad internal factors that exist in companies (and in your own circumstances) that might make particular actions difficult or not ideal timing. But here are some possibilities, in case they inspire action in your persuasive conversations:

> *I'm really energized to take on the vice president role—thank you. Given that I'll now be doing his role in addition to my own, I'd like to schedule a conversation about what my new salary and title will be. Perhaps we could find some time tomorrow?*

This gives your manager time (scheduling the meeting tomorrow, not today) but also doesn't lose momentum. You also signal in the language that your understanding is that you are taking on the vice president role. It's not semantics.

> [If refused]: *Thank you for that context—that's helpful. I'd like to do the role for one quarter and at the end of that quarter, I'd like to have the title and salary promotion conversation again. I want to do the best job for you that I can and that involves me knowing I have the faith of the executive team.*

Here you are compromising and asking for that conversation after you've had a chance to prove yourself in the role. You're firmly signaling that you intend to have that conversation in three months' time, and implying that if you don't have the faith of the team—in the explicit form of a promotion—you won't stay.

[If refused again]: *I understand your position, and of course that's your prerogative. It won't be something I can get on board with, and I want to be transparent about that. I'll loop back with my next steps.*

Working two jobs for the price of one might be untenable for you, and you may want to leave the company entirely. This is one of the ways you could make that clear.

But of course, these are a few responses out of an endless list of possibilities—and all of them will depend on what you want out of the exchange. Do you not care about the title, but do care about managing a team? Are you more concerned with financial stability right now than management? Thinking through your own priorities and then creative possibilities is a great way to begin. Even when it feels too hard to have the conversation or you think there is only one possible outcome, it's always worth digging into all the imagined options.

Listing them out gives you a greater sense of possibility and creativity when it comes to dreaming up an acceptable counter: many times you might bring an interesting perspective or idea that the other party may never have thought of.

And of course, this is another genre of persuasion: bringing an interesting, reasoned perspective to someone can convince them, especially if they haven't considered that idea before. It's important to understand their motivations and what solution they're solving, too. In the example with my friend, it would have been expensive and time-consuming to find and onboard a new hire who could step into those two roles quickly, so they may have been more willing to hear out a proposal from her instead of her quick acquiescence to do both for unchanged salary and title.

While we're on the topic of job negotiations, one of the most common questions I'm asked is about negotiating for a job offer *before* you start at a company. In some ways, this is the moment that feels like it has the highest stakes: you have to persuade a future colleague or recruiter that you're worth more than they have offered. But it's only the first difficult conversation you're going to have in that role, not the last, so it's worth using it as a litmus test of how well you're able to work with that person or organization.

For instance, it's a great opportunity to spot red flags that may signal to you that this organization isn't for you. Are they slow to respond and need consensus from too many people to decide? Are they aggressive in the conversation? Do they ask you how much your husband earns? (This was an actual question I got once when negotiating, and I should have paid more attention to what it said about the person and company. Unfortunately, I did not, and though I didn't reveal my partner's salary, I did take the job. Sigh.) Or, on the contrary, are they empathetic and trying to advocate for you from the outset? Creative and flexible in trying to help you achieve what you need to take the role? Generally communicative about their reasons? Depending on myriad factors you might be solving for in that situation, these conversations are so useful and re-vealing that it can be a blessing that it's part of the job-finding process at all.

My own approach in these moments is to be honest and collaborative up front. I'll always have in mind what I'm after or the salary I need as my minimum and know clearly what my walkaway moments will be. I'm never afraid to ask for time to reflect and think about something (it can be a red flag for me if I'm asked to give an answer immediately, depending on the circumstances). While there isn't a perfect formula for these conversations, I usually start with a lot of enthusiasm if I want the role or job ("Thanks so much for thinking of me, this looks incredibly exciting!"), then express what I need to make it work ("I'll need to reach X as a floor here—is there anything you can do to help me get there?") and then add a little counter-urgency ("If we can make X work, I can sign today"). If some-one thinks asking for what you reasonably need is "difficult," then that's likely someone you shouldn't want to contract with.

If I can tell you anything about difference and negotiation, it's this: we don't negotiate only when we buy a house or take a job. Negotiation includes things like asking for a bigger budget or more resources, getting approval for a project, del-egating work, having dinner with a toddler (just me?), and so much more. It's not useful to think of it occupying a stressful and unusual place in our lives. It's much more productive to think about negotiation as a calm, everyday thing that you do all the time. For one thing, reframing it this way removes the stress when you must do it. And it also lets you become highly skilled at it because you realize you're using those muscles every single day.

> **Try this:** If the word *negotiation* feels antagonistic or adversarial to you, consider thinking about it as an everyday practice, rather than a one-off, scary activity that you save for job promotions or buying a car.

Our difference is a beautiful and powerful thing. It means we can give something to a team they may have been missing, and our perspectives are critical and need to be heard. On occasion, we might question—or have others question—our tone or even physical presence, like me on the plane. The powerfully likeable answer is to find a place on the spectrum that feels like it speaks to our own sense of self: *Who am I, and how would I like to come across? How would I be proud to come across?* If you find deference sneaking in as an uninvited and unwelcome visitor, think through ways you can rephrase or reposition your ask and your presence and see if that feels, well, different, to you.

EIGHT

The Downsides of Preparation
and the Importance of Rest

In which we discuss why we experience a Preparation Expectation, point out how overpreparation can mire us in specific problems, explore how lighter preparation frameworks help us show up with more impact (and less worry), examine how rest can unlock our strongest communication, and discover strategies to cut through a lot of noise.

When I was getting my PhD, I was a teacher's aide for a literature class. This meant I facilitated tutorials for small groups of students from the main lectures, helping them to understand the texts better. I was twenty-three at the time, so I guess I still looked like an undergraduate. For the first tutorial, I was early to class and sat down near the end of the table, where the tutor usually sits. I was reading through my notes when a student named Dylan sat down near me. "Hey, cutie," he whispered. "I haven't done the reading for this class. Do you have any notes I could look at? I really want to make a good impression with this tutor. What's your name, by the way?" I smiled and told him I'd tell him in a few minutes. He looked confused. A few min-

utes later, when everyone else was seated, I welcomed everyone
to the class and introduced myself. Dylan's face fell as he realized I was the tutor, and a good impression he had, in fact, not
made.

The tricky thing about preparation is that for many of
us—unlike Dylan—it can be never-ending, and we often
overrely on it. Many of us maintain extremely high expectations instilled deep within us that we will be—must be!—
prepared for every single possible scenario that might occur. I
call this the Preparation Expectation—and by now you won't
be surprised to learn that in my experience, it is a deeply gendered phenomenon. It's reasonable to be prepared for the job
you want to do; it's another thing altogether to expect yourself
to know every possible variable in the universe. And that's the
pressure women often feel. The high preparatory burden we
place on ourselves is extraordinary and can be deeply exhausting. Many women I work with will tell me they intuitively
feel they need to have more evidence, to be more prepared, to
have done more homework than their peers in their efforts
simply to feel *competent*. Think about that for a moment. More
work than anyone else not to shine or to win but just to be
standard? It doesn't seem right.

Of course, there are men who prepare or overprepare, too,
but the preponderance of my clients' experiences suggests a
different story. I've wondered whether the gendered component of preparation stems from our socialized ideas about
motherhood, where idealized mothers are always ready with
the Kleenex, the Band-Aid, the water bottle, or snacks when a
child is in need. Is preparation encoded for maternality and all

its associations? Even those of us who aren't mothers, do we take this on as a coded pattern and construct from our own experiences of being mothered? If you have ever given a friend a tampon, a nail file, some gum, or anything else when they've asked—this might be what we're dealing with. Many of us have observed mothers, aunts, and grandmothers—both our own and around us in the culture—show up as dependable, prepared, and forward-thinking, and this has naturally affected the way we show up at work: the supplies might be different, but the impulses are not. Deeply ingrained in us is the instinct to make ready and arrange things to provide for the broader group around us.

Crucially, preparation and its expectation are often also seen by women as an inoculation against possible attacks or as armor when we feel vulnerable. Sherry, one of my clients, says, "My absolute kryptonite is being put on the spot." She hates almost above all else the idea that she will be shown up by a lack of preparation. Similarly, Karina, one of my former colleagues, says, "I feel this pressure to prepare for every possible scenario, question, pushback. I have seen many women, myself included, be punished in the meeting room for not doing so."

Certainly, the Preparation Expectation impulse tries to protect us from feelings of being caught out, vulnerable, and exposed. This inclination—*let me prepare myself so that I don't have the wind knocked out of my sails in an important moment*—is understandable. Most of us wouldn't think twice about preparing for a job interview, for instance. Rehearsal is a reasonable and often necessary thing to do.

OVERPREPARATION CAN BE OUR WORST ENEMY

You might be interested to know that almost everyone I work with in my coaching practice says some version of "I feel powerful when I am *prepared.*" The expectation of preparedness is motivating for some and an overwhelmingly disabling idea for others. Now, to be clear, preparation is not evil. Being prepared for a call means you know what you're going to say or how you're going to pitch something, and in many instances it's generous to stakeholders, who are likely to appreciate you coming to them with fully baked thoughts and a detailed agenda. Preparation can feel like the secret sauce to make us feel more comfortable, and there's no denying it can move you up the impressive scale. When you feel better about your work, you're likely to present it with more authority, too.

It's also important to remember that different contexts will require different types of preparation. Two of my close friends are lawyers and much of their job anchors on their preparation. They look at the legal documents supplied by their teams, strategize, and try to prepare for every single possible argument that might be made by the opposing counsel in each case. In fact, the expectation to prepare is absolute; it's literally much of their whole job before arguing a case in court. When I spoke to one of them, Natasha, about the idea of preparation, she said with firm conviction, "Preparedness is everything." In her situation, she and her colleagues prepare for every possible eventuality, and the costs for not doing so can be high.

The Preparation Expectation also has a cute double bind of its own: if we're perceived as being prepared or overprepared, we're often singled out for being too ambitious, too *thirsty*. We all remember when Hillary Rodham Clinton was accused of being "overprepared" for one of her presidential debates and, indeed, for her presidency itself. One would think this a fairly uncontroversial action to take when planning to assume the highest elected office. A *Washington Post* article even went back to her high school days to show Clinton had a long history of being . . . prepared? The temerity! It should go without saying, of course, that if she had the audacity to be *underprepared* on any question in that debate or even campaign, the headlines would never let her forget it.

In 2010, after finishing my PhD, I started working for Google. I left the small, sleepy, "let's take months to complete a chapter" academic enclave to join a start-up world that was so starkly different I may as well have traveled to the moon. My old academic world—think beige filing cabinets and a clunky desktop computer the size of a small horse—felt alien next to the bright, primary-colored fever dream of free gourmet food and beanbags at Google. It was profound sensory whiplash on every level. I felt like I had stepped out of a black-and-white photograph and into the future.

After five years focused on one enormous thesis, at Google I'd write thousands of words in emails, blog posts, plans, and more, all usually due that day or, sometimes, that *hour*. People walked from meeting room to meeting room with their laptops open, as if the time it'd take to close and open them would be an efficiency loss (and it probably was). It wasn't the pace of the work that surprised me. I was hungry for the quick hit of completion and rapid context-changing. What was challenging was that there was no opportunity to think deeply or polish a sentence until it was perfect. I had to get used to an entirely different paradigm of work. I had to get used to releasing work into the wild despite knowing I hadn't had much time with it. I had to be comfortable with being underprepared.

Working in such a new environment was a profoundly liberating experience—eventually—and it made me realize a new mode of working and communicating. The phrase "drinking from the fire hose" is usually employed when you go into situations like these where the sheer pace and amount of information can quickly become overwhelming. Even though I wanted to be super prepared for every interaction I'd have, it just wasn't possible to get the job done in that way. I would not have enough hours in a day—and the days were already crushingly long.

Without consciously realizing it at the time, I began to use a technique I was familiar with from debate, specifically when I competed at the World Universities Debating Championships. This is the tournament that has the shortest preparation time I've ever experienced, and it's where I learned the most about what my limits are and what my capacity is. Here, teams are given an unseen topic fifteen minutes before the actual debate begins—and each speaker must speak on it for ten minutes.

As if this wasn't scary enough, a serious complicating factor was that my beloved debate partner, Vanessa, usually had to go to the bathroom ("Nervous wee!") during that same fifteen minutes. It was a chaotic quarter of an hour, but by practicing having so little time, we became fluent in creating mental models of issue summary, speedy note-taking, and rapid shorthand between us. We also, of course, had to become more comfortable with a half-written speech, having to make it more polished in the moment. While what I've just described might sound like a stress dream to you (and sometimes it was for us, too), it gave me an enormous insight into just what you could achieve in fifteen minutes: sometimes talking to each other through a bathroom stall door. (Among the many pleasures of being the highest-ranked all-female team at that tournament was that Vanessa and I could freely use the women's bathroom as our prep room—there was usually no one else in there!)

Flexibility and the Fifteen-Minute Rule

An excellent way to combat overpreparation is to make your mindset flexible about preparation in general. When I first started working with Sherry, she told me emphatically, "Kate, when I have time to memorize a presentation, I do well. When I don't have the time to do that, I know I'm going to fail epically." It's as if she had decided this in absolute terms and wouldn't budge. Unfortunately, the scope and pace of her job as a senior leader in a big tech company meant that it was nearly impossible to memorize everything she needed to say.

Many of us hit various impasses like this one: a tool we may have relied upon successfully for many years (in this case, memorization) becomes less and less tenable as our career and responsibilities grow. As far as her Preparation Expectation went, I encouraged her to prepare *slightly* less for everything. Even just 5 percent less. Each time she gave herself a slightly shorter time to prepare, slightly more license to show up prepared but not to the fully memorized extent she was used to. And over time, she has found it easier to rely on her innate ability and knowledge in the moment. This is not to say she doesn't prepare at all anymore, but she's given herself an op-portunity to rely more on her capacity and experience in the moment. And she has learned that she's more robust than she had previously believed.

For you, this might look like writing fewer notes for a pre-sentation: relying, say, on the headline and the data point and speaking more off the cuff for the rest. It'll vary depending on your circumstances and the type of interaction for which you're preparing. Keeping a flexible mindset about your Prep-aration Expectation can also open you up to opportunities and even the delights of answering something impromptu or feel-ing proud of an answer you delivered in the moment.

Here's where I directly drew the idea for my fifteen-minute rule. I'll be honest with you—this exercise doesn't have a fancy name or a cute mnemonic. It is exactly what it sounds like, which is investing fifteen minutes into the logic of the project. Fifteen minutes doesn't seem like a long time at all, but it can be such a generative time if you structure it well. Say you have a big meeting or speech coming up—maybe you've even been putting off thinking about what it should be about or how you're going to approach it. This is a fast exercise that helps shape what you need to do, and you'll find by the end of it that you'll have an excellent way to move forward.

0–1 min. What is the aim of what you're trying to achieve?

You'll likely know this when you sit down, but take a minute to clarify it in your own mind. This should be quick: "get buy-in from my stakeholders" or "make people want to talk to me about the company after the speech" or "outline speech for summit."

4 mins. What could the content of this presentation look like?

The operative word here is *could*. All arguments are valid. Write them down and cross them out later. This is not data; rather, these are the arguments you need to make to succeed, and you'll want the most compelling ones you can think up. This should look like "If we invest in the hiring process now, we'll be able to free up more marketing dollars in Q3 when we need them" or "The electrification of the house should be our first priority when scaling state government programs" or "Please fund this program for the love of potatoes."

4 mins. Edit, prioritize, and decide.

Some of your arguments might not be amazing—be ruthless and cut them here. Prioritize them in order of excellence and relevance: think which needs to come first for the others to rest on, later. Decide on an order and an approach you're happy with.

2 mins. Run through for fluency. What have you missed?

When you know too much about something, you often miss a logical joining idea, or your explanation is too vague. So do a quick gut-check as if you're telling this to a friend or someone smart who is outside of your industry. What might they need to know, and do you have it down on your paper?

5 mins. What are the data points, pieces of research, or precedents you need to make this bulletproof?

You can't win debates with no data. Think about your most persuasive data points or references that you can include in order to back up each idea. You might not have them yet, so note where you need to dig in and find something.

There. In fifteen minutes, you've more than broken the back of that difficult upcoming thing: you've given yourself a road map to begin with, which is what my debate notes looked like. It's the best way to get through a mental block, and you'll be surprised at what you can achieve in that time. Many of the women I coach find that after ten minutes or so, they feel prepared enough to stop: it's not an impossible pattern to adopt and can save hours of back-and-forth and panic.

Keep in mind that your fifteen minutes can be twenty. There's no hard-and-fast rule about this. It doesn't matter the quantity you ascribe—some things might need a great deal more time or less—but it does matter that you put a limit on it and to be content with the outcome. Something like, "I'll spend fifteen minutes getting my thoughts together for that presentation" or "I'll allow myself one or two rehearsals of my speech." If the outcome shows you that you should have prepared more, that's good data for next time, and not an outright failure, but you do not need to overprepare to the point of exhaustion.

Slow Time Down in Order to Find Your Direction

The part of the Preparation Expectation I haven't mentioned yet is what happens when you are caught out by an incoming question, and you really, truly haven't thought about it before. First, we have to internalize that this doesn't mean we're a bad person or a negligent employee. It's okay not to have a perfect answer always at the ready. You can always say, "I'd love to take some time to dig into that and I'll follow up after this meeting," especially if the question requires specific research or data that isn't at your fingertips. But for other occasions, I'll share one of my tricks.

One of the highest-adrenaline debate styles is called British Parliamentary, in which your opposition can ask you multiple questions while you are talking. Yep, that's right, they stand up and interrupt you, saying, "Point of information!" and the rules dictate that you must accept two questions during your ten-minute speech. Absolute sadists, we are, for loving this, right? The double intention of asking a question of a speaker mid-sentence is both to ask you a difficult question about the topic and to make you uncomfortable and rattled.

Now, not all work-related questions are going to feel as adversarial or as Machiavellian as these are, but many can, so I think this is a good analogue to think through in terms of corporate life. Initially, I was terrified of points of information and would feel like I was in front of a fast-moving train, and I had no choice but to lie down and let it run over me. And for sure, in the beginning I was not good at answering them. I'd falter, lose my momentum, and sometimes be stuck for a few seconds—which felt like hours. But over time, I began to enjoy the challenge and got much more practiced in the strategy of answering a difficult question, even if I wasn't prepared for it in the first instance. Your mileage will vary depending on the situation and what sort of a conversation you're in—for example, it'll be different if it's with a stakeholder who's your manager than it would be in a highly adversarial negotiation with an outside party, but let's get into it.

So, what's the trick? It has to do with slowing down time. I know that sounds crazy, but hear me out. Sometimes our adrenal response can be super high when we know we haven't prepared (another cute side effect of the Preparation Expectation). We're ready to run away from the question or put up our defenses and often don't stop to listen properly. Did you ever get the feedback (I know I did) in math class, where a teacher would say, "Stop and read the question carefully"? Sometimes I'd see numbers and quickly jump to a conclusion, missing important information. (It's also possible I was very bad at math, but let's go with conclusion-jumping. It is my book, after all.) I'd suggest breathing deep and letting the questions come—welcome them, in fact. See them slowly lay themselves out and see that they're just component words that can't hurt you—and, in fact, might even contain some assumptions or assertions that don't help the questioner.

Determine the Type of Question Being Asked

Second, this might be a controversial take, but many questions—even when asked aggressively—aren't *that* hard to answer. That's because there are two main kinds of questions you can get in these sorts of situations. The first one asks for a specific number or fact (for example, "What's the capital of Japan?" or "How many sign-ups have we had so far?"). There is usually an objective right or wrong to these sorts of questions, and in these instances, you simply either know or don't know the answer, and you can say as much. You can even pose a guess and flag that you'll follow up later: "I think it's around five hundred, but I'll check and let you know after this meeting."

The second main type of question asks for your perspective or opinion (for example, "Will we be ready to launch in time?" or "Do you expect us to sell the product for more or less than our other offerings?"). When giving an opinion, the main thing that your manager or stakeholder wants is a sense that you can *find* the answer, not necessarily that you have it right now. The worst thing you can do in debate or in life is falter for a long time: it's optically a real bummer. So have a good go-to planned. You could use something like this:

> "That's a great question. My sense is that it'll launch in
> September, but I've made a note to check with the
> engineering team."
> "I want us to sell the product for less because of A, B, and
> C, so it's important we get some clarity on that over the
> next few weeks. I'll update you as soon as I know more."

When you start seeing patterns to questions, you can also often see the emotion behind them: sometimes it's a projected anxiety from them that they must have an answer for their manager or client, and it's being transposed over to you. Validating that concern—"I know it's frustrating to wait to figure this out, I'm hoping to have this sorted by Friday"—can go a long way to alleviating some of that stress. Crucially, it can help you close some of those open mental tabs for yourself as well as sometimes for the person you're speaking with.

Not to sound like the pointy-eared guy from *Star Trek,* but strong emotions can often cloud reasoning and good logic. Listening to the question carefully and trying to determine the real reason behind why it's being asked can go a long way to giving a good answer. Is there anxiety there? Resentment? Is this person trying to show you up? Remember, too, you can always frame it like this: "I get the feeling that I haven't answered what you're looking for. Can you tell me any specific concerns you have, so I can speak to them?" That way, you look open and allow them to reconfigure the question and maybe make it more precise for you to answer.

Perhaps they are someone who feels comfortable with numbers and stats, and your first answer referenced the emotion (it's going well!) or the status update (it's on time!) but not the specific metrics. Or vice versa. Over time, you'll start seeing more pattern recognition with the types of questions you can get and feel more equipped to know how to handle or delegate them in the moment. And it follows that when you know people better, too, you can start to get a feel for what type of answer they care about or are looking for. After all, the worst thing that can happen is that you don't know the answer or don't want to hazard a guess, which is okay. Stay the course: hunt it down, follow up on it, and move along.

Try this: If you find yourself stuck or feeling a preparatory crisis, slow down time and focus on what exactly is being asked. Do you know the answer or something adjacent that would add value? Could you offer to follow up later, instead?

THE NEGATIVE SIDE EFFECTS OF OVERPREPARATION

So, what's so bad about overpreparation? I hear you ask. Surely it means I've done my homework, I'm more prepared than everyone else, and I'm going to get a proverbial gold star. Well, *overpreparation* can actually cause you to have specific problems. The most significant is that overpreparation can stop you from listening. For instance, if you've prepared a slide deck, you often want to dive right into it and show the other person immediately. You've spent weeks on a proposal for a meeting, and it looks exceptional. Not only are your visuals popping, but there is careful thought and intelligence applied to each slide. You're a golden slide deck genius! But if you don't have a conversation first to discover what that client needs or what that stakeholder is struggling with, persisting with your deck can lead to frustration on their part.

This is not to say that you never want to have a slide deck prepared—in many situations, it's crucial. But *clinging* to that preparation when the meeting shifts organically to something else can be disastrous: it can signal that you're intransigent or simply not on the same page. The global consulting firm McKinsey & Co. coaches their first-year analysts to "release your agenda"—that is, to prepare appropriately for a meeting but to let it go if it feels like the client is directing them to different terrain. Remembering to release your agenda, even if you have done an extraordinary amount of work on it, can be frightening, but I want to explain five things here in relation to overpreparation.

First, consider the sunk cost fallacy, which you may have also heard described as "throwing good money after bad."

The sunk cost fallacy describes a tendency to commit to an action if we've already invested time or money or effort into it, often overlooking whether it still makes sense to do so. Now, it can feel that you've sunk so much energy into something, you'll hold on to it for dear life. But the opposite can often be true: understanding you've done the work and then choosing to go another direction is a meaningful and helpful path forward. Why? You look agile and flexible in the moment, happy to leave the safety of your known work and venture out into something that might be new and challenging. Your audience will appreciate you not clinging too firmly to a now-outdated idea or presentation if it's clear that you've both moved on.

Second, know that the work you've done is rarely wasted. Doing work and preparing adds to your mental frameworks of understanding the world: it might not be useful in this particular meeting, but it might be extremely handy elsewhere. You've just gathered and researched a lot of helpful context, which might be beneficial to you even though the question itself may have changed.

Third, overpreparation—doing more than you needed to— is a symptom of having porous boundaries in other areas of your life. It means you've set yourself up with extraordinarily high expectations, which might lead to exhaustion or even burnout if you keep it up consistently. True overpreparation time and time again is not sustainable. Learning to right-size your preparation for the right reasons and opportunities can be hugely liberating. So while preparation is integral, we must be flexible when it comes to letting go of it and creating our own mental models in the moment.

Fourth, overpreparation can mire you in too much information, losing the actual point of what you set out to do in the first instance. Remember in debate when I'd perform the worst on topics I knew the most about? It can be complicated to be subjective about a topic about which you have a deep amount of knowledge. It can also be hard to move away from the script you have in your own mind: you are less nimble and flexible when you have the verbatim words—sometimes folders full of words—in your mind. There's a tendency to cling to that prepared material instead of moving deftly through the conversation. If you do like to prepare, don't do it in full sentences: write down the bullet points of the arguments you'd like to make so you can talk to them, but also walk away when you need to.

Fifth, preparing lightly can mean it's easier to meet people where they are. Which is to say, some work is far better served if you listen, observe, and then come back with some ideas and recommendations. This is clear when talking to customers—taking the time to hear their pain points before launching into your solution is critical, because you might otherwise be answering a question they do not have in the first instance. My friend Erin once pointed out to me, too, that preparing lightly is imperative when you're doing community work. In her case, she works with Indigenous people who don't need or want her version of a solution at the outset. Instead, they want her to listen and then apply her specific expertise in service of *their* agenda, an act that she says requires her to be responsive, pivot quickly, and be unafraid to say she doesn't know but will find out. Preparing lightly makes her an invaluable (and likely rare) resource.

> **Try this:** If you find yourself overpreparing, consider the costs you're incurring and think about which flexible approaches from this chapter you might adopt, instead.

FINDING A MORE PRODUCTIVE AND LIGHTER-TOUCH FRAMEWORK

In life, we spend a lot of time running from back-to-back meetings, scribbling to-dos and action items, getting little time to consider the strategy for each one. When we move at this pace, it's easy to become overwhelmed and unfocused—which means our communication can suffer, too. It helps for us to define our foundations in order to create focused and easy-to-understand communication.

1. Determine Your Win

Determining your win is the first step to getting what you need out of an interaction and also reducing your preparatory burden. Think about what exactly you need from an upcoming interaction. What is the win I am seeking at this moment? Is it the approval of a next step? To plant a seed for another meeting? To get buy-in on a general idea? To agree to reassess in a few weeks? Amidst the speed of our lives, we get overwhelmed about what we need to achieve and when. It's often not possible (or even necessarily advisable) to get a big project green-lighted in one meeting. On a smaller, more personal level, it also might not be reasonable to think you'll be able to write four chapters of your book before lunchtime (ahem). Maybe instead, you only need to get the go-ahead for, say, the ability to research what that activity might cost and save your gunpowder for the next meeting, where you can move the project forward another step.

When I think about knowing what the win is, I'm reminded of one of the first things that made an impression on me from debate: learning I didn't have to prove *everything*; rather, I just needed to argue the strategic points that would win that specific debate. In fact, in debate, this is called the "burden of proof," a term that lawyers will recognize, which refers to the idea that you only have to prove the elements that are relevant to the topic you're debating. No more, no less. For instance, if you're debating whether social media negatively affects teenagers, you don't have to prove it affects adults or toddlers, too. Your burden begins and ends with teens, if that's what your topic states.

Applying this to a work and life context, how might our interactions and communications go if we could think about what our win is—what do we need to prove or get out of a particular interaction? Sometimes your win is just getting someone to reconsider something new or to add you to a meeting next week. Understanding what our win is and working out the most appropriate way to get it will help shape and focus our energy. And sometimes it brings a sense of relief: oh, I don't have to solve this *whole project* today, I just need to work out what the next step is. We stop being worried about the minutiae; we know we're in service of our win. I think about framing up my wins in a few ways.

2. Do Your Research

It's important to think about the research that you could do, for instance, before walking into a conversation or meeting. What other preparations could serve you well? Not too many or too much, you understand, but what should I arm myself with, at a bare minimum? Is it collecting more information, talking to other folks who do similar things, or studying a particular area? It's hard to focus your energy around a win if you don't know the landscape you're stepping into in the first place. Sometimes this is as simple as some quick online research before a meeting or looking up some relevant news articles about a company or person so you're up-to-date.

Having even a small degree of context for a conversation makes it much easier to form an opinion about *their* opinion, because you're able to highlight to yourself what a win could look like, which might just be getting a read on something from others. Research gives you helpful blinders so you're not distracted by anything extraneous. (And remember our earlier point about overpreparation—not *too* much research.)

3. Get Others Excited About Your Win

Getting other people excited about your win is an underrated talent. I've seen so many clients overprepare to the point of exhaustion, yet they haven't even told anyone else about the project they're working on. It's a lost opportunity because you won't get good data on what might improve your project and you also might be working in a silo, unaware of something else useful that could help you. It's also really hard to move anything forward if no one else knows or cares about it in the first instance. If you can demonstrate the value of your project to others, you might be able to secure traction and supporters, which might help you get it across the line: ideally, your win might be someone else's win as well. Imagine putting yourself in another stakeholder's shoes: if their motivations, incentives, and priorities line up with yours, you might have found yourself an ally in making the ask. If all your arguments center around your win, they become even more persuasive when your counterparts start to believe in them as well.

When your own language of the win is mirrored back to you, you know you're succeeding in getting others to think about the win favorably. For instance, if someone else says, "I'm eager to get a sense of timing—when can we expect launch timing?" and you've been pushing to know that exact same thing—that's perfect! You can amplify that—"To Vivek's point, I'd also love to know about launch timing, as that'll affect my team's priorities over the next two weeks." You only need one win on one project at a time for it to work. If everything is pushing forward slowly, you'll find yourself on track. This is preparation of a kind, but it's light and friendly. It's designed to be more communal and collaborative than slaving away in a dark room by yourself.

4. Let Go of Things That Don't Matter

Be prepared to be generous on anything that isn't mission-critical to you. This can be a game changer when it comes to bargaining or negotiating on something: if you're able to give something away or let someone else take a leadership role with it (and you don't actually want that thing, anyway), that can create a strong sense of communality and goodwill, which can make your own win feel like a win-win for you and others around you.

In using a lighter-touch framework for preparing, these steps can actually help move you forward in your interaction or project and can help position your actions in their most persuasive light. Knowing and isolating your win is a profoundly helpful way of listening to your body and your true self's needs. It helps catalyze your energy around one thing and push it forward so that you don't lose focus or worry about what other people think of it. Instead of expending energy on the whole scope of the project you're handling, think about distilling your win for *right now*: the most important thing you need to get consensus on so you can move forward.

Try this: Try applying the four-step framework outlined previously to something you may have been overpreparing or at least investing very deeply in. Can you hold it more lightly and see the progression of steps and how they apply to you?

SLEEPING WHEN WE'RE TIRED: HOW TO AVOID BURNOUT BY BEING SMART ABOUT OUR COMMUNICATIONS

One beautiful spring day in May, I was in Paris with my friend Jodi walking along the Seine, probably with a buttery croissant in hand. She had just flown in from San Francisco and I from Sydney, Australia, and we were talking about the most efficient way to handle jet lag. Was it having a brisk walk in the morning to get sunlight? A complex timetable of melato- · nin and sleeping tablets? Adjusting your watch on takeoff to the local time zone? If you couldn't already tell, I am someone who likes a plan. Amid obsessing about finding the best, most optimized program, Jodi stopped and looked at me. Or, she said slowly, we could just sleep when we're tired. I was stunned. Sleep? When you're tired? *Mon dieu.* It seemed so obvious. The phrase stuck with me in the weeks after I returned home (incidentally, quite jet-lagged).

Taken literally, of course, "sleep when you're tired" means listening to your body and acting on its behalf. And I wondered why this was so revelatory for me. The number of times I've stayed up late or struggled to focus when I was tired—especially with the advent of young children in my life—is too high to mention. I could always justify not having a nap or powering on, because there always seemed to be so much to do. Or because I didn't think I had "earned" it. Or because I thought someone else—my boss, my partner, my friend—expected something from me. The Preparation Expectation has never yelled louder: I would drive myself so hard that eventually my inner tyrant just went on autopilot—*You can do this, other moms do this, no one else is out here napping in the middle of a workday.* And in fact, they probably weren't: "Women are nearly twice as likely (31%) as men (17%) to rarely or never feel well-rested, and report sleep deprivation more frequently, too." I never even thought "sleeping when I'm tired" was an option—and it probably would have been the best medicine for me.

What I'm even more interested in, though, are the *meta-phorical* implications of this rather radical idea. What if the notion of "sleeping when you're tired" could mean that we more fully listen to what we need, without overthinking, guilt, resentment, or overpreparing a solution? In other words, if we could communicate our needs and desires, would we in fact have more energy and power to show up in the moment in just the way we wanted? What if we ate when we were hungry? Spoke when we had something to say? Stood up for an injustice when we felt shocked by it? What if we had frameworks for explaining and articulating what we needed so we could save energy and use it for . . . whatever we wanted to? "Sleeping when you're tired" became, for me, in the months and years after that magical Paris trip, a kind of shorthand to encourage myself to actively check in with exactly how I wished to expend and manage my energy, prepare appropriately, and, importantly, communicate those needs to others.

HOW TO BE PERSUASIVE WHEN YOU'RE TOO CLOSE TO THE TOPIC

If our energy is finite and our capacity has natural limits, it makes sense that we'd want the meetings and conversations that we do make time for to shine. But it's often in them, ironically, that we can appear unpersuasive and de-energized about our own work, which is weird, because you'd think that would be what we're most excited about.

For many of us, the initial shininess of our passions or areas of work dulls quickly once we've thought about it a few (hundred) times. We can become detached from and frustrated by it, which makes communicating all the harder. This is made clear to me when I'm working with founders of tech companies. I'm generalizing, but these founders are usually extremely bright, often deeply technical, and hard on themselves. I'm sure that's how they've managed to get where they are. And yet when I speak with them about what they're building, they often give me their spiel with a sort of resigned air—sometimes verging on being embarrassed. And it's because they're so deep in the weeds that they've lost what it is that's exciting about their project; they bury the lede so far down it's almost completely obscured.

My job is often to help them pull out what's interesting about their project: you're building a new version of the internet with privacy at its core? Creating the biggest network of gig economy workers in Indonesia? Changing the way we diagnose diseases with liquid biopsy? These are incredible things, and it's helpful to remember how transformational our work might be, even if it feels ordinary to us. In fact, nothing is boring if we rediscover what drew us to it in the first place: perhaps the opportunity to work with a certain leader in the field or to be fulfilled creatively in a new way for you. Whatever it is, try to remember your original motivation and summon it to the fore.

Tell It to a Smart Twelve-Year-Old

Gwen, a close friend of mine, is a brilliant professor of law, and she told me one night over dinner that she was frustrated that her ideas weren't being taken up by other academics and the media. I asked her what specifically she was writing on, and she sighed before explaining her work in a deeply theoretical way. I asked her, when you get home, send me a voicemail about your recent research and what you're trying to achieve with it as if I'm a smart twelve-year-old.

The Smart Twelve-Year-Old frame is one I use a lot when the work is complicated, or when I've spent too long in the company of others who take my work for granted. It's not a burn to clever preteens: it's actually a shortcut to remembering the sense, logic, and excitement behind what you're working on. Sure enough, a few days later I got some super energized messages from Gwen, breaking down the concepts simply and highlighting the most interesting parts of them. Right away I could hear a different energy in her voice. She took a lot of joy in the process of distilling her ideas, and it also reconnected her with the fun of communicating her work.

As Gwen told me afterward, "Even the imaginary audience sparked my preference for communicating with people more interactively about my work." And the interactive part is key. So much of our work, whether we are energized by it or not, happens in isolation, and there's true delight that can come from showing and telling it to others. The fictional twelve-year-old listener encourages us to simplify but also to remember the shiny bits.

This frame also can help you articulate the value of your work and how it fits into a larger notion or the mission of your organization. That can help others feel the momentum and excitement in your work, too. In debate we call this a case line: a recurring idea that we can come back to, to pitch our case— a through line that helps draw everything together for clarity and impact. Our work isn't boring; we just have to rediscover what's exciting about it.

Getting excited about our own material is so critical for persuasion because we often find ourselves having to lobby external clients or even internal stakeholders to give our projects time, money, or attention, or sometimes all three. You can't expect anyone else to be energized about what you're doing unless you are, and often, that excitement can lead to allocating you and your team budget, resources, praise, and much more. There is often an interesting nugget that might allow you to persuasively position your project to teams and to others in a way that has momentum and helps propel you forward.

Being excited about your own domain can also happen in conversations, especially those in public fora, such as panels, media interviews, and conferences. In these cases, I often coach people to shift the emphasis of a question if they feel like a straightforward answer would otherwise be boring (so they don't carry boring energy into the room).

For example, one of my clients, Anika, hates getting asked about one of her main areas of expertise. That feels counterintuitive—it's what she knows the most about!—but when she's asked about Indian capital markets she finds the question too broad to be interesting, and it is hard for her to appear excited about her answer. In instances like these, it's useful to think about pivoting and answering a question where you think you can add the most value and interest to a conversation. So instead of accepting the boring and clichéd premise of the question, which might be too vague and amorphous, for example, she could say something like, "The fascinating thing about India right now is . . ." and add the most intriguing or delightful thing she's recently seen or heard in her job. This way, she can frame her answer to something specific she knows about and include some colorful examples. This is not to say don't answer the question; you absolutely should answer it, but think about also sidestepping into an adjacent interesting space about which you are curious.

If we think about activating our own interest areas, we're much more likely to light up and give more thoughtful, interesting, and creative answers. If you can manage to do so, I guarantee your answer will be more fully realized, and your own energy and power in that interaction will increase, too. In this way, "sleeping when you're tired" can mean finding out where else you can find energy or fuel. It's not always the first place you might look.

> **Try this:** What is the big, cool takeaway of what you're working on right now? What's jaw-dropping or intriguing? What's the lede, and have you buried it? How might you articulate what's interesting to a family member? Your best friend? Your boss?

Assume a Mental Promotion

You know those lessons that you learn and can't believe you didn't figure them out sooner? This is one of those for me. Many years ago, I got a promotion when I worked at a fairly hierarchical tech company. I moved from being a level four to a level five and felt elated that I had made this jump. I have a distinct memory of sitting at my desk and thinking, *Well, now I can finally act like a level-five person*—and then promptly realizing my error. Can you spot it? As many of us realize too late, you likely only get a promotion when you're already acting like the next level up, which means that by the time you are *actually* promoted, you usually have been displaying the capabilities and characteristics of that higher level for some time. The idea that I thought I now had permission to behave like the next level up was a total illusion: I was *already doing it*. If I did want to change my behavior, then I could have already been acting like a level six or level seven if I had wanted to. In my case that would have meant being decisive, not waiting for permission, and bringing my new ideas to my manager far sooner than I had before. I wished someone had told me that truly listening to my body and myself could also mean that I could assume ownership, assume a mental promotion, and just show up with more authority.

Now, I don't mean that you should gaslight yourself about the level you're at. It's more like, what would happen if we all gave ourselves a secret, internal promotion? What would change in the way we worked and communicated? Run the mental experiment: *What would I do differently, and how? Is it worth incorporating any of those aspirational future-self goals into my present-day work life?*

For me, I had unconsciously decided that I had a present-day work mode and another future-aspirational one—kind of like an unopened present under the Christmas tree—that I'd only be able to access once a promotion was bestowed on me. But I've rethought that framing and now I see that any delayed gratification when it comes to stepping into a more authoritative or powerful version of yourself is just plain back-to-front. *We* are the present under the tree. We just have to show it off in the right circumstances and show the people around us just what we can do.

> **Try this:** Have you followed through on the job or idea you were tasked with? Have you decided which preparation framework to use? Which one will help lighten your load the most effectively?

Overpreparing might feel like a safe or prudent option, but it's likely to hamper your impact and longer-term sustainable work patterns. More productive and light-touch frameworks help us get to a place where we can lightly prepare and then give energy to responding in the moment, showing up in a more fluid and fluent way. Couple this with great rest practices and understanding when you need to take your foot off the accelerator, and you have the key to finding a place where you can show up with more energy—by having conserved some of it in the first instance.

NINE

Overcoming Fear:

Navigating Conversations Under Threat

In which we learn how to recognize and respond when we are under threat, discover that hard conversations are the key to overcoming fear, recognize that calm communication can help us find our antidote state, and grasp that physiological safety might be our best key to communications nirvana.

It's circa 2010, and I'm standing on the eightieth floor of one of the biggest banks in the world, with an intimidatingly expensive view out over Sydney Harbour. My aspirationally professional outfit is somewhat undermined by the fact that I can't walk very well in my new, too-squeaky heels and am carrying a fancy leather folder in the hopes that I will look like I work here. Everyone I've met so far on this sunny day is a man wearing a suit and tie, and I'm clearly not that. I'm about to co-facilitate a workshop with ten bankers who range from a bit introverted to that guy who always talks about marathons. They are all a lot older than I am. I'm mainly feeling excited—I know we're here to help workshop the art of storytelling, and it's a topic I love—but also I feel weird. I feel obvious and noticeable in this room full of all men. (My mental open tab: *Oh God, what if someone asks me to get coffee? Did they ask me because I'm a woman or for some other reason?*) In fact, I have about a hundred mental tabs open, all of them scanning for threats and questioning everything from my expertise to my very existence.

My colleague kicks off his presentation and begins with a kind and generous introduction to me, and I'm starting to feel more self-assured and happier to be here. I tentatively start closing a few of the pessimistic mental tabs. And then my colleague gets to the part about me having a world ranking in debate and *just* as I was beginning to feel a glimmer of growing courage, a man seated near me says, quite loudly, "Ha! Lucky I didn't marry you, then!"

It's no exaggeration to say it felt like I melted through eighty floors back to sea level and lost every drop of meager self-assuredness I had summoned. I may as well have been a small buoy, bobbing out there in the harbor, anchored to the ocean floor.

I felt my cheeks burn, and I smiled, and then I immediately hated myself for smiling. I was so far away from debate-mode Kate—this comment had come out of nowhere, and it was personal.

This man, who was about twenty-five years my senior, reveled in the guffaws from the group that his comment elicited while I marveled at how he even *got* there. We are in a work meeting, talking about work! The idea of a professional achievement even connecting to marriage only revealed that he hadn't seen me as an executive but as a card-carrying dowry recipient. Had he not *seen* my fancy leather folder?

And of course, his comment was not about real marriage at all. It was intended to undermine my credibility in front of his buddies. After all, what easier way to quickly demean a woman than to insult her marital eligibility? It was quick, cost him nothing, got a laugh, and critically pitted me against the room. I've taken great pleasure wishing him painful toe funguses ever since.

So, let's freeze-frame on toe fungus guy for a moment (sorry) and consider communicating under threat. One of the things that has always appealed to me about debate is that it was an opportunity to be given the floor for ten whole minutes and plead my case. Debaters essentially get permission to give a full-throated defense or attack, and everyone else has to listen. For someone like me who was just dying to explain all the ways in which something was too impractical or too expensive or whatever the topic demanded, this was a dream come true. Ten minutes of structured, logical, neatly persuasive material was all mine to present. And I knew what I was up against. Debates are so organized and the expectation is that they are often hostile, hard, and fast—unlike real life where weird personal comments or situations can crop up with little warning.

Of course, much of debate—and especially the styles I participated in—was extremely adversarial. It wasn't just about persuading an audience of my side of the case; it was also about tearing into the opposition's case. In fact, many people who first met me in a debate context confided many years later (and usually once we were friends) that they had been intimidated and terrified by me. Terrifying? *Moi?* Well, debate often show-cased my aggression, and as a woman, that rarely brings people closer to you. In fact, it does something like the opposite. It's hard to reconcile *that* Kate with the Kate I self-identify with today. We all contain multitudes, but maybe we don't show off the 100 percent adversarial version very often.

CALM RESPONDERS AS FIRST RESPONDERS

Being a calm responder can help us stay grounded and fo-cused, cutting through the noise and drama that swirls around us—and, hopefully, helps us achieve impact and change where we want to see it. I'm a firm believer that people don't truly accept or acquiesce to new ideas unless they feel calm or set-tled about them. Now, you could persuade someone with fear and panic, and they might accept your argument, but I sus-pect they're likely to feel resentful or uncomfortable later. That might be a workable short-term strategy, but I think over the longer term it's foolish. What we seek in persuasive communication is for our partner or recipient to let down their defenses—and maybe some long-held beliefs or delusions—and come to accept a new idea or reality. So it's incumbent on us as people who care about effective longer-term persuasion to engender a calm, meaningful authority as we engage in in-fluencing others.

The most powerful, unarguable form of influence comes when we can find our calm.

Of course, telling someone—yourself or anyone else—to "calm down" might be the worst advice you could give, ever, so I promise not to do that in this chapter. From experience, I know that calm does not—shall not!—come by invoking its presence: it comes when we can get our bodies and our minds to a place where we can focus, breathe, and let ideas come to us freely and without constraint. Similarly, we can influence others with more clarity and impact when we are calm: we think better, we reason more easily, and we have more elasticity in our mood. When we are calm, our stakeholders receive and perceive us as less threatening, less adversarial, and more collaborative. Calm communicators are more influential and impactful: we prize their rationality, thoughtfulness, and levelheadedness. In short, in work and in life, calm can help us convince, persuade, and connect.

A common misconception about communication is that it happens from the neck up. I am here to tell you it happens in our whole body, whether we're aware of it or not. It's literally my job to help people's full selves appear when they present, and I'm always alert to the signals their bodies might be giving—good and bad—and whether it's supporting or undermining their message.

In fact, back when I was training in the Australian debating team, our beloved coach, Rob—who was way ahead of the curve and still is today—was one of the only coaches I remember who taught us about our bodies and mental states as much as he did the debate strategy itself. For instance, he'd advise us to eat high-protein meals before each round to avoid sugar and carbohydrate mental crashes and even lead us in tai chi sessions before each debate at the World Championships.

I had never done tai chi before—my only reference point was having watched elderly people swaying gently in parks—so

I knew it looked restful, but I didn't understand what it had to do with my communication. It turned out this gentle, meditative, and focused movement was just the thing for us as a team: we'd find a quiet place before each debate, and Rob would lead us in a short practice session. I'd find that my breathing would slow, my mind would become a little clearer, and while I was still nervous, I would feel energized and activated rather than terrified. Toward the end of the tournament, when Team Australia had been on a strong winning streak, we had other teams ask to join our tai chi sessions, too, which was incredibly sweet. When we won the Grand Final and all ranked in the top ten individual speaker rankings, I had little doubt that this practice had helped us locate our level-headed responses onstage.

What about our breathing changed our cadence, presence, and impact as debaters, individually and collectively as a team? I've spent many years since wondering and studying exactly how calming the body effected change in our minds. And outside of debate, I find that similar ideas are relevant to corporate contexts, too. Why then does calm have such an effect on how we speak and respond?

CALM AS YOUR BEST LEADERSHIP STRENGTH

By now, you won't be surprised when I tell you: emanating calm can be one of the most powerful and likeable things you can do at work. Truly calm, self-assured, and grounded leadership, whether you're a CEO or a new hire, means few things rattle your cage. You're not scared by what's in front of you, and your mind can be open and ready to be its most creative, flexible, and collaborative. If you're calm, you're not worried about competition with peers; you're just creating excellent work. If you're calm, you're not agonizing over a mistake you made; you've moved forward and can figure out how not to make it again. And the real secret? If you're calm, other people will want to work with you and for you, and will encourage others to do the same.

In fact, calm leaders are often our favorite leaders. If you think about your preferred teachers, managers, or mentors, they are usually grounded and unlikely to demonstrate persistent chaos and stress. A study by the University of California found women who displayed calmness and positive emotions tended to get higher ratings for effective leadership as compared with men. So, it's not terribly surprising that we would seek out a predictable, consistent calmness from our leaders, for the fewer threats we experience, the better our sense of stability, safety, and security.

When it comes to how this calm can emanate from us, there has been much written on the connections between our mind and our body, so this certainly isn't a new idea. In fact, it's an ancient one. It just so happens our brain's limbic system hasn't evolved much since we were early humans: the same brain mechanics that used to save us from sneak attacks from cave lions now get activated in modern-day boardrooms and video calls across the world. Being calm in our communication feels somewhat counterintuitive because we think persuasion needs to be passionate and energized. But that's not always the case: calm can be deeply effective. Staying calm can signal that you feel your argument is incontrovertible—it's solid and stable, and so are you.

What Happens When We Forget to Be Calm

So, what happens when we're not calm? Much of the communication we do at work can provoke mental and physical responses within us: we are incensed by an email, defensive in a conversation, and avoidant in a meeting. And our internal monologues are similarly visceral: *I hate that guy* or *I wish she'd stop talking* (and oftentimes at nighttime, our partners and friends hear all about the idiots we work with, knowing them like characters in a play). It's a lot like road rage, but all of us are the cars on a busy corporate road. When we're not calm, we don't listen well to others, and we can override social cues or ignore them completely. (I'm reminded of one of my favorite studies, which found that people often were more excited to tell others about themselves than they were to receive money!) When we're not calm, we fail as leaders, managers, colleagues, and contributors every day.

You might have experienced that feeling of being made up of two beings: a work self ("I've got to get online!" or "I've got to be at that meeting!") and a true self ("But I'd love to lie in the sun and snack" or "Just ten more minutes in bed, then I'll try to get up"). Coach and author Martha Beck calls them our "computer" and "creature" selves, acknowledging that we all work between these two selves, inhabiting one and then the other throughout different parts of the day.

In a work context, we're so habitually used to forfeiting the creature in favor of the computer that it has, for many of us, become harder to check in with what would make us more comfortable and cared for at work. Add this to being a woman where our acculturated sense of putting others first (whether it's children, partners, co-workers, aging parents, or all four), there's a particular type of "I know I should look after myself, but I have to look after everyone else first" reality that emerges for many.

Not convinced? You only have to look at the many expressions about having energy or managing a lot of different things at once that come from the domestic sphere: "You've got a lot on your plate," having your "hands full" or "having your work cut out for you" from seamstresses' work, or even the oft-referenced "you can't pour from an empty cup." As women who must communicate our own needs and wishes at work, it seems at the outset that we're already coming from a place where we might know we need to be calm, but we can't find the words to make it happen.

Physiological Safety: Find Your Comfort, Find Your Calm

Work self-care is critical to being comfortable, which I want to suggest is in large part how we can get to feel powerful at work. You might be familiar with the concept of "psychological safety" at work: the "belief that one can speak up without risk of punishment or humiliation," as explained by leadership and organizational professors Amy Edmondson and Mark Mortensen. To be psychologically safe at work is one of the factors most proven to drive good decision-making, healthy interpersonal relationships, and generally effective ways of working. In a survey of employees at Google in 2014, psychological safety was found "more than anything else . . . critical to making a team work." I argue that psychological safety is key, but that we should also consider the idea of physical or *physiological* safety: how we can make our bodies comfortable at work to step into our own most powerful and calm self.

In the pursuit of finding our own best working self, we must remember that we have power over how we respond. And part of recognizing this is remembering that communication happens from our whole body, not just our face. You know, that aspirational, calm, interesting, great communicator who shows up and does a great job? She's likely been able to regulate her emotions, find comfort in her body, and have a good mental framework for how to approach what she's going to say. Want to meet her? Let's dive in.

Finding Your Antidote State

For me, I find when I am deep in thought, usually writing, I focus so intensely that when I stand up, I'm likely to trip over or clumsily bump into a doorway. (As I write this, I am nursing two badly bruised shins from not noticing a low coffee table at my son's school. Not the highlight of my week, for sure.) There was a period, too, when I was finishing my PhD that I had bruises on my body that came from not watching where I was going after long stretches of writing. It was a weird time. My partner joked that I was "just a head," meaning I spent so much of my conscious energy inside my head that the function of my legs and torso was solely to carry around my brain.

I don't think I'm alone. I've noticed many of us can drop into a similar state, even for short bursts, when we are under pressure in a meeting or conversation. That is, we get so focused on the brain and our thinking that we forget about consciously leveraging the rest of our body to help guide us through the moment.

What do I mean by "leveraging our bodies"? That's a fair question. Think about it like this: we often unconsciously use our body to get us through a tricky moment: we might swing back on a chair, jiggle our knee or foot, click on a pen, chew gum, fidget, or doodle. Why do we take these actions in the first place? My hypothesis is that we have a lot of nervous energy coursing through us, and sometimes it's soothing to have a sensory stimulus to channel that to feel more regulated. Now, there's nothing inherently *wrong* about any of these actions, but many of them can make you appear nervous or as if you're not taking the proceedings seriously, which might be undercutting the message you're trying to communicate. What we forget amidst the pen clicking and the chair swinging is that there are other ways to regulate our bodies that can help us change the way we communicate and respond to others.

Regulating our body before we respond looks radically different for all of us: there's no one way of being that is going to suit everyone, but I'll work through an example here so you can see what I mean. One of the women I coach, Shuvi, is highly credentialed and has probably never been outside of the top three in any given context. She is an intellectual power-house, and yet despite this, she often found herself deeply stressed and what she called "constricted" in conversations and meetings, almost stepping outside of her body to police what she was doing and how. It was exhausting and didn't feel like her. She came to me asking, How do I stop experiencing this and start talking with more authority?

Over subsequent weeks working together, I noticed

similar variations of the words *constrained* and *constricted* coming up in Shuvi's conversation with me. I wanted to find what I thought of as an antidote state for her: How could we reimagine a new mental state or posture to find a truer, freer feeling, a direct antidote for constriction or constraint?

Shuvi described this new imaginary state as a place where she was "comfortably sharing her thoughts, testing hypotheses, curious," and where her ideas were "free-flowing," which I thought was such an elegant and beautiful articulation. We ended up calling this a space of "relaxed curiosity with spacious knowledge"—an idea countering the feeling of constraint she was experiencing. Once we had named this state, I asked her to practice "stepping into it" each time she had a conversation or interaction at work. Could she imagine herself in her new relaxed, spacious state and then proceed? It might feel a little clunky at first (A relaxed, imaginative state? Oh please!), but it's been a small revelation for her. A week or so later I got an email from her saying that this was the first time in a long while that she had been "enjoying conversations" and felt comfortable "voicing my thoughts, even the more confrontational and provocative ones." What a win! The physical constraint she experienced has vanished in favor of seeking out her curiosity.

Why an antidote state works so well is because there's a power in leaning in to the idea of a mental state or posture in which you feel comfortable and then taking your most comfortable self into the meeting. It's an immediately actionable and practical reframe that helps us literally envision a new state and let it seep into our communication. If you're interested in constructing a similar one for yourself, list out the words that you currently feel or experience in a difficult conversation or meeting. What feelings come up in your body? Your mind? Are there critical, disparaging voices you hear? List them all out, and then, in another column, list out the feelings you would like to have. Your imagination here is your only guide. It doesn't matter that these might be super aspirational; it matters that they feel resonant with you. They might be opposite where you are currently, or they might be a little closer by. Then think up what your phrase might be (remember Shuvi's was "relaxed curiosity with spacious knowledge") and try it out in your next interaction. You'll likely be so much less reactive and more focused on a thoughtful response, instead. The only thing you need to practice is time and opportunity—a free, invisible, and useful space that's just for you.

Try this: Describe to yourself or someone else what your ideal communicative headspace might look or sound like. It might be an antidote to any current communicative issues you're experiencing. Decide on a shorthand name for this space and remind yourself of it when you're feeling under threat.

THE FOUR PATTERNS OF RESPONSES UNDER FIRE

It was back in the early 1900s that neurologist and physiologist Walter Bradford Cannon coined the phrase "fight or flight" to categorize the largely physical changes that people undergo in their nervous systems when they are threatened.

From Bradford Cannon's perspective, the fight response referred to an aggressive reaction, the desire to attack, retaliate, or get angry. On the other hand, the flight response is the wish to run: to get away from the situation as soon as possible.

In the late 1970s, psychologist Gordon Gallup added the third response: to freeze, which feels like a counterintuitive survival strategy, but can be indicated by feeling stiff and immobile. Much more recently, psychotherapist and trauma survivor Pete Walker added a fourth to this set of trauma responses: to fawn, where the individual ingratiates themselves and makes themselves small to avoid further conflict.

Importantly, these four responses to threats are and were critical for our survival. If we had no limbic system in our brain to respond, we wouldn't be able to protect ourselves from impending danger. In chapter 3, we explored how communication is intimately connected with our bodies. This makes sense on a visceral level: we know this when we stammer, blush, sweat, feel sick, and so much more; our words and our bodies obviously come together. While communication at work isn't traumatic per se (Although, in some instances? Girl, *absolutely*.), it's illuminating to use the frameworks of the fight-or-flight responses to see how our communicative reactions can follow certain patterns of responding to threats and why this often makes our communication harder in the moment.

While the four threat responses are grounded in sensible survival modes, they often show up and hinder the way we communicate, when, in fact, we're rarely under imminent physical threat. Put another way, it's not so much a lion stalking us on the savannah, it's just an email from some guy called Greg. On the other hand, some of the bosses I hear about from clients are aggressive, insecure, worried about their place in the corporate hierarchy, and so on and turn to shaming, condescension, hostility, passive-aggression, and many other actions. It takes less of a mental leap to understand why people in these categories would trigger a threat response.

We all move between fight, flight, freeze, fawn, and a fifth state of calm or equilibrium throughout our working careers—and sometimes, even during one workday. We might experience certain contexts or people that bring out some of these reactions, but it's fair to say we often react using a mix of them all. These reactions inform how we feel when we speak and how we can make others feel. Because that's one of the real tricks of calm: if we can model it, others will feel it, too. It is, of course, their choice as to whether to pick it up and run with it, but at least you gave them the opportunity, an immensely generous gift in a busy workday.

Modeling Calm in the Face of Fight

The fight impulse when it comes to communication can be something you experience yourself (a frustration or anger at someone's behavior or decision), or you could be on the receiving end of aggression, or passive-aggression. Honestly, neither situation is fun. My father-in-law, Bob, tells a story when, many years ago, he once went into his boss's office, sat down, and the boss began shouting at him. Bob picked up his chair, moved it into the doorway, and sat down again. The boss stopped short, looked confused, and asked him what he was doing. Bob replied, "Please keep going. It was just hurting my ears, so I had to move back a little."

I love this story, because sometimes it takes a big swing to disrupt a pattern. If that boss was used to yelling at people in that chair, for example, then changing it up by moving the chair literally intercepts the message and alters the outcome. When you're faced with a fight communicator, there's of course not always a chair to move, and when you add gender into the mix, male aggression especially can be flat-out scary, triggering, and even dangerous to navigate.

I once worked with a CEO who said he used to like seeing the "whites of people's eyes" in meetings. It wasn't so much that he wanted to be so close that he could see them, as in the Revolutionary War admonition, but rather he enjoyed seeing people get freaked out when he berated them in public—so much so that their eyes would go wide with terror. Totally normal-and-not-at-all-sociopathic behavior, amirite? The fight impulse can manifest in ways that range from mildly disconcerting to downright awful. And if we're on the receiving end, it can often rattle us for a long time afterward, feeling the aftershocks of the encounter hours or even days later. For what it's worth, it's interesting to note the gendered double standard here: women are allegedly "too emotional," but as tennis legend Billie Jean King said, "When a woman is emotional, she's 'hysterical' and she's penalized for it. When a man does the same, he is 'outspoken' and there are no repercussions."

So, what to do if you're experiencing a colleague in a fight mode and you have to be in close proximity to them? It's hard to be near someone who is frazzled or openly panicking, especially when you must take instructions from them. Child psychologist Rebecca Kennedy aka Dr. Becky notes of parenting—a different type of leadership to be sure, but managerial nonetheless!—that parents must be "sturdy" leaders. She draws the analogy of what sort of pilot's voice you want coming over the intercom when you're experiencing turbulence in a plane: Pilot One, who is angry and minimizes the threat of turbulence; Pilot Two, who is frazzled and asks if anyone else can pilot the plane; or Pilot Three, who emphasizes that it's a scary situation and calmly explains that there's some turbulence, so fasten your seatbelt and she'll get us to land safely because she's done it before. Sturdy, calm leaders can be present for their team and handle crises; they can show up with warmth or focus when their team needs them and also regulate their own nervous systems. It can be hard, but we owe it to ourselves and our colleagues to try.

In my experience, the more nerve-racking the work problem is, the calmer you need to be in the face of it. High-stakes situations at work often feel like life or death, and they're often the ones that trigger a fight response. If you run into a workroom with high levels of noticeable and contagious anxiety, you are doing a disservice to your team and peers. When the proverbial house is burning down, you need to be a firefighter, not an arsonist. Modeling calm and sturdy leadership in these types of situations is not only valuable to those around you but also lets you access an unrattled part of your own brain that is immune from panic so you can make better, more rational decisions and help others see through the smoke and flames.

Planting Roots in the Face of Flight (or the Super Fun Desire to Run Away)

The flight impulse, on the other hand, is when you feel like escaping the situation altogether. Think, *I just wanted to get out of there as soon as possible,* or *I ran from the room because I knew I was going to cry.* We might experience the flight response ourselves and feel like we want to escape a particular moment, and we might also work with people who are experiencing it who might seem in some way avoidant or distant. There's even a physical flight response I often see in my work: some folks exhibit what I think of as "runner's pose" where they're sitting or standing and their whole foot isn't in contact with the ground, as if they're on a metaphorical runner's starting block, ready to bolt out of the room. It's an easy signal to me that we need to do some work together to get comfortable in that space before they speak.

Communicative flight responses can also be demonstrated through anxious fidgeting or dilated, darting eyes looking about the room, as if on high alert for an imminent threat. And in practice, communicative flight responses are often shown by avoidance, procrastination, or prevarication: we put things off, or we make the greatest distance between ourselves and the thing of concern. This sort of hypervigilance is exhausting and has the bonus of making us look avoidant or as if we're concealing something.

I once worked with a woman called Gabrielle, who was a big externalizer of her own flight response. She would come to the office each day with her head down, walk right past me, not say hello, and just start typing frenetically, eyes wide with panic. I would cheerfully say, "Morning!" to ease what I perceived as tension, but she was so focused on her work that she would not respond. Now while she technically did nothing wrong (she was probably writing something brilliant and concentrating hard), the impact of someone literally not even saying hello in the morning made everyone on the team feel like we were all at a code red, panic station level. Even if the team was just doing our everyday, non–panic station jobs, her flight energy pervaded every room and email; it made us feel like we, too, should be on edge. Flight energy feels contagious more than the other responses. It's as if one animal senses danger, and then the rest of the herd feels precarious, too.

So, what do we do if we feel flight impulses when it comes to how we're showing up at work? One of the reasons it occurs in the first instance is that we go into silent spirals of self-doubt and crises of confidence. When you start to feel a flight impulse, I want to suggest you try this reframe with your body. This is something I learned from debating and something I still do today. Think of those moments when you want to flee a situation; speaking from my own experience, those were the moments I felt as if a strong gust of wind might blow me over. It's a deeply disconcerting feeling, and for many of us, it can bring us back to childhood or to a moment of vulnerability where we feel uncertainty or a lack of autonomy, hence the wish to run away.

Now, here's where it gets a bit woo-woo, but stay with me. As a debater, I usually stood in front of an audience, occasionally with a lectern or desk in front of me, but mostly just by myself. I had spent so long working on my posture, vocal levels, and gestures, but still, sometimes, the flight impulse would rush over me. As I imagined everyone in the audience looking at my whole body—you can feel exposed on a stage— I felt a strong rush to run, which often manifested in swaying or moving too much, distracting the audience. I needed to think of being more grounded, to keep myself steady and strong, but I also didn't want to feel like a robot, rigid and stuck to the floor. So what was I to do?

Over time, I began to think of my body as a tree. (Told you it would get weird.) I would picture myself with my feet firmly anchored in the ground. Not on it but *in* it, deeply rooted in the earth. No one can hurt me or knock me over— I am part of the ground, and my imagined roots reach out far beyond this moment in time. My roots, I would imagine, ran all the way from where I was standing (in another country, usually far from home), and they would travel to other people and other places, which gave me strength. The roots from under me reached to my family, my friends, laughter, my favorite beach, freshly squeezed orange juice—it didn't matter what it was in the moment. It just had to connect me to places or things that gave me connectedness and calm. This secret meant I could reach out and find comfort whenever I needed. In whatever country or city I'd come to find myself, I carried with me all my sources of calm. Whatever metaphor helps you—you can borrow the tree, if you'd like—think about ways to be connected, even just mentally, with things and people you love when you're under the spotlight. It's a helpful way to situate yourself with power and unassailable courage when you otherwise feel alone or singled out.

Whatever way you have to ground yourself (literally, I guess, in the tree example) is a useful stabilizing and calming mental exercise. Importantly, a tree isn't locked—it can bend and sway, and its leaves rustle. It's very much alive, but it's present, tall, and strong. A tree's leaves and branches respond to external conditions, such as wind, which meant that I could feel fluid in my body, not locked in or prisoner to a certain piece of carpet, which felt relieving for me. All we want to do with our body here is to get out of the communicative flight response and back to a place where we're not rushing for the door, where we can say our piece and be heard.

Reconnect with Your Body to Thaw Your Freeze

When I was about thirteen, I was in a debate, and I forgot how to speak. Well, that's how it felt at the time. My team and I were up against a boys' school, and I just remember being so frustrated by their arguments that I literally lost my words. I stood in the middle of the room and just couldn't finish a sentence. Nothing. *Nada. Niente.* I looked around at the faces in the audience—of course, that was the night a big crowd had turned up—desperately searching for clues on how to find a segue or anything, and it never came. I managed to claw my way to the end of the speech, and those few moments—about twenty seconds, realistically—truly felt like twenty years. When I was debating, the freeze impulse meant death. This was when I would falter the most, struggle to find the word, or realize my best refutations were locked away, only to be annoyingly discovered later that night or, even worse, weeks later.

We all fear the freeze. No one wants this to happen, especially in front of a big or important audience. The freeze impulse is one that many of my clients are familiar with, too, every idea immediately vanishing from your head when you're called on or put on the spot in a stressful situation. Oftentimes, you actually do know the answer: it's just not available to you in the moment. It's like suddenly all your good data is locked in a vault and even though it's your vault, you don't have the password. You might experience a strong soundtrack of your own heartbeat or blood rushing in your ears. The big adrenaline dump you get in a freeze response unhelpfully doesn't invoke action; it just feels like it circulates around your body, faster and faster, keeping you held in your chair or your sentence. You might also experience everything as if in slow motion; that you count time differently. You are so tense that no good ideas come, and your words dissipate into the ether. The vast blankness of the freeze response is often the spot of true terror and answers the question, *What if I forget everything when I'm there?* Welcome to the silent scream of freeze.

Shuvi, whom we met earlier, emailed me one night, perplexed that in a meeting that day, she suddenly realized she wasn't breathing—and then, unsurprisingly, felt a strong sense of constriction and anxiety. When we caught up later in person, she explained that it's also something she does when she's working out: if she's stretching herself to manage a specific lift of weights, she'll stop breathing then, too. A freeze can happen in lots of different ways—and can often involve feeling breathless, out of breath, or immobile. In her case, I suspect her breathlessness came from being overwhelmed—too much pressure in the meeting (or in the gym, literally too much pressure of the weights) would cause her just to stop breathing. It was likely a message from her brain to take a break and refocus later.

If you find yourself in communicative freeze mode where you freeze under pressure or attention, your body can feel locked and stuck. And it's cruel, because you're alive to the sense of imminent danger but also unable to move out of its way. It's truly an awful, gut-wrenching feeling. Think about how your body feels in those moments and notice the bodily reactions you experience.

For example . . .

- Are you holding your shoulders around your ears?
- Is your jaw locked and clenched?
- Are your lips dry?
- Is your mouth parched?
- Are your thighs clenched?
- Is your breath shallow?
- Are your palms or underarms sweaty?

Many of these feelings result from an adrenaline dump under pressure, and they make us feel as if we're destined to underperform from the outset. As with the flight response, the way I always teach clients to get through the freeze response comes from the body, too. You know by reading this far in the book by now, our bodies are key to how we show up: they're the vehicle for your head and the site of a lot of pain and power. We feel things viscerally—a stress migraine, a nervous wee, stomach flutters, cramps, a seized back, an eye twitch—often, our body is the truth-teller our brain would like to ignore. So, instead of thinking about the negative signals our body can send us that spark fear or make us experience panic, what are the proactive, positive signals we can send to our body?

Choosing your own favorite type of sensory stimulation is a great way to remember you have a body and to help yourself out of a freeze response. Before a situation that might otherwise cause you to freeze, it's helpful to give your body signals that you are safe, comfortable, and alive in the world. Going for a run, having a shower, listening to music, gently rubbing your fingers against each other, or scrunching your toes against the floor are all examples of subtle (and not-so-subtle) ways of reconnecting with your whole body and breathing to bring a groundedness and solidity to your communication. If you like yoga or tai chi, some movement can be a great way to give some flow to your communication, too—there is something about flowing movements that can help unlock our speech and language. If someone is consistently freezing when they speak, I suggest thinking through their upcoming meeting while doing movement, such as walking or a sun salutation; giving movement to it while thinking through your ideas seems to connect the two and helps move you through the meeting, too. I used to do this in debate postmortems: I'd walk and walk, mentally re-experiencing the debate and moving through the stuck parts to the other side.

Ask a Counterquestion to Stave Off the Fawn

Finally, the fawn communicative response is a doozy. It essentially removes the word *no* from our vocabulary and doesn't give us a replacement. If you identify as a people pleaser or someone who has difficulty in certain instances establishing and maintaining boundaries, this might be you. Fawning communicators overrely on deference, laughter, minimization, and flattery, which we discussed in chapter 2. You might also spot your inner fawn if you acquiesce quickly to something that you know you don't want to do, but the pressure in the moment causes a fast reaction that feels inexorable.

When we're fawning, we're in a low-status position in relation to another person. Linguistics professor Deborah Tannen notes that whereas "girls tend to learn conversational rituals that focus on the rapport dimension of relationships . . . boys tend to learn rituals that focus on the status dimension." In my experience, this childhood acculturation Tannen writes of means that when women are faced with status situations, we often defer and make ourselves small, especially when we sense a threat.

A mental framework here that can be useful to avoid the fawn impulse is to ask yourself a counterquestion. We often start with negative self-talk: *This is going to be a disaster,* or *I'm going to fail,* our helpful internal monologue might suggest. So, a counterquestion could look like, for example, *What if this goes better than I could ever expect?* or *When are the other times I've had success in something similar?* or even *What would it look like if I shoot the lights out with this?* Imagining a world in which you are better than you think you are can help you envision more creative, more exciting outcomes, and even if they all don't come to fruition, it can be a helpful exercise to imagine and shift your focus from tight, constrained nerves to expansive, creative energy. Here, consider presenting facts to your internal monologue: there will be a hundred people in the audience, or there will be five vice presidents on the call, for example. Facts like this can help ground you in a reality rather than an imagined catastrophe, which is helpful for our communication because you can begin to speak to the real issues instead of the nervous, anticipated ones. And imagining catastrophe only leads to paralysis—it's too much, so we do nothing at all. So instead, what's the absolute best that could happen here?

One of the things you might have noticed reading thus far is that the fight, flight, freeze, and fawn responses will happen, whatever we do. First, we need to be aware of their presence and then work on how we'd like to show up instead. Less at their mercy and more like a knowing, experienced frenemy: *Ah, flight, it's you again, you filthy old so-and-so.* Once we can recognize our own triggers and notice their presence, we can start to work out our action plans to mitigate them in the moment. This is with a view to our own words being able to come out without hostility, avoidance, panic, or deference.

For all four types of communicative threat responses, there are two more exercises you can try that can fit a variety of situations.

DISCOVER YOUR BASELINE: BREATHING TO REGULATE FOR CALM

When I run workshops in my coaching practice, I always get participants to do a breathing exercise at the beginning of each session, and you can see their initial skepticism. *She's asking me to . . . take deep breaths? Revelatory.* But after the first one, they're usually insisting we start every session together like this.

Think of breath as the constant thread between you and every interaction you'll ever have—it's your constant companion. Understanding its potential can be so helpful. It can feel like a secret superpower. So, here's a simple practice for when you're about to have an interaction that feels intimidating or threatening. Or whenever you just want some calm. You can do it invisibly and with no equipment except your breath, making it portable, straightforward, and free. Sometimes I do it when I'm dropping the kids off at school or trying to get to sleep at night—it's never failed me yet. And more critically, it can be done before a big meeting or even during the meeting: it's a silent, secret weapon for overcoming tension.

Here it is: take a nice deep breath and whatever you count in for (say, three beats), breathe out for twice as long, say six beats. Repeat as needed—you can do at least five in-and-out breaths and see how you're feeling. Another variation is called "box breathing" where you inhale for four counts, hold your breath for four counts, and then exhale through your mouth for four counts. I've found both to be effective and helpful; it's personal preference as to which you pick.

Research suggests that the longer exhalations in this type of breathing cadence help stimulate the vagus nerve, which basically kicks us out of "fight or flight" and into "rest and digest," something that yoga, tai chi, and meditation have known for centuries. And even if you have no background in those practices, it makes intuitive sense: when you are under threat, you're not doing long, relaxed exhales, you're breathing fast and ready to act. This breathing exercise can functionally help hijack a body's stress response, and research even suggests that it can help us make better decisions, allowing for more time and space to think and be creative under pressure.

A breathing practice lowers that initial adrenaline rush that can come when I go to speak and helps me find the words I'm looking for when under pressure. Activities like heavy exercise—(lifting weights, for example), singing loudly, scuba diving, going for a run—all of these can feel good in part because they're regulating your breath. Once your breathing is more regulated, you can trick your body out of a threat state and into a calmer one. And it's not to say you have to start scuba diving on your way to work. Doing a silent, intentional breath practice before your meeting or on your commute can be impactful, too. If you're not convinced, test it when you need focus or some more regulation in your life and see what happens. You literally have nothing to lose.

Try this: Pick a breathing practice that feels comfortable to you and get into the habit of doing it before big conversations or meetings that you may have been dreading. You might even find you look forward to it as a routine to prepare, calm down, or focus.

Talk with Your Anxiety Like an Old Friend

When you're feeling a communicative threat arise in *anticipation,* another general way to find a calmer space is to open a literal dialogue between you and your feelings of anxiety or disquiet. This isn't for responses in the moment. It's for the ones we dwell on, anticipate, and sometimes dread. Many of the people I work with say they're hard on themselves when they feel nervous. *Don't feel anxious!* they'll say. *I need to stop being so tense!* Paradoxically, by saying these things, we tend to feel even worse. And conversely, if you try to ignore that voice, it tends to make everything worse because then we feel anxious *about being anxious.*

I'd suggest framing up your nerves as a simple message that your body is giving you: maybe you've had a bad experience with speaking before, and it's trying to protect or remind you that the stakes are high. If nerves are the messenger, or so we say, they're hardly going to hurt us, right? You could say, for example, "Thanks so much for letting me know, body. This *is* a big deal. And you're right, I hear you." I then like to present a plan back to the voice. If you can structure a logical argument against your own warning system, it can help ground what you're doing in the realm of the rational. For example, you could say, "Despite the high stakes of the day, I am going to present onstage and I've done what I need to prepare myself." You might be surprised at how often this works to quell nerves before a presentation: just letting your body know you heard it prevents it from upping the ante with more feelings of dread and agitation. Talking to your anxiety like a friend can be a great first step toward channeling the self you *want* to bring to that meeting—one who isn't defensive, angry, frightened, or constricted.

Try this: When you feel a threat response arise, can you imagine a conversation with the anxiety you're feeling? This works when you are anticipating something coming up and perhaps are dreading it. In the conversation, you may reveal the core reason or be able to isolate what part is especially unnerving and how to mitigate it.

Being calm. It's one of the most powerful and likeable assets you can cultivate in how you bring yourself to work and, indeed, the world. Our own energy is contagious, and if we can bring more calm to our conversations, our ability to connect, cut through, and communicate only gets stronger. Remember: many times we'll be in a situation where we are not the ones who are nervous or skittish, but we're working with someone else who is. Here's where it's integral to remember that, and we can help them calm down with our own sense of calm. If you can listen, observe, and try to understand where your colleague or client is coming from, you can try to help them alleviate their fears and concerns, too. And that's perhaps the biggest gift you can give: to help someone else to come back into their own bodies and to see the world a little differently, too.

Influencing with calm is the radical idea that paying better attention to our mental and physical states can help us get to a communicative self that helps us get what we want and need in a given moment. It helps us *respond* and not *react*. As Mary Oliver puts it so beautifully in her poem "Wild Geese," "You only have to let the soft animal of your body love what it loves." It's not a failing to pay attention to what our creature self might be hinting toward: it's a true gift to hear it and then to act on its behalf. On the quest for powerful likeability, it's also key to finding your own sense of power in how you show up at work and beyond.

Failure Privilege:

Why It's Not Available to Women
and What to Do About It

In which we experience an epiphany about failure, understand that much fascination with "failing fast" is super gendered, explore how we often miscategorize experience as failure (and why that hurts us), and examine why the real issue that hurts women the most is the expectation that we won't fail at all.

When I was in my first year of law school, I walked out at the end of a three-hour exam, absolutely distraught, and convinced I had failed. We had been given a case study to analyze about an accident between a driver, a cyclist, and a bystander. While I thought I had adequately responded to the relevant legal issues in the case, for the life of me I couldn't remember the word *pedestrian* and instead had used *walker* throughout the entire paper. In hindsight, this is hilarious ("In the event the walker had seen the cyclist, the walker would have had to yield" and so on), but at the time I was certain an examiner would think I was too stupid for law school. Spoiler: against the vocabulary odds, I did fine in the exam, but years later decided I didn't want to practice law. Look who's walking now! But back to the point: very often our perception of failure can be a devastating feeling and can lead to us wanting to have endless do-overs and chances to make good on a missed opportunity. And many times, we over-correct, thinking we failed when we have not.

The way women perceive and understand failures of communication intersects squarely at the powerful/likeable binary. Real or perceived failure can make us feel powerless and unlikeable, sometimes at the same time. When failure diminishes even the small amount of power we might have held in a situation, it can be devastating. Failure is the opposite of power. And failure is always at the front of our minds when we're thinking about likeability, too. If you've ever policed your accomplishments in front of others for fear of coming across as too successful to be easily liked, you've run up against exactly this.

THE GENDERED NATURE OF ACCEPTABLE FAILURE

Getting comfortable with failure is important: the ability to "fail fast" or "launch early and iterate" in a tech context means a team should aim to go live with the most basic product they can build and get feedback from the market to course-correct and change as they go. But this brand of failure extolled in Silicon Valley—failing fast, failing often, and failing in front of people—isn't an inclusionary one. In fact, it's one that seems to extend only to men. I've come to term this gendered aspect of failure the *Failure Privilege*: the idea that only some of us can afford to fail or embark on an adventure for which we know there will be a safety net waiting to catch us if we fall. And it's a deeply masculine privilege at its core. If, as a man, you haven't earned your failure badge, you haven't completed a core rite of passage in the eyes of the establishment. And as a woman, you'd better not fail, because no one will catch you if you do. In an interview with tech reporter Kara Swisher, former tennis champ Martina Navratilova notes, "When a women's endeavor fails, it's because it was women doing it, and you're done *forever,* whether it's business, sports, or entertainment. Women can't afford to fail." The idea that women can't *afford* to fail connects the idea of failure to an imagined budget—that some people have enough failure currency, and others do not.

WOMEN ARE EXCLUDED FROM THE FAILURE PRIVILEGE AND ACCULTURATED TO ANTICIPATE FAILURE

In tech fundraising, even before they get the chance to become titans of industry, we know women founders are subjected to harder and more risk-averse questions from investment firms, which tend to "ask men questions about the potential for gains and women about the potential for losses," meaning the male entrepreneurs were asked about their hopes, achievements, advancement, and ideals, while female entrepreneurs were asked questions oriented around topics like safety, responsibility, security, and vigilance. This lens automatically restricts a woman's answers to smaller, detail-oriented, shorter horizons while allowing men to paint big, visionary, blue-sky aspirations.

Here, the Failure Privilege is not extended to women: women were *expected* to fail, while men were *predicted* to succeed (and, watching how the world works, were protected if they did fail). While men were essentially asked to share their hopes and dreams for their company, the questions directed to women in those same meetings boiled down to this: "Before it's even happened, what are you doing to mitigate your imagined, imminent, and inevitable *failure?*" It's not a long bow to draw to hypothesize that this type of questioning pattern also directly impacts how much funding the founders eventually receive, too—if they even get funded at all.

Many women are subjected to a high degree of imagined and anticipated failure beginning with our early upbringing. From being raised more cautiously as children ("Be careful! Don't fall!" and so on) to constantly being made aware of danger as teens and young adults ("Don't wear that! Don't walk down that alley! Hold your keys as you walk to your car!"), we are more likely to believe we have limitations, are less capable, and are inherently vulnerable. In fact, research demonstrates parents are four times more likely to tell daughters than sons to be more careful after incidents that lead to the emergency room. It isn't unreasonable to think that an early acceptance of physical harm or injury can correlate with a later belief in our own culpability and result in a low risk tolerance (and therefore, a high failure aversion). And, of course, in a culture of wanting both power and likeability, where both require women not to alienate those around us, *inviting failure in*— which seems for women to preclude future opportunities, resources, and success—is alien and, frankly, insane. *Why, if likeability and power give me permission to succeed, would I choose failure—and public failure!—as a next stepping stone?* we reasonably think. We know we have only a scarce amount of risk capital to spend before we go over the limit. Where is that limit? We are often not sure, but you should assume it's out there and stay underneath it, sensibly, cautiously, often moving away from it far before we're even close to crossing it. So let's explore how to get comfortable with failure, *powerfully likeable*-style.

Don't Lose Before You Play

The trouble is, the pursuit of success often involves failure. And when we shy away from the idea of failure itself, we definitionally allow for ourselves a much smaller world of opportunity. I see so many women in my coaching practice who are so fearful of failure that they self-limit in myriad ways. And in many instances, not only is the risk of failure very small, sometimes it's even unnoticeable when it happens. When I left corporate roles to start my own company, I remembering saying to my friend Jessica, "But what if no one wants to hire me?" She gave me such a valuable answer. Instead of dismissing me with a pat "of course they will!" she thought a moment and said, "I think that is an unlikely outcome. But if that actually comes to pass, you'll just go and get a new job, and no one will ever know." No. One. Will. Ever. Know.

My suspicion here is that we spend so much time being the object of the gaze, we forget not everybody is actually watching us. By which I mean, most people are so caught up in their own careers and lives that your own actions just aren't in the center of their thoughts at all. And worst case if they do know, they're likely not to care nearly as much as you do. The most important thing is to understand your own capability—and to bet on it. We fail when we don't actively believe in our own power to do the thing in the first place. Take Rebecca, a brilliant early-career manager who works at a big tech company. She'll often say, amidst displaying the most perfectly articulated or organized thing, "I'm the worst!" or "I'm so hopeless!" or "Trust me to make a mistake like that." Imagine interacting with that level of self-minimization if you didn't know her. It'd be so striking to see someone be so cruel and give voice to those negative voices many of us have in our heads about our performance and how we show up. In this type of example—and extrapolating from it—we can sometimes see an overt signal of failure (and oftentimes not even an accurate one) effectively help us *lose before we even get a chance to play*. If we truly recognize our own value, then we need to do a good job of communicating it to others. Not necessarily by singing about our accomplishments with a trumpet fanfare, sure, but at least by not undermining ourselves before anyone has had a chance to see what we have to offer.

Willing Our Failure into Being with Our Words

People can smell self-doubt from miles away. If you're feeling it, you're likely *being* it, too: your communication will seem tentative, unsure, and wavering. You'll put failure as an option on the table, and your counterpart will see it. Body language, your voice, your ideas—everything will seem doomed from the outset if you're already emanating failure. It's like you know it's over—yet it hasn't even begun. Over the years, I've interviewed dozens of candidates for jobs, and I can see it all over their faces when they think they have given a bad answer and their affect changes for the worse.

One of my clients, Lily, is a coach, and she noted to me that she had a lot of trouble with charging the rates she wanted to work for. When I probed on this, it turned out that after an initial conversation, her follow-up emails would contain her quoted price but then immediately add a caveat: "If that doesn't work for you, please let me know—I'm sure we can work something out." Unsurprisingly, a lot of people asked for a discount, to which she always acquiesced immediately.

Lily ended up being in a position where she failed, time and again, to make her earnings goals. In this instance, my client put *her* failure—in this case, earning a lower rate than she believed she was worth—as an option for the other person to choose, and choose it they did. Her wish for likeability and collegiality ("Look how chill I am about money, you guys!") overrode in that moment her true feelings about her worth and value as a coach. Lily felt—and likely imagined—that she didn't have Failure Privilege with her prospective clients. She feared they would judge her or find her rates too high and not proceed with an engagement with her. But the flip side was that she then had to live with the fact she had undercharged her client for the rest of their working relationship: an uncomfortable truth and a difficult one to change.

Being able to determine what's at the root of your indecision, paralysis, or apprehension can help more easily isolate what's happening, and then you can move it forward and work through the difficult conversation or take the leap you were fearful about. Or not! But the point is, gently interrogating whether you're stuck in a failure mode helps work out the next step.

> **Try this:** It's helpful to run a quick audit on where you think the failure idea might be coming from and ask yourself, *What is the reason behind my failure thinking? Is it a rational concern? Would someone else consider it a failure, or just me?*

Course Correction Isn't Failure

As women, we tend to classify trial and error or course correction as failure, when it actually isn't. Now, it's not necessarily surprising why we'd do this with the exclusionary Failure Privilege looming large in our minds, but here's where it gets interesting. We feel as though we aren't allowed to fail (no Failure Privilege or free pass) and at the same time *bestow* failure on ourselves when it isn't applicable. Another cute double bind, eh? To better illustrate this point, here are three stories of women I know that might resonate with you, and as you read, think about how you might describe their experiences and why.

My brilliant friend Katherine wanted to leave the media industry and make a career change. She researched a wide range of options and ultimately took a job as a curator at a cultural institute. I called her a few weeks in to hear how it was going, and she told me that she had quit, already. In the first three weeks, she had decided that the institute's culture wasn't for her; it was intransigent and lazy, and she could see only frustration ahead. We spoke about it, and she told me she lamented her mistake—and that she had failed in taking the role.

Another friend, Monica, had a great idea for a start-up. She gave herself five months to research the idea, prototype the software, and line up prospective investors. I was blown away by the amount of work and the sheer speed at which she worked. By the end of that time, she decided that the product wasn't right for her market and that she'd be unlikely to pay back potential investors on time. She, too, told me casually of her failure and how she was embarrassed that she had put her weight behind the idea.

A third friend, Emma, took on a role at a nonprofit organization and quickly realized that the extremely toxic workplace culture and the excruciatingly long hours were both unsustainable and undesirable. She left after a few months, as did five out of the eight other employees—a real indictment of a culture that overworked, underpaid, and otherwise exploited its employees. Despite that validation of her own move, she told me she had "big failure feelings" and felt disheartened by the whole experience.

Three different women, three different scenarios—all with a similar judgment of their own paths. I would suggest that in all three cases, the woman *didn't fail.* She experimented with something new, she came to the conclusion that it wasn't for her, and she course-corrected. The learnings they had in each situation are immense—whether it was about how to assess a workplace before you start working there or understanding how a business idea will or won't come to fruition—this is such rich and important information. The biggest failure in all three scenarios would have been *inaction,* staying and choosing to ignore the realizations gained during the time in the position.

For Katherine and Emma, leaving their jobs meant it was better for their own career trajectories (they're both in jobs they love now) and better for their respective organizations, who could find someone who would be a better fit. Monica's discontinuing investment in her idea also worked out better, because she understood the business wouldn't be viable before she began. I've met so many founders who would pay a lot of money for this type of insight before they took on an investment, and they wouldn't think of it as a failure, either.

So why did all three women conceptualize these moves and choices as failures? These weren't rash decisions in which the women went in blind. All three made strong, brave decisions that were pivots in their lives and threw themselves into the tasks with full vigor and ambition. That they realized they weren't exactly right and course-corrected should be championed—by them and by all of us. What we can learn from them is to describe what happened with a broader definition rather than through a lens of failure.

Think back to those men in funding meetings being asked about their vision and not about their limitations: what could the big-vision version of your experience be, and how would we tell it? I'd suggest that the language of experimentation or prototyping could be helpful here: "*I tried working at a new organization, but their negative culture meant that I left quickly and moved on to the next thing.*" With an honest assessment, you'll often find that the thing you're calling a failure or a mistake could actually be redefined as a valuable experience or experimentation. Even if you're only talking about this to yourself, it matters. Feeling like you're coming off the back of a learning experience rather than a crisis of self can only help with whatever the next step forward will be.

A/B Test Your Life

Tech companies might be a little too extreme with their failure talk, but one thing they love to do is A/B testing, which I think can be useful as we think about being more flexible when it comes to classifying our experimentation. A/B testing is the process of comparing two different things to determine which one performs better. For example, you might A/B test the language on a website to see what a consumer will choose or, more to the point, click on. So, teams will run variables of language ("Sign up now!" versus "Learn more!") and, over time, learn which ones get the most clicks or purchases. Putting some language or a particular design into the market and understanding how people react to it is the best way of informing their decisions. This type of testing happens more informally, too. Think about a store owner putting different things in the window and seeing which items drive more foot traffic into the store than others. While the results of an A/B test show you which words or designs have failed to convert customers, it's critical to understand that *the test itself is not a failure.* The test is the mechanism to reveal which way to proceed. I think this is such a valuable framework for us to apply to our own decisions. We often need more data and inputs to know which way to jump, and sometimes A/B testing isn't available, so we have to do the damn thing in the meantime. But *doing* the thing isn't the failure; not learning from it is.

Liberation from Failure

Early in my career, I had a memorable public failure when I sent an invitation to reporters for a tech launch. Now you might think—as I did—how hard can sending an invitation be? Surely, I don't need to run that past my manager? Well, as it turns out, launches are hard. Tech company invitations never tell you what the event will launch, just that there will be a launch, and reporters accept this and attend to see the big unveiling. In my case, I had effectively broken the global secrecy of the launch by telling more than thirty reporters exactly what was coming in a week's time. Insert melty-face emoji times a thousand. My manager excoriated me, and I remember hiding in a conference room ugly-crying, genuinely worrying that I was going to be fired. Afterward, I got to work, and I followed up with each reporter individually, explaining that there would be a lot more to write about at the event itself, and that I was looking forward to seeing them there. As it happened, those reporters happened not to write about the product early and most still attended the event—a huge relief. So the point is obviously that it worked: the launch was successful, no one died, and I kept my job. Perfect. *No, wait!* My point is that sometimes the worst failure can liberate you. If you are comfortable with that, it means you can be quick to call out your failure (or in my case, have it called), make amends, and move everything along, and even lead to a better outcome.

Owning failure and being honest about it are at the core of a powerfully likeable communication style. Accepting that failure might happen—will happen!—and knowing you'll be okay one way or the other is such a liberating position to be in. Indeed, perhaps the biggest failure of all, and the one that hurts women the most, is the expectation that we won't fail. Whether we have this idea projected by others or believe it ourselves, it can be so detrimental to our sense of being and happiness in the world. You *will* fail at some things, and at others you will succeed. And that's actually a reasonable outcome of a life lived putting yourself forward for bigger opportunities, many of which might carry a degree of risk.

In fact, a question I get asked a lot is "What happens if I fail?" and I always counter with "*When* you fail" because you will, if you haven't already. This is different from believing that everything you might attempt will fail. It's a more subtle acceptance that if you're trying and experimenting at everything, not every outcome will be perfect. Not to be a downer, but you will fail a hundred different ways, and in one way or another, all of them are recoverable, I promise. The best way to fail is to tell someone immediately about it. Explain your failure calmly and concisely. This is extremely important if you're in a larger team or have a manager; they need to know fast so that they, too, can help correct what's happening. Being embarrassed and quiet about it is the fastest path to trouble. Ideally, come to the group with a solution for how you will remedy the situation and then also how you will try to ensure it never happens again.

Communicating that you *own* a failure—like I did with my launch event—is a key step in recovering from it. Speak up early and quickly when you've realized something has gone awry, and take responsibility if that awry thing was, well, you. I'm hypersensitive to owning a failure when it is mine. I try to recognize it immediately, communicate it, and offer what I can do to remedy the situation. It's not always perfect, but it's a start, and I think people respond to me with more grace when they see I'm trying to get in front of it and be account-able. Importantly, don't own someone else's failure—it might be tempting as you wrestle with your inner likeability inclina-tion, but only accept responsibility for that which you call your own. And that includes not just big failures, like a bad launch or malfunctioning product, but little ones, too.

LEARNING TO BE AN OPERATOR FOR ALL SEASONS

One of the most critical ways we can get out of failure-mode thinking and communicating is to stop deciding that we only succeed in one type of environment. Mary, a senior leader at a bank, tells me that she's fine so long as she knows who's going to be in the room for a sales pitch. Anjali, a junior web developer, says she thinks she'll succeed if she has enough time to code—but the minute she's rushed "I know I'm going to fail." You might have similar thoughts about your own work: *If X conditions are met, I will be okay,* or *I will defi-nitely fail if Y conditions happen.* When did we start deciding that failure is guaranteed if and when particular conditions are met?

Is there a perfect season or type of weather you enjoy? Let's imagine someone out there who only likes the weather when it's eighty degrees. Warm, sunny, not too hot—just perfectly delicious. Eighty-degree days, forever, amirite? Now, while it's perfectly acceptable to have preferences like these, and it's not controversial to enjoy a sunny day, if that person *only* considers a day a success if it's eighty degrees, you'd probably agree that she's conceding failure on many days of the year at the outset. Even if it's a few degrees off, it won't hit the bar in a way that feels just right. That's a lot of days to leave on the table as failures when something productive or positive could be done with them.

You can see where I'm going here, but we ascribe work with perfect conditions in a similar way: *I will succeed only when I know everyone in the room.* Or when I'm an expert in the field. Or whatever your pet favorite condition might be. And when these conditions aren't met—even if they're only a few degrees off what we wanted or expected, we sometimes feel enormously let down: I didn't do a good job. I didn't know anyone there. I felt totally out of my depth. I *failed.*

Time and again, I work with women who may have left a meeting or presentation just a few degrees off their perfect expectation and feel like they have failed by a significant margin. Natalia, a CFO, tells me, "I feel like I need to be more than perfect to be credible, and I have a hard time exteriorizing assurance." Of course, the expectation to be perfect or, in Natalia's words, "more than perfect" is an extraordinary baseline. And "more than perfect to be credible" almost definitionally means there won't be a time when you're believable, let alone amazing! The side effects of this type of all-too-common mindset are various and all equally damaging. For one, when this thinking happens in a meeting and you realize one of your arbitrary conditions isn't being met, you can lose a lot of energy, trail off, or not make the impact you had hoped for. But more critically, when this thinking is pervasive, you might find you don't bring up a point, run a project, or take an opportunity at all.

I recognize this phenomenon well. In fact, it speaks to my soul, because it used to be me. In my years debating, I used to have the most impossibly high standard for my performance and the conditions surrounding it. If I hadn't given the *exact* right performance, I'd often assume it was a total flop—which it rarely was. One time I was wrong-footed in a really high-stakes debate being recorded for televised broadcast. I wasn't expecting the debate to take the direction it did, and I ended up having to give my ten-minute speech with no notes, thinking up arguments about free trade and tariffs on the fly. Inside, I wanted to die. How mortifying to be shown up like this, I thought. Afterward I explained to my friends who had been in the audience what happened, and they were completely unaware I didn't have any notes. One friend, Dave, said, "I didn't think it was your best debate ever, but it certainly wasn't bad at all." This comment has stuck with me, because it made me realize that what I had mentally defined as a catastrophe was actually just a few points off my normal.

I want to suggest that even though we might have strong preferences for the perfect conditions at work, we must get used to being an operator for all seasons. Hot? Windy? Unfamiliar terminology? High stakes? No notes for your speech? Part of fully embodying our power is to understand our preferences and *be flexible to operate outside of them*. It's not to say we can't have preferences—it's just that we can summon our courage and potential and operate even when they're not met. To continue with the metaphor, the weather is largely out of our control. Sure, you could choose to live in a temperate climate if that's your thing, but you'll still get the odd cold day or scorching hot day (especially in our climate-changing world). The analogy here is that you could still find a workplace that is largely suited to your preferences and still have an off day here and there.

A key part of embodying powerful likeability is both to understand what your favorite preferences and behaviors actually are and then also to know how to still bring your full self when those preferences aren't being met. It's not good if you are able to present only to, say, a room when you know everyone there. In order to succeed you must be able to present to strangers with the same level of impact and authority because there's no doubt that that day will come, if it hasn't already. If you're someone who says, for example, "I'm only good when I . . . ," try loosening up that formulation for yourself. Maybe it's as simple as trying to be gentler to yourself when your conditions aren't met, advocating for something to help you have a greater sense of authority in the moment, or thinking differently about failure, too.

Try this: What are your preferred conditions in which to operate? Do you find yourself having to operate outside of them very often? What advice would you give yourself to reimagine what success could look like in imperfect conditions?

APPLY THE SAME RIGOR TO IMAGINING SUCCESS AS YOU DO FAILURE

We're so used to thinking about the possessive risks and pitfalls that we forget that success could even be a possible outcome for us. We naturally think through possible points of failure with a frenzied fervor but don't often sit down with the same rigor and apply it to a list of reasons you might succeed and think whether there's reasonable merit to them, too.

To that end, the question "What would it look like if I succeeded?" is a most useful one. Sometimes giving ourselves permission to imagine the best case can be a powerful lever in shifting our own energy around the event or experience. I realize I just used the word *energy,* but I'm not talking about practices of manifesting or vision boards or tarot cards (although if those work for you, brava!). I'm rather suggesting that you employ the same rigor to imagining success as you do failure.

Take the same brain that so easily wanders into the failure domain, that sees every possible variable, land mine, and flaw, and then train it on a success model. Ask yourself, *Where are the moments that I can leverage? Do I know someone I can talk this through with?* Your communication around whatever you're dreaming up will change considerably if you've been thoughtful with engaging through the success frame. It's not to say this always guarantees success, but it definitely will have a positive effect on the way you talk about your projects and work, and this counts for an enormous amount. If you consistently question about success rather than failure, you might just find yourself surprised by the answer.

Try this: Is it possible that success could be an outcome? Why or why not? What might you do to mitigate the situation and change the outcome? Consider asking yourself one of my favorite questions: *What would this look like if I succeeded?*

FAILURE IS OFTEN AN EXCELLENT AND
POIGNANT TEACHER

I know, I know, none of us want to hear this, but it can be painfully true. My partner talks about truly memorable failures as "school fee moments"—sometimes we must pay for a lesson, and it's usually one we will never forget. I'm sure you've experienced those moments at work when you'd get a "special opportunity" (that is, you've been assigned to a shit show of a project because they needed safe hands for it). You might even realize it wasn't that special and sometimes wasn't even that much of an opportunity, but that's the nature of work, sometimes.

My friend Annie used to call those situations AFGOs, which stands for "Another Fucking Growth Opportunity," which at least made us laugh. And despite groaning about these moments under our breath, we still knew we'd likely come out of it in a better place and with more than we had before. Because that's ultimately the aim, right? To come out of a dismal experience with more data than we had before. Sometimes that knowledge might result in you coming to an understanding that you have to leave a particular job, and at other times, it may be a nice surprise to have learned a new thing in order to make a more informed decision going forward. Either way, more knowledge is more power, not failure.

Connect with Your Community

One of the very particular modes of female failure is to feel shame or disconnection when we fail. I want to suggest that connecting with your community while creating something—

even if it's failed—will be core to getting you through that moment. Research suggests that women are less likely to use their "weak ties" (think: long-lost LinkedIn connections or old school friends) when they have questions or favors to ask. Men are more comfortable reaching out to an old friend or acquaintance they haven't spoken to in a long time to make an ask. We're missing an immense opportunity here to use the networks we have, and we might be surprised who can help us or connect us to someone we hadn't been contemplating who can open a useful door for us.

Many of my clients have told me of cold-calling someone in their trusted, extended circle in moments of doubt, and I think it's one of the most beautiful aspects of vulnerably sharing your experiences with another. Trusted advisors, mentors, confidantes, and sometimes even friends only become those roles for us because we've asked for their guidance: they're key for self-assurance or for reinforcing we're doing the right thing. (Or telling us when it's the wrong one!) And if that still feels difficult, remember that you probably like to help others, and you might even be flattered if someone asked you for some advice.

In a similar vein, research about how women network shows that women are about one-third *more* likely than men to form high-status connections via a third-party tie. When introducing another woman to a connection, the introduction itself serves as an amplification, legitimizing and vetting the person you're introducing. This means that we take introductions and the idea of vetting very seriously, which consequently means we can be powerful levers for each other in sharing our community when asked or offering to make an introduction in the first instance.

Communicative inclusion is helping all voices feel welcome in a space. Try it and see how much you can get out of your colleagues (or yourself, if you're naturally shy). It automatically works against feelings of failure, as it helps people contribute, ask, and engage in an entirely different-feeling way. The culture you create in so doing is warmer and easier for an outsider or new team member in which to feel welcome. Remember Gina from chapter 2? We spoke a few weeks after the "Just Gina" conversation, and she expressed so much relief that she doesn't feel small on those calls with the CEO anymore. But she did tell me our conversation had made her rethink many other situations at work, including self-deprecatingly calling herself Negative Nelly when she gives presentations at all-hands meetings! I was pleased that our workshopping the problem had helped her see her other interactions through a new perspective—and my hope is that we can show up without preemptively giving others a reason to doubt ourselves or our capabilities.

One of the most valuable lessons is to believe in your own potential and excellence while also knowing that there might be failure ahead. I believe we'll have true parity with men only when we can fail in public and then rebound with few repercussions the way they do, when we can experience an equal Failure Privilege. This would mean that our failures don't define our total value but are a small blip in our chronology of life events. I, for one, very much look forward to that day.

Beautiful Works in Progress:

Living a Powerfully Likeable Life

In closing, I want to tell you a story. This time it's not about debate or even work. The setting is a hospital many years ago, which I appreciate might be jarring, but stay with me. I don't remember the first thing I noticed when I woke up from the surgery, but I do recall the tubes. There seemed to be so many of them, running in and out of my body, each one with a different job to do. In particular, I could see bright, red-colored drains poking out from bandages, not revealing their entry or exit points. Groggily but with much painkiller-induced authority, I told my partner, James, how fortunate it was that they painted those drains red so that I—squeamish since forever—didn't have to see the blood within. It wasn't until a few days later that I realized that those tubes were, in fact, transparent and that I had been observing my own blood. I almost passed out.

It's fair to say that there's a lot to process in big life events like these. When this surgery was over, I remember being so relieved and happy to move on with my life. But in 2020, I found out I had to have another operation on the same scale, and I was terrified. This was weird, because up until then, I had always self-identified as being brave. I told my friend Minh that I was scared, and how deeply *annoyed* I was that I was scared. I was almost more annoyed about being scared than I was actually afraid. And he looked at me and asked, "Do you think warriors in battle didn't feel scared? Think about everyone who has ever shown bravery. Do you think they had no fear at all?"

And that's when it hit me: fear is a necessary precondition for bravery. In fact, you can't be brave if you're not scared, because otherwise you're just, you know, alive and doing stuff. We cannot be brave unless there's something to overcome or to face down. This was the unlock I was looking for: oh, I'm scared, so it means *now I get to be brave*. In fact, the adjective *brave* means all the things you'd expect, such as plucky, heroic, adventurous, gutsy. But remember that the verb *to brave* means to withstand, to bear with, to face up to, to confront. We have to *do the thing* in order to be brave. We have to live the verb, not just throw around the adjective.

Living a powerfully likeable life is much the same. It requires a rethinking and maybe a re*doing* of so many things we've done before. For me, realizing that my next surgery offered the *opportunity* for bravery gave me a whole different way of looking at and experiencing the event. (And I was super brave, in case you were wondering—even about the drains.)

Powerful likeability suggests that it is through *doing* things differently that you'll find the space to speak from your most authentic, powerful place. And it might require bravery from you, too. It might require some rethinking, reimagining, and recalibrating exactly how you communicate. My hope for you is that it offers you an opportunity for bravery or newness in your own lives, even in the more mundane moments of giving a presentation or running a meeting. For me, the opportunity to be brave has profoundly changed the way I communicate and also how I coach others on it. When you have the opportunity to do a hard thing, you have a chance to be delighted with the outcome.

I wrote at the beginning of this book that the myriad ways women show up at work and in life are changing. If some of the discussions in this book resonated with you, I welcome you to experiment and play with those ideas. Take them for a walk, try them on, let yourself roll around in a new concept or framework, and see what fits or feels good to you. Please don't attempt to be a Whole New Person in a week, because that's not ideal for a lot of reasons. What we're trying to do is to learn to flex some powerfully likeable muscles (and maybe unlearn some flexing of others—deference, I'm talking to you). It's much less about changing the person you are and instead about unfurling a sense of power that was always there but until now perhaps only tentatively grasped. Or maybe it's about letting go of over-indexing power and coming back to a more balanced mix to feel more like yourself.

The pattern matching and archetypes we have learned for so many years can and will recede if we want them to. The most important thing to remember is that none of those communicative binaries actually exist; they're only drawn in pencil. We are all works in progress, so all in good time. If we continue to tell ourselves that there are so many more options for how we show up and communicate in the world, people will see our example and change will come.

With flexible, inventive reimagining of our communication, we can operate outside many of the restrictive and constraining binaries, archetypes, stereotypes, and more that have defined us, up until now. Dismantling communicative binaries can lead to much more fluid, expressive, creative, and powerful ways to show up at work and beyond, and allow women to unleash their creative power and energy, something I've believed in forever.

Go get 'em.

—KATE xx

ACKNOWLEDGMENTS

I never miss reading an Acknowledgments section. It's a magical thing to appreciate all the work, thoughtfulness, and sometimes even serendipity that have to converge for a thing to get made.

An increasingly common pattern I have noticed in pages like these, however, is the propensity of authors to apologize for their burdensome selves or their unavailability throughout the writing process: "Thanks for putting up with me" or "Sorry I was away a lot and didn't do [a household chore]." You will not be surprised, dear reader, after reading *Powerfully Likeable,* that I will not be doing that. As I informed my partner yesterday, I have been nothing but a "total delight" during the writing of this book.

And that's really because I *adored* writing it. It was such a pleasure to have the space to capture some ideas I care deeply about. All mistakes are mine alone, and I'm grateful to have this opportunity in which to wholeheartedly thank some special people who were, in different ways, very present with me during the process.

To my dear friend Katherine Stirling, for gently insisting that I write this book since we first met. Thank goodness I gave you my card that fateful day in SF.

To Chris Keneally, for being such a generous and incisive friend—I cherish our conversations. Also, I promise to never use the word *elide* ever again.

Early and beloved co-conspirators include Kathryn Apte, Annie Buckman, Sarah Darmody, Sam Duboff, W. David Marx, Rachael Neumann, Jodi Olsen, Jessica Powell, Tash Simonsen, Gel Vicencio, Alex Vikmanis, and Vanessa Collins, for buying me that stamp in Paris.

My agents, the brilliant duo Mollie Glick and Kari Stuart, for their unwavering faith in and support of both me and this book. You are both living examples of the title.

To Shannon Welch, for your early and heartfelt championing of the book.

To my inimitable editor, Marnie Cochran, for being just as excited as I am to bring this book into the world (which is no small feat). Your joy, smarts, and energy have been such gifts—thank you.

Thanks also to the broader team at Harmony, which has worked so hard to make this book shine.

To the Penguin Australia team—the wonderful Isabelle Yates, Madison Gu, and Kaelee Aboud—thank you, too, for your warm embrace of this book.

To Karen Wickre, who literally wrote the book on networking, for being so generous with her network.

To the beautiful Team Pourquoi Pas, the Kyoto Krew, and the Neckerbockers—thank you for literal and metaphorical adventuring with me.

To Mes Olives and to Lamb Dinners, for literal and emotional sustenance along the way.

To my very special family, in particular my mum and dad, and my beautiful sisters, Em and Bec. I lucked out beyond measure when I got you all in my corner—thank you for everything.

To my beloved grandpa, who will turn one hundred the same year this book comes into the world.

To my boys, Charlie and Leo.

And to James, my biggest champion.

NOTES

vii **"We spend too much time"**: Chimamanda Ngozi Adichie, *We Should All Be Feminists* (Fourth Estate, 2014), 24.

vii **"One of the criticisms I've faced"**: Jacinda Ardern, quoted in Maureen Dowd, "Lady of the Rings: Jacinda Rules," *The New York Times,* September 8, 2018, www.nytimes.com/2018/09/08/opinion/sunday/jacinda-ardern-new -zealand-prime-minister.html.

INTRODUCTION

xx **likeability as something to avoid**: See, for example, Lois P. Frankel, *Nice Girls Don't Get the Corner Office: Unconscious Mistakes Women Make That Sabotage Their Careers* (Grand Central Publishing, 2004).

xx **negotiate intensely**: See, for example, Alicia Menendez, *The Likeability Trap: How to Break Free and Succeed as You Are* (Harper Business, 2019).

xxi **inequitable salaries**: Maria Konnikova, "Lean Out: The Dangers for Women Who Negotiate," *The New Yorker,* June 10, 2014, www.new yorker.com/science/maria-konnikova/lean-out-the-dangers-for-women-who -negotiate.

xxi **never-eventuating promotions**: In a study, men rated their own performance 33 percent higher than equally performing women. Christine Exley and Judd Kessler, "Why Don't Women Self-Promote as Much as Men," *Harvard Business Review,* December 19, 2019, https://hbr.org/2019/12/why -dont-women-self-promote-as-much-as-men.

xxi **endemic lack of funding**: Women received a whopping 2.3 percent of all venture capital funding in 2020. Ashley Bittner and Brigette Lau, "Women-Led Startups Received Just 2.3% of VC Funding in 2020," *Harvard Business Review,* February 25, 2021, https://hbr.org/2021/02/women-led-startups -received-just-2-3-of-vc-funding-in-2020. They're also systematically discriminated against through being asked different, penalizing questions. Dana Kanze, Laura Huang, Mark A. Conley, and E. Tory Higgins, "Male and Female Entrepreneurs Get Asked Different Questions by VCs—and It Affects How Much Funding They Get," *Harvard Business Review,* June 27, 2017, https://hbr.org/2017/06/male-and-female-entrepreneurs-get-asked -different-questions-by-vcs-and-it-affects-how-much-funding-they-get.

xxi **believe expert testimony:** Mariam Younan and Kristy A. Martire, "Likeability and Expert Persuasion: Dislikeability Reduces the Perceived Persuasiveness of Expert Evidence," *Frontiers in Psychology* 12, article 785677, December 23, 2021.

xxiv **"public speech was":** Mary Beard, *Women & Power: A Manifesto* (Liveright, 2018), 17.

xxiv **"nice girls don't get the corner office":** Frankel, *Nice Girls Don't Get the Corner Office.*

CHAPTER ONE

4 **communicate in a compelling manner:** For an extensive and compelling deep dive into the topic of authority, see Mary Ann Sieghart, *The Authority Gap: Why Women Are Still Taken Less Seriously Than Men, and What We Can Do About It* (Transworld Digital, 2021).

7 **fall off the glass cliff:** Michelle K. Ryan and S. Alexander Haslam, "The Glass Cliff: Evidence That Women Are Over-Represented in Precarious Leadership Positions," *British Journal of Management* 16, no. 2 (2005): 81–90.

7 **bump into a glass wall:** Amy Diehl and Leanne M. Dzubinski, *Glass Walls: Shattering the Six Gender Bias Barriers Still Holding Women Back at Work* (Rowman and Littlefield, 2023), chap. 1.

7 **"Women are expected":** Elise Loehnen, *On Our Best Behavior: The Seven Deadly Sins and the Price Women Pay to Be Good* (Dial Press, 2023), 18.

8 **our health, sanity, and career:** Maytal Eyal, "Self-Silencing Is Making Women Sick," *Time,* October 3, 2023, https://time.com/6319549/silencing -women-sick-essay.

14 **"When a woman made a key point":** Juliet Eilperin, "White House Women Want to Be in the Room Where It Happens," *Washington Post,* September 13, 2016, www.washingtonpost.com/news/powerpost/wp/2016/ 09/13/white-house-women-are-now-in-the-room-where-it-happens.

CHAPTER TWO

28 **Pauline Rose Clance and Suzanne Imes:** P. R. Clance and S. A. Imes, "The Imposter Phenomenon in High Achieving Women: Dynamics and Therapeutic Intervention," *Psychotherapy: Theory, Research, and Practice* 15, no. 3 (1978): 241–47.

28 **imposter phenomenon:** Leslie Jamison, "Why Everyone Feels Like They're

Faking It," *The New Yorker,* February 6, 2023, www.newyorker.com/
magazine/2023/02/13/the-dubious-rise-of-impostor-syndrome.

28 **"Imposter syndrome directs our view":** Ruchika Tulshyan and Jodi-Ann
Burey, "Stop Telling Women They Have Imposter Syndrome," *Harvard
Business Review,* February 11, 2021, https://hbr.org/2021/02/stop-telling
-women-they-have-imposter-syndrome.

31 **"Almost all voice assistants":** "Artificial Intelligence and Gender Equality:
Key Findings of UNESCO's Global Dialogue," United Nations Educational,
Scientific and Cultural Organization, 2020, 2, https://unesdoc.unesco.org/
ark:/48223/pf0000374174.

32 **"the kind that is important":** Linda Babcock, Brenda Peyser, Lise Vester-
lund, and Laurie R. Weingart, *The No Club: Putting a Stop to Women's Dead-
End Work* (Piatkus, 2022).

38 **"untitling":** Amy Diehl and Leanne Dzubinski, "We Need to Stop Untitling and Uncredentialing Professional Women," *Fast Company,* January 22,
2021, www.fastcompany.com/90596628/we-need-to-stop-untitling-and
-uncredentialing-professional-women.

48 **"reclaiming my time":** Vanessa Williams, "Maxine Waters Inspires a New
Anthem: 'Reclaiming My Time,'" *Washington Post,* August 1, 2017, www
.washingtonpost.com/news/post-nation/wp/2017/08/01/maxine-waters
-inspires-a-new-anthem-reclaiming-my-time.

50 **including by other women:** A study found that "73% of the women sur-
veyed expressed fear over how women are perceived when self-promoting."
See Caroline Castrillon, "How Women Can Embrace Self-Advocacy at
Work," *Forbes,* June 21, 2023, www.forbes.com/sites/carolinecastrillon/
2023/06/21/how-women-can-embrace-self-advocacy-at-work.

51 **"accomplished, high-potential women":** Herminia Ibarra, Robin J. Ely,
and Deborah M. Kolb, "Women Rising: The Unseen Barriers," *Harvard
Business Review,* September 2013, https://hbr.org/2013/09/women-rising
-the-unseen-barriers.

51 **people choose their colleagues:** Tiziana Casciaro and Miguel Sousa Lobo,
"Competent Jerks, Lovable Fools, and the Formation of Social Networks,"
Harvard Business Review, June 2005, https://hbr.org/2005/06/competent
-jerks-lovable-fools-and-the-formation-of-social-networks.

CHAPTER THREE

57 **"Communication isn't as simple":** Deborah Tannen, "The Power of Talk:
Who Gets Heard and Why," *Harvard Business Review,* September–October
1995, 138.

58 **"With men, we listen":** Lakoff quoted in Ann Friedman, "Can We Just,
Like, Get Over the Way Women Talk?," The Cut, July 9, 2015, www.thecut
.com/2015/07/can-we-just-like-get-over-the-way-women-talk.html.

59 **pertaining to their voices:** Emma Gray and Claire Fallon, "Want a Lesson

in How People Judge Women's Voices? Start a Podcast," *Huffington Post,* July 13, 2015, www.huffpost.com/entry/how-people-judge-womens-voices -podcasts_n_55a01ae9e4b0a47ac15c893c; Terry Gross, "From Upspeak to Vocal Fry: Are We 'Policing' Young Women's Voices?," *Fresh Air,* July 23, 2015, www.npr.org/2015/07/23/425608745/from-upspeak-to-vocal-fry-are-we -policing-young-womens-voices.

59 **"I get criticized for a lot"**: Glass, quoted in Gray and Fallon, "Want a Lesson in How People Judge Women's Voices?"

60 **"Girl Finally Speaking"**: "Girl Finally Speaking Up Enough for People to Critique Her Speaking Voice," *The Onion,* October 5, 2015, https://theonion .com/girl-finally-speaking-up-enough-for-people-to-critique-1819578264.

60 **"low-pitched voice indicated"**: Beard, *Women & Power,* 19.

61 **vocal tone grew increasingly masculine**: Jennifer J. Jones, "Talk 'Like a Man': The Linguistic Styles of Hillary Clinton, 1992–2013," *Perspectives on Politics* 14, no. 3 (September 2016): 625–42.

69 **known as the chameleon effect**: Tanya L. Chartrand and John A. Bargh, "The Chameleon Effect: The Perception-Behavior Link and Social Interaction," *Journal of Personality and Social Psychology* 76, no. 6 (1999): 893–910.

70 **"Smiling doesn't win you gold medals"**: "Simone Biles Tells Dancing with the Stars Judges: 'Smiling Doesn't Win You Gold Medals,'" *Sports Illustrated,* May 9, 2017, www.si.com/olympics/2017/05/09/simone-biles -smile-dancing-stars-response-video.

71 **more than spiders or, literally, death**: Kaya Burgess, "Speaking in Public Is Worse Than Death for Most," *The Times* (London), October 30, 2013, www .thetimes.com/article/speaking-in-public-is-worse-than-death-for-most -5l2bvqlmbnt.

CHAPTER FOUR

93 **"traditionally expected to be caring"**: Pragya Agarwal, "Not Very Likeable: Here Is How Bias Is Affecting Women Leaders," *Forbes,* October 23, 2018, www.forbes.com/sites/pragyaagarwaleurope/2018/10/23/not-very -likeable-here-is-how-bias-is-affecting-women-leaders/?sh=5668f34e295f.

94 **as "feminine" attributes**: I'm using "masculine" and "feminine" in an academic sense only and write with an awareness that gender isn't a binary, and in fact many folks move between multiple different communication modes all the time.

106 **a client named Matt**: There is *always* a Matt. See Madison Malone Kircher, "Tesla Used to Joke About Having More Employees Named 'Matt' Than Women," *New York Magazine,* November 13, 2017, https://nymag.com/ intelligencer/2017/11/tesla-had-more-employees-named-matt-than-women .html.

109 **"best alternative to a negotiated agreement" theory**: Margaret Neale

writes extensively and persuasively on negotiation. Her book is an incisive and helpful read; see chap. 2 in Margaret A. Neale and Thomas Z. Lys, *Getting (More of) What You Want* (Basic Books, 2015).

CHAPTER FIVE

113 **"tiara syndrome"**: Deborah M. Kolb, Judith Williams, and Carol Frohlinger, *Her Place at the Table: A Women's Guide to Negotiating Five Key Challenges to Leadership Success* (Jossey-Bass, 2010), 174.

126 **Bridgewater:** Alexandra Stevenson and Matthew Goldstein, "Bridgewater's Ray Dalio Spreads His Gospel of 'Radical Transparency,'" *The New York Times,* September 8, 2017, www.nytimes.com/2017/09/08/business/dealbook/bridgewaters-ray-dalio-spreads-his-gospel-of-radical-transparency.html

126 **Netflix:** "Netflix Culture—the Best Work of Our Lives," memo, Netflix, https://jobs.netflix.com/culture.

CHAPTER SIX

147 **tall poppy syndrome:** Bert Peeters, "Tall Poppies and Egalitarianism in Australian Discourse: From Key Word to Cultural Value," *English World-Wide: A Journal of Varieties of English* 25, no. 1 (January 2004): 1–25.

147 **around the world in other guises:** Japanese, for instance, has a comparable phrase, "the nail that sticks up gets hammered down" (出る釘は打たれる, deru kugi wa utareru), referring to the relative safety of homogeneity. See John Simpson and Jennifer Speake, eds., *The Oxford Dictionary of Proverbs,* 5th ed. (Oxford University Press, 2008), 410. The well-known German word *schadenfreude,* meaning the pleasure derived from the misfortune of another, is also related to tall poppy syndrome.

147 **4,710 respondents:** Rumeet Billan, "The Tallest Poppy: How the Workforce Is Cutting Ambitious Women Down," Women of Influence+, March 2023, www.womenofinfluence.ca/wp-content/uploads/2023/02/tp-whitepaper.pdf.

147 **"indicated that at some point"**: Billan, "Tallest Poppy," 4.

CHAPTER SEVEN

150 **"role incredulity"**: Amy Diehl and Leanne M. Dzubinski, "When People Assume You're Not in Charge Because You're a Woman," *Harvard Business Review,* December 22, 2021, https://hbr.org/2021/12/when-people-assume-youre-not-in-charge-because-youre-a-woman?s=03.

151 **all the research:** See, for example, David Rock and Heidi Grant, "Why Diverse Teams Are Smarter," *Harvard Business Review,* November 4, 2016, https://hbr.org/2016/11/why-diverse-teams-are-smarter; Sundiatu Dixon-Fyle, Kevin Dolan, Dame Vivian Hunt, and Sara Prince, "Diversity Wins: How Inclusion Matters," McKinsey & Co., May 19, 2020.

159 **"ritual apologies"**: Tannen, "Power of Talk," 143.

160 "The world would be a much": Cindy Gallop and Tomas Chamorro-Premuzic, "7 Pieces of Bad Career Advice Women Should Ignore," *Harvard Business Review,* April 15, 2021, https://hbr.org/2021/04/7-pieces-of-bad-career-advice-women-should-ignore.

166 *because* as a key to influencing: See chap. 6 in Robert Cialdini, *Influence: The Psychology of Persuasion,* rev. ed. (Harper Business, 2006).

166 copy machine experiment: E. J. Langer, A. Blank, and B. Chanowitz, "The Mindlessness of Ostensibly Thoughtful Action: The Role of Placebic Information in Interpersonal Interaction," *Journal of Personality and Social Psychology* 36, no. 6 (1978): 635–42. See also James Clear, "The One Word That Drives Senseless and Irrational Habits," https://jamesclear.com/copy-machine-study.

168 "When selecting metaphors": Suzanne de Janasz and Beth Cabrera, "How Women Can Get What They Want in a Negotiation," *Harvard Business Review,* August 17, 2018, https://hbr.org/2018/08/how-women-can-get-what-they-want-in-a-negotiation.

169 women negotiate less than men: Linda Babcock and Sara Laschever, *Women Don't Ask: The High Cost of Avoiding Negotiation—and Positive Strategies for Change* (Bantam, 2007).

169 "hurt to ask": Hannah Riley Bowles, Linda Babcock, and Lei Lai, "Social Incentives for Gender Differences in the Propensity to Initiate Negotiations: Sometimes It Does Hurt to Ask," *Organizational Behavior and Human Decision Processes* 103, no. 1 (May 2007): 84–103.

169 lose hundreds of thousands: Linda Babcock and Sara Laschever, "The Costs of Not Negotiating," *Harvard Business Review,* January 29, 2009, https://hbr.org/2009/01/is-talent-going-to-waste-in-yo. Women are also slightly more likely than men to say they didn't feel comfortable asking for higher pay (42% vs. 33%). See Kim Parker, "When Negotiating Starting Salaries, Most US Women and Men Don't Ask for Higher Pay," Pew Research Center, April 5, 2023, www.pewresearch.org/short-reads/2023/04/05/when-negotiating-starting-salaries-most-us-women-and-men-dont-ask-for-higher-pay.

169 same-sex groups negotiating: Uta Herbst, Hilla Dotan, and Sina Stöhr, "Negotiating with Work Friends: Examining Gender Differences in Team Negotiations," *Journal of Business and Industrial Marketing* 32, no. 4 (May 2017): 558–66.

169 "women negotiate better outcomes": Herbst, Dotan, and Stöhr, "Negotiating with Work Friends," 559.

171 a new title but not a raise: Ray A. Smith, "Your Promotion Doesn't Come with a Raise. Should You Take It?," *Wall Street Journal,* March 11, 2024, www.wsj.com/lifestyle/careers/that-new-job-comes-with-a-bigger-title-and-no-raise-whats-your-move-b79c919d.

Chapter Eight

181 **Clinton was accused:** John Nichols, "Hillary Clinton Prepared for the Debate, and Showed She Is Prepared for the Presidency," *The Nation,* September 27, 2016, www.thenation.com/article/archive/hillary-clinton-prepared -for-the-debate-and-showed-she-is-prepared-for-the-presidency; Dan Primack, "Hillary Clinton Defends Her Debate Preparations: 'I Also Prepared to Be President,'" *Fortune,* September 27, 2016, www.thenation.com/article/ archive/hillary-clinton-prepared-for-the-debate-and-showed-she-is-prepared -for-the-presidency.

181 *Washington Post* article: Dan Zak, "Always Running, Always Prepared: Hillary Clinton as a High School Politician," *Washington Post,* October 17, 2016, www.washingtonpost.com/lifestyle/style/hillary-clinton-high-school -years-always-running-always-prepared/2016/10/17/35dd9e4a-8c08-11e6 -bf8a-3d26847eeed4_story.html.

199 **"Women are nearly twice as likely":** Barbara Rhoden, "Women Feel Guilty About Getting Enough Sleep—and It's a Public Health Emergency," *Fortune,* March 6, 2024, https://fortune.com/2024/03/05/women-feel-guilty -getting-enough-sleepand-public-health.

Chapter Nine

213 **A study by the University of California:** Thomas Sy and Daan van Knippenberg, "The Emotional Leader: Implicit Theories of Leadership Emotions and Leadership Perceptions," *Journal of Organizational Behavior* 42, no. 5 (September 2021): 885–912.

213 **the connections between our mind and our body:** On the mind/body connection as it pertains both to trauma and illness, see Bessel van der Kolk, *The Body Keeps the Score: Brain, Mind, and Body in the Healing of Trauma* (Penguin Books, 2015); Gabor Maté, *When the Body Says No: Understanding the Stress-Disease Connection* (Wiley, 2011).

214 **one of my favorite studies:** Frank Rose, "The Selfish Meme," *The Atlantic,* October 2012, www.theatlantic.com/magazine/archive/2012/10/the-selfish -meme/309080.

214 **our "computer" and "creature" selves:** Martha Beck, *The 4-Day Win: Change the Way You Think About Food and Your Body in Just 4 Days* (Piatkus, 2007), 57.

215 **"belief that one can speak up":** Amy C. Edmondson and Mark Mortensen, "What Psychological Safety Looks Like in a Hybrid Workplace," *Harvard Business Review,* April 19, 2021, https://hbr.org/2021/04/what-psychological -safety-looks-like-in-a-hybrid-workplace.

215 **"more than anything else":** Amy Gallo, "What Is Psychological Safety?," *Harvard Business Review,* February 15, 2023, https://hbr.org/2023/02/what-is -psychological-safety.

219 **neurologist and physiologist Walter Bradford Cannon:** Walter Bradford

Cannon, *Bodily Changes in Pain, Hunger, Fear, and Rage* (Martino Fine Books, 1929).

220 **psychologist Gordon Gallup:** Gordon Gallup, "Tonic Immobility: The Role of Fear and Predation," *Psychological Record* 27, series 1 (1977): 41–61.

220 **psychotherapist and trauma survivor Pete Walker:** Pete Walker, *Complex PTSD: From Surviving to Thriving: A Guide and Map for Recovering from Childhood Trauma* (CreateSpace Independent Publishing Platform, 2013).

222 **"When a woman is emotional":** King, quoted in Tracey Packiam Alloway, *Think Like a Girl: 10 Unique Strengths of a Woman's Brain and How to Make Them Work for You* (HarperCollins Religious, 2021), 4–5.

223 **Child psychologist Rebecca Kennedy:** Jessica Winter, "Dr. Becky Kennedy Wants to Help Parents Land the Plane," *The New Yorker,* October 22, 2023, www.newyorker.com/culture/the-new-yorker-interview/dr-becky -kennedy-wants-to-help-parents-land-the-plane.

231 **"girls tend to learn conversational rituals":** Tannen, "The Power of Talk," 140.

233 **Research suggests that the longer exhalations:** Roderik J. S. Gerritsen and Guido P. H. Band, "Breath of Life: The Respiratory Vagal Stimulation Model of Contemplative Activity," *Frontiers in Human Neuroscience* 12 (2018): 397.

233 **can help us make better decisions:** Marijke De Couck, Ralf Caers, Liza Musch, Johanna Fliegauf, Antonio Giangreco, and Yori Gidron, "How Breathing Can Help You Make Better Decisions: Two Studies on the Effects of Breathing Patterns on Heart Rate Variability and Decision-Making in Business Cases," *International Journal of Psychophysiology* 139 (May 2019): 1–9.

CHAPTER TEN

238 **failure extolled in Silicon Valley:** Tech leaders wax lyrical about having a culture of failure, with Mark Zuckerberg's well-known "Move fast and break things" mantra at Meta, and Spotify founder Daniel Ek's quote—or strange flex?—that "We aim to make mistakes faster than anyone else."

239 **"When a women's endeavor fails":** "Martina Navratilova on Transgender Athletes, Pay Equity, and Trump," *On with Kara Swisher,* November 30, 2023, www.podchaser.com/podcasts/on-with-kara-swisher-4865725/ episodes/martina-navratilova-on-transge-193604682/transcript.

239 **"ask men questions":** Kanze et al., "Male and Female Entrepreneurs."

240 **Hold your keys:** Of course being assaulted is no failure on the part of women, but depressingly the research suggests victim-blaming is still in full force. See, for example, Renata Bongiorno, Chloe Langbroek, Paul G. Bain, Michelle Ting, and Michelle K. Ryan, "Why Women Are Blamed for Being Sexually Harassed: The Effects of Empathy for Female Victims and Male Perpetrators," *Psychology of Women Quarterly* 44, no. 1 (2020): 11–27.

240 **that lead to the emergency room:** Elizabeth E. O'Neal, Jodie M. Plumert,

and Carole Peterson, "Parent-Child Injury Prevention Conversations Following a Trip to the Emergency Department," *Journal of Pediatric Psychology* 41, no. 2 (March 2016): 256–64.

256 **"weak ties":** Jerome A. Katz and Pamela M. Williams, "Gender, Self-Employment, and Weak-Tie Networking Through Formal Organizations," *Entrepreneurship & Regional Development* 9, no. 3 (1997): 183–98. Thanks also to Margaret Neale and Deborah Gruenfeld, who introduced me to this idea in their Stanford University Executive Program in Women's Leadership in 2014.

256 **Trusted advisors, mentors, confidantes:** Tara Mohr has an excellent chapter on identifying great mentors, creative ways to consider mentorship, and even discovering what she calls an "inner mentor." See chap. 3 in Tara Mohr, *Playing Big: Practical Wisdom for Women Who Want to Speak Up, Create, and Lead* (Avery, 2015).

256 **connections via a third-party tie:** Carla Rua-Gomez, Gianluca Carnabuci, and Martin Goossen, "Research: How Women Can Build High-Status Networks," *Harvard Business Review,* March 20, 2024, https://hbr.org/2024/03/research-how-women-can-build-high-status-networks.

INDEX

A/B testing, 247
accomplishments, owning, 37–41,
    52–54
acquiescence, 8–9, 70, 231
action mode, 164–65
affect, xiv
AFGOs, 255
Agarwal, Pragya, 93
agreeableness
    exhausting nature of, 3–4
    influences of, xxvii
ambivalence in others, 105–8
amenability, 5–7
amplification, 14–15
antidote state, 216–17
anxiety, 152–53, 234–35
apologizing, 158–61, 164, 167
arguments, persuasive, 128–33
artificial intelligence (AI), 31
asks of others, 32–35, 139–40, 161,
    164–65
assets inventory, 16–20
assumptions, challenging, 49–50
attributes, 94–95, 169–70
"audience friends," 75–76
authority
    body language and, 57–58

communicating with, xv
    masculine coding of, 93
    reinforcing, 13–15
    signposting, 141–45
    voice and, 58–66

ballgame metaphor, 168
Beard, Mary, xxiv, 60
"because," use of, 166–67
Beck, Martha, 214
best friend voice, 100–102
Biles, Simone, 70
bodies
    calm in, 211–12
    communicating with, 57–58, 68,
        220
    fawn response, 220, 230–32
    fight response, 219–20, 221–23,
        233
    flight response, 219–20, 224–27,
        233
    freeze response, 220, 227–30
    leveraging, 217
    mind-body connection, 211–12,
        213
    nerves, 234–35
    threat responses, 219–21

boundary setting
  communicative self-care, 21–25
  difficulties with, 230–31
  overpreparation and, 192
  saying "no," 9–10
box breathing, 233
bravery, 260–61
breathing exercises, 232–34
Bridgewater, 126
British Parliamentary debate style, 187
burden of proof, 195
Burey, Jodi-Ann, 28
burnout, 198–200

Cabrera, Beth, 168
calm
  in the body, 211–12
  breathing to regulate, 232–34
  influencing with, 236
  as a leadership strength, 212–13
  loss of, 214–15
  modeling, 221–23
  responding with, 210–12
Cannon, Walter Bradford, 219–20
caveats, 35–37
chameleon effect, 69
Clance, Pauline Rose, 28
Clinton, Hillary, 61, 181
clothing, 80–85
collaboration
  competitive, 95–96
  fostering, 44
colleague archetypes, 51
color of clothing, 84
communication
  asking questions, 115–23
  body language, 57–58, 68
  crisis, 23–24
  defending ideas, 123–26
  deference, 158–64, 165
  facial expressions, 66–71, 77–79
  inclusive, 136–39, 255
  intelligence, 35

managing up, 121–23
masculine coding of, 93
masculine vs. feminine styles,
  xiv–xv
negotiation, 167–76
non-goals, 21–23
people-pleasing, 8–12
persuasive, 128–33, 141–45,
  200–206
powerful/likeable binary, 4–5
reasoning, 166–67
self-care, 20–25
signposting, 141–45
Smart Twelve-Year-Old frame,
  202–4
smiling, 69–71
Sushi Train Logic, 130–33
taking time, 23–25, 47–48
unfair expectations on women, 6–7
verbal expressions, 68
voice, 58–66
  warmth in, 164–65
  while female, 4–5, 70
  See also conversations; public
    speaking
community, 255–56
competence, 51
competitiveness, 95–96
computer self, 214
conciseness, 128–30
confidence
  assuming appropriate responsibility,
    104–5
  building, 100–102
  Confidence Combination exercise,
    xxvii, 93–96
  detective mindset, 105–8
  embracing hesitation, 108–110
  executive presence, 97
  feedback on, 88–91, 97
  internal voice of, 100–102
  masculine coding of, 92–93
  over-indexing on, 91–92

presence dysmorphia, 97–100
valuing own expertise, 102–3
connections, 255–57
conversations
about money, 170–71
with anxiety, 234–35
context for, 196
de-escalating, 124–25
difficult, 3–4, 74, 111, 145–48, 174, 219, 243
impromptu, 114–15
ritual apologies, 159–60
shaping with question-asking, 117–18
See also communication
counterquestions, 231–32
course correction, 244–47
creature comforts, 83–84
creature self, 214, 236
credibility, 42–44, 207–210
crisis communications, 23–24

debate, xiii–xv, xvii–xix, xxvii, 37–38, 69–70, 128–29, 182–83, 187, 195, 209–212, 225–27, 252
defending ideas, 123–26
defensiveness, 123, 125–26
deference, 158–64, 165, 167, 231
dehydration, 88
de Janasz, Suzanne, 168
detective mindset, 105–8
determining your win, 194–95
Diehl, Amy, 150
diet culture, 33–34
differences
anxiety about, 152–53
deference and, 158–64
embracing, 154–56
in negotiation, 167–76
opportunities and, 156–57
powerful/likeable binary, 151–52
as strengths, xxvii–xxviii, 153–54
upsides of, 152–56
"difficult" label, 5

discomfort, 29
distrust/dislike from others, 145–48
diversity, 151–52
"Does that make sense?" usage, 42–44
Dr. Becky. *See* Kennedy, Rebecca
"dress codes," 82–83
drive, 95
dry promotions, 171
Dzubinski, Leanne, 150

Edmondson, Amy, 215
Ely, Robin, 51
emotions, 135–36, 189–90, 213, 216, 222
empowerment, xxi
encouragement, 13–15
energy
attitude as, 135–36
calm, 236
expressions about having, 215
levels, 56–57
load-sharing, 136–39
nervous, 217
projection, 85–86
shifting, 254
engagement, 157
excitement, 196–97, 203–4
executive presence, 97, 151
expectations, 21–23
experimentation, 246–47
expertise, 102–5
eye contact, 75–76

facial expressions, 66–71, 77–79
failure
acceptance of, 249
anticipation of by women, 239–41
course correction vs., 244–47
Failure Privilege, xxviii, 238–40, 243, 244, 255
fear of, 241–42
gendered nature of acceptable, 238–39

failure (*cont'd*):
learning from, 255–56
as opposite of power, 238
owning, 248–50
perceptions of, 237–38
perfectionism and, 250–53
willing into being, 242–44
fast-talking, 62–63
fawn response, 220, 230–32
fear
of asking questions, 120–21
of failure, 241–42
necessity of, 260
of public speaking, 71–72, 115–16
responding calmly to, 210–12
feedback
on communication style, xiv–xv
on confidence, 88–91, 97
pain of giving/receiving, 126–28
solicitation of, 113–14
fifteen-minute rule, 184–86
fight response, 219–20, 221–23, 233
flexibility, 183–84, 194
flight response, 219–21, 224–27, 233
flow, 230
framing language, 42–44
freeze response, 220, 227–30
Frohlinger, Carol, 113

Gallop, Cindy, 160
Gallup, Gordon, 220
gender biases
in AI, 31
role incredulity, 149–51
generosity, 139–40
Getting on the Same Side framework, 124
Glass, Ira, 59
Google, 13–14, 181–82, 215
grief, 160–61
grounding, 226–27
group sessions, 134–35

Harvard Business Review, 51
hedging, 161–63, 167
Holmes, Elizabeth, 56
hypervigilance, 224

Ibarra, Herminia, 51
Imes, Suzanne, 28
Imposing Syndrome
caveating to avoid judgment, 35–37
challenging assumptions, 49–50
defined, 30–32
"Does that make sense?" usage, 42–44
minimization, 32–35
owning accomplishments, 37–41
pushing back on, xxvii, 44–54
reframing "how things are usually done," 45–47
self-advocacy, 50–54
taking up space and time, 47–48
imposter syndrome, 28–30
inauthenticity, 91–92
inclusive communication, 136–39, 255
inexperience, 29–30
information-sharing, 121–23
inner monologue, 231–232
insecurities, 146–148
intelligence, communicative, 35

jargon, 119–20
job negotiations, 171–75
judgment, avoiding, 35–37

Kennedy, Rebecca, 223
King, Billie Jean, 222
Kolb, Deborah, 51, 113

Lakoff, Robin, 58
Langer, Ellen, 166–67
leadership
calm as a strength, 212–13
power assets, 17–18

letting go, 197–98
likeability
    conceptualizing, xx
    as criteria in colleague choice, 51
    failure and, 238, 240–41, 243
    imposition as a threat to, 30–31
    perceptions of for women, xx–xxi
    power vs., xv–xxiv
    "yes" as a signifier for, 8, 12
listening, 118, 191
Loehnen, Elise, 7
logic, xxvii, 130–33

managing up, 121–23
manner, xiv
McKinsey & Co., 191
memorability, 155
mental promotions, 204–6
mind-body connection, 211–12, 213
minimization, 26–28, 30, 32–35, 242
Mnuchin, Steven, 48
money talk, 170–71
Mortensen, Mark, 215

Navratilova, Martina, 239
negative self-talk, 231–32
negotiation, 167–76
Netflix, 126
networking, 256–57
newscaster, 57–58
"no," saying, 9–10
non-goals, 21–23
non-promotable work, 32

Obama, Barack, 14
Oliver, Mary, 236
Opera Incident, 9
operating conditions, preferred, 250–53
opinions, 189
opportunities, 156–57
overpreparation, 180–83, 191–94, 206
overt cues, 157
overwhelm, 194, 228

participation, 137–39
people-pleasing, 8–12, 230
perfectionism, 250–53
personality, 56–57
persuasion, 128–33, 141–45, 170,
    173–74, 200–6, 213
physiological safety, 215–16
pilot's voice analogy, 223
pitch, 59
power
    assets inventory, 16–20
    deficits, 158–63
    as defined by men, xxiii–xxiv
    embodying, 252–53
    failure as opposite of, 238
    likeability vs., xv–xxiv
    perceptions of for women, xxi–xxii
    physical considerations, 19
    reinforcing with question-asking,
        117
    as a verb, xxvii
    voice and, 58–66
    warm, xxv–xxvi
    women positioned as outside of, 7
powerful/likeable binary, xv–xxv, 4–5,
    151, 170, 238, 261–62
preparation
    determining type of question being
        asked, 188–90
    determining your win, 194–95
    excitement about your win,
        196–97
    fifteen-minute rule, 184–86
    flexibility, 183–84, 194
    letting go, 197–98
    light-touch frameworks, 193–98
    maternal coding of, 178–79
    overpreparation, 180–83, 191–94,
        206
    overreliance on, 178
    Preparation Expectation, xxviii,
        178–79, 180–81, 183–84, 188,
        199

preparation (*cont'd*):
    research, 196
    slowing down time, 186–88
presence dysmorphia, 97–100, 101–2
presenting. *See* public speaking
promotions, asking for, 50–54,
    171–74
prototyping, 246–47
psychological safety, 215
public speaking
    as an attribute of maleness, xxiv
    clothing, 80–85
    disconnected audiences, 77–80
    educator mindset, 80
    energy projection, 85–86
    eye contact, 75–76
    fear of, 71–72
    practicing, 72–73
    recovery mode, 87–88
    talismans, 73–74

question-asking
    checking your credit, 116–17
    communicative inclusion, 137–38
    conversation-shaping with,
        117–18
    counterquestions, 231–32
    determining type of, 188–90
    fear of, 115–16, 120–21
    making asks, 32–35, 139–40, 161,
        164–65
    "why" questions, 118–19
    of yourself, 119–20

raises, asking for, 50–54, 171–74
reasoning, 166–67
recovery mode, 87–88
reframing
    accomplishments, 37–41
    detective mindset, 105–8
    flight impulse, 225–27
    "how things are usually done,"
        45–47

language, 47–48
presence dysmorphia, 101–2
regulation
    of bodies, 217–19
    breathing exercises, 232–34
    of emotions, 135–36, 216
releasing your agenda, 191
research, 196
resting concentration face, 67–68
risk tolerance, 240–41
ritual apologies, 159–60
role incredulity, 149–51

safety, 215–16
self-advocacy, 50–54
self alignment, 56–57
self-care, 20–25, 215–16
self-consciousness, 153
self-doubt, 242–44
self-presentation, 38–39
self-promotion, 50–51
self-talk, negative, 231–32
sense-making, 42–44
sensory stimulation, 230
sexism, 59
shouting, 93
signposting, 141–45
"sleeping when you're tired,"
    198–200, 204
Smart Twelve-Year-Old frame,
    202–4
smiling, 69–71
speaking
    communicative inclusion, 136–39
    public, xxiv, 71–80
    as sign of engagement, 157
    speed, 61–63
    volume, 59–60
speed, talking, 61–63
stage makeup metaphor, 85–86
stepping on toes, 34–35
strengths
    calm, 212–13

differences as, xxvii–xxviii, 153–54
power assets, 16–20
success
    calling out, 13–15
    hostility towards, 146–48
    imagining, 253–54
    imposter syndrome, 28–30
suggestions, 36–37
sunk cost fallacy, 191–92
Sushi Train Logic, 130–33
Swisher, Kara, 239

tai chi, 211–12, 230, 233
talismans, 73–74
tall poppy syndrome, 147–48
Tannen, Deborah, 57, 159, 231
terminology, industry, 119–20
threat responses
    about, 219–21
    anxiety about, 234–35
    breathing to regulate, 232–34
    fawn, 220, 230–32
    fight, 219–20, 221–23, 233
    flight, 219–20, 224–27, 233
    freeze, 220, 227–30
tiara syndrome, 113
time
    reclaiming, 47–48
    slowing down, 186–88
    taking, in communication, 23–25
tone of voice, xiv, 63–66
tree metaphor, 226–27
trial and error, 244–47
true self, 214

Tulshyan, Ruchika, 28
Twain, Mark, 143

UNESCO, 31
University of California, 213
unlikeability, xxi
untitling phenomenon, 38–39
upspeak, 59, 64–65

vagus nerve, 233
value, communicating, 40–41
verbal expressions, 68
vocabulary of communication, 6
vocal fry, 59
vocal projection, 60
vocal timbre, 60–61
vocal variance, xiv, 63–66
voice, xiv, 31, 58–66, 138
volume, speaking, 59–60

Walker, Pete, 220
warmth, 164–65
Waters, Maxine, 48
weak ties, 256
weather metaphor, 250–51, 252–53
weight-loss language, 33–34
"why" questions, 118–19
"Wild Geese" (Oliver), 236
wins, 194–97
working relationships, 126
work self, 56, 214

"yes," saying, 8, 10–12
YouTube, 112–13

ABOUT THE AUTHOR

KATE MASON, PHD, is a communications expert and world-champion debater who has spent her career working with founders and executives from tech start-ups to major global brands. She coaches executives on actionable skills to become the leaders they wish to be and to amplify their voices, reach, and impact at work. Kate lives in Sydney, Australia, with her partner, James, and their two sons.

This book was set in Garamond, a typeface originally designed by the Parisian type cutter Claude Garamond (c. 1500–61). This version of Garamond was modeled on a 1592 specimen sheet from the Egenolff-Berner foundry, which was produced from types assumed to have been brought to Frankfurt by the punch cutter Jacques Sabon (c. 1520–80).

Claude Garamond's distinguished romans and italics first appeared in *Opera Ciceronis* in 1543–44. The Garamond types are clear, open, and elegant.